NEW PROCLAMATION

Year B, 2002–2003

Advent through Holy Week

Frederick Houk Borsch

James M. Childs Jr.

Philip H. Pfatteicher

Martin F. Connell

FORTRESS PRESS

Minneapolis

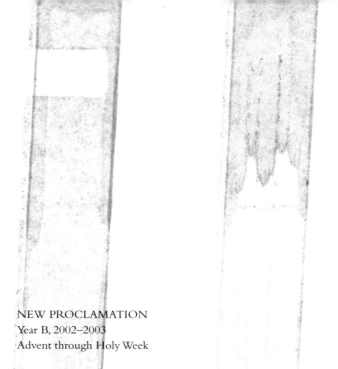

NEW PROCLAMATION
Year B, 2002–2003
Advent through Holy Week

Scripture quotations, unless otherwise noted, are from the New Revised Standard Version Bible and are copyright © 1989 by the Division of Christian Education of the National Council of Churches in the United States of America and are used by permission.

The poem "The Bright Field" by R. S. Thomas from *Collected Poems: 1945–1990*. London: J. M. Dent, 1993, appears courtesy of J. M. Dent/Orion Publishing. Used by permission.

Cover and book design: Joseph Bonyata

Illustrations: Tanya Butler, *Icon: Visual Images for Every Sunday,* copyright © 2000 Augsburg Fortress.

ISBN 0-8006-4247-3

The paper used in this publication meets the minimum requirements of the American National Standard for Information Sciences—Permanence of Paper for printed Library Materials, ANSI Z329.48-1984. ∞

Manufactured in the U.S.A.   AF 1-4247

06   05   04   03   02   1   2   3   4   5   6   7   8   9   10

CONTENTS

The Season of Epiphany
James M. Childs Jr.

The Season of Lent
Philip H. Pfatteicher

HOLY WEEK
MARTIN F. CONNELL

FOREWORD

New Proclamation continues the venerable Fortress Press tradition of offering a lectionary preaching resource that provides the best in biblical exegetical aids for a variety of lectionary traditions.

Thoroughly ecumenical and built around the three-year lectionary cycle, *New Proclamation* is focused on the biblical text, based on the conviction that those who are well equipped to understand a pericope in both its historical and liturgical contexts will be stimulated to preach engaging and effective sermons. For this reason, the most capable North American biblical scholars, theologians, and homileticians are invited to contribute to *New Proclamation*.

New Proclamation is planned and designed to be user-friendly in a variety of ways:

- *New Proclamation* is published in two volumes per year, designed for convenience. The volume you are holding covers the lections for approximately the first half of the church year, Advent through Holy Week, which culminates in the Great Vigil of Easter.
- This two-volume format offers a larger, workbook-style page with a lay-flat binding and space for making notes.
- Each season of the church year is prefaced by an introduction that offers insight into the background and spiritual significance of the period.
- How the preacher can apply biblical texts to contemporary situations is a concern of each contributor. Exegetical work ("Interpreting the Text") is concise, and thoughts on how the text addresses today's world and our personal situations ("Responding to the Texts") have a prominent role.

- Although they are not usually used as preaching texts, brief comments on each assigned psalm ("Responsive Reading") are included so that the preacher can also incorporate reflections on these in the sermon.
- Boxed quotations in the margins help signal important themes in the texts for the day.
- The material for Year B is here dated specifically for the years 2002–2003, for easier coordination with other dated lectionary materials.
- These materials can be adapted for uses other than for corporate worship on the day indicated. They are well suited for adult discussion groups or personal meditation and reflection.
- A calendar for December 2002–April 2003 is included at the end of the book for quick reference and notes.

We are grateful to our contributors, Frederick Houk Borsch, James M. Childs Jr., Philip H. Pfatteicher, and Martin F. Connell, for their insights and for their commitment to effective Christian preaching. We hope that you find in this volume ideas, stimulation, and encouragement in your ministry of proclamation.

THE SEASON
OF ADVENT

FREDERICK
HOUK BORSCH

Introduction

"Hark! a thrilling voice is sounding. 'Christ is nigh,' it seems to say." I loved hearing this Advent hymn as a child. "Christmas is coming!" it seems also to say. I could not wait. But I had to wait, even while something of the spirit of Christmas spilled over into the weeks before.

"The kingdom of God has come near," Jesus proclaimed (Mark 1:15). One can still hear a breathlessness in that message. The ways of God are so near they can be anticipated now. The new time is already begun. The kingdom is not way off in a distant heaven nor in a faraway future. It is upon us and among us even while its fullness is yet to be realized.

"Cast away the works of darkness, O ye children of the day," the hymn continues. "Prepare the way of the Lord, make his paths straight," calls out the prophet (Mark 1:3). It is time to get things straight. It is a time of judgment. *Judgment* may seem like a harsh word, but who would want a world where evil was not judged and the good defended and cherished?

A lot is happening during this Advent season, and a lot is about to happen. This is a solemn time of waiting and expectation, of hope and also fear. Are we ready for this coming? Are we already now beginning to live by the ways of justness and God's love?

"See, I am coming soon; my reward is with me, to repay according to everyone's work" (Rev. 22:12). "Amen. Come, Lord Jesus!" calls out the seer (Rev. 22:20). One prays, not without trepidation, for the return of the Lamb that was slain and to hear the voice from the throne saying,

"See, the home of God is among mortals.
He will dwell with them as their God;

they will be his peoples,
and God himself will be with them;
he will wipe every tear from their eyes.
Death will be no more;
mourning and crying and pain will be no more,
for the first things have passed away." (Rev. 21:3-4)

A new age will dawn.

Advent may seem a welter of messages about already, almost, and not yet. Jesus has come, is near, will come. The kingdom is nigh, is begun, is coming. All this can sound mysterious and even confusing, especially to the linear-minded. But then what else should we expect? This is about God. This is about God, who is the creator of innumerable galaxies and in whom we live and move and have our being. This is God beyond all understanding, who yet draws near and even enters into human life—Alpha and Omega who was and is and is to come. How can we do more than begin to know this presence? How can we be other than in fear and longing, in wonder and thanksgiving?

"Hark! a thrilling voice is sounding." It is our task as preachers, standing before the bright eyes of children and the cautious eyes of grownups, amid all the pageantry and gladness, the hopes and heartbreaks of our lives, to catch expectation and awe in our words and to tell again of the nearing God.

FIRST SUNDAY IN ADVENT

DECEMBER 1, 2002

REVISED COMMON	EPISCOPAL (BCP)	ROMAN CATHOLIC
Isa. 64:1–9	Isa. 64:1–9a	Isa. 63:16b–17, 19b; 64:2b–7
Ps. 80:1–7, 17–19	Psalm 80 or 80:1–7	Ps. 80:2–3, 15–16, 18–19
1 Cor. 1:3–9	1 Cor. 1:1–9	1 Cor. 1:3–9
Mark 13:24–37	Mark 13:(24–32), 33–37	Mark 13:33–37

FIRST READING
ISAIAH 64:1–9 (RCL, BCP);
ISAIAH 63:16b–17, 19b; 64:2b–7 (RC)

Interpreting the Texts

Isaiah 63:7—64:12 is like a psalm of lamentation and prayer. (See particularly Psalm 74 and this Sunday's Psalm 80.) It reverberates with the tone and themes of the book of Lamentations. While we cannot be certain of the time when the passage was written, it is likely (in its first use) to come from the period of return from exile when there was disappointment that the hopes for restoration and a new community of faith had not been fulfilled. Like much of the book of Isaiah, this section was no doubt used as a running commentary, referentially aware of earlier parts of the book and the people's history, and still being added to by words and nuance right up to the time of the final shaping of the book around 200 B.C.E. Even after codification, Jewish and then Christian interpretation and response continued.

Isaiah 63:16 both calls upon God and reminds God of God's role as Father (again in 64:8) and that the Israelites are God's people (63:18; 64:9). But 63:17–19 recognizes and confesses how far the people have strayed from a faithful relationship with God ("like those not called by your name") and assumes that this is part of the plan of an almighty God. This sense of God's abandonment and so of God's anger (see again 64:9) must be a result of Israel's sinning (64:5), while there is at least a hint that the transgression also is a response to the hiddenness of God's presence ("face" in 64:7). The comparison to a filthy cloth (64:6) implies ceremonial and cultural shame and uncleanness.

As in many a biblical lament and plea, there is also praise for what God has done in the past. God's righteousness and willingness to work for those who wait for him are remembered. The plea that God would now act again recalls the fire and mountain of the exodus and Sinai. This imagery and "that you would tear open the heavens" (64:1) are suggestive of apocalyptic language of destruction and new creation.

RESPONSIVE READING
PSALM 80:1-7, 17-19 (RCL);
PSALM 80 OR 80:1-7 (BCP);
PSALM 80:2-3, 15-16, 18-19 (RC)

Here is another communal lament that takes up the tone and several of the themes of this Sunday's first reading. The references (v. 2) to the northern tribes may suggest a northern kingdom provenance for the psalm, possibly before 722 B.C.E. If so, however, the lament was reused in other times of distress (no doubt after the fall of Jerusalem), and the psalm and its last verses look forward to the restoration of a united Israel. "The one at your right hand, the one [son of man] whom you made strong for yourself" is its king or chosen one representative of all Israel.

God is appealed to as shepherd (see Ezek. 34:11-31 et al.) who, also as Israel's true king, is enthroned on the cherubim—an allusion to the figures on the legendary Ark of God (see 1 Sam. 4:4 et al.). But in God's anger God resists the people's prayers and, instead of a shepherd's good food, gives them the bread of tears. "Restore us," the people plead over and over again (vv. 3, 7, 19). "Let your face shine, that we may be saved," continues the petition. In other words, "Smile upon us." Your caring presence is what we ask and need.

SECOND READING
1 CORINTHIANS 1:3-9 (RCL, RC);
1 CORINTHIANS 1:1-9 (BCP)

Interpreting the Text

This letter's opening prayer of thanksgiving and praise also describes a people in waiting (v. 7), in this case for the "revealing [Greek *apokalupsin* = apocalypse = revelation, disclosure, often used in this period with an allusion to the last days] of our Lord Jesus Christ." This will be a time of judgment. Paul sees the Corinthians' great hope as being found "blameless [a word used often by Paul] on the day of our Lord Jesus Christ." This "day" derives much of its significance from "the day of Yahweh" or "day of the Lord" in the Hebrew scriptures. The day of the Lord would be, first of all, a time of retribution, destruction, and justice. In Jewish apocalypticism, on that day this evil age would come to an end. This "day of the Lord" was readily transferred to be "the day [implying or linked frequently with the idea of the return] of the Lord Jesus" (or "of Jesus Christ" or "of Christ"). This phrase is employed a number of times by Paul and others in the New Testament (and see below "on the days of the Son of Man"). Corinthian Christians, however, are to have hope while awaiting this day, because they have been enriched and strengthened for this "end"—this ending or goal (Greek *telos*). They may trust that the God who has called them into the fellowship *(koinonia)* of his Son will be faithful in this calling.

Readers familiar with the Corinthian correspondence can hear in almost every word of these opening verses allusions to the teaching and admonitions to come later in the letters. Prone to divisions, the Corinthians have to be reminded that "not lacking in any spiritual gift" does not mean that some are superior to others. Speech *(logos)* and knowledge *(gnosis)* will have to be defined as a wisdom that is a kind of foolishness (1 Cor. 1:18-31) and a proclamation that is not "in lofty words or wisdom" (1 Cor. 2:1). Enrichment (1:5) is not known in the ways of this world or worldly religion (see 1 Cor. 4:8-13). This time of being strengthened is to be one of disciplined waiting—not a time of exalting selves because of (or otherwise misusing) the charismatic spiritual gifts (Greek *charisma*) that have been given.

THE GOSPEL
MARK 13:24-37 (RCL);
MARK 13:(24-32), 33-37 (BCP);
MARK 13:33-37 (RC)

Interpreting the Text

Early Christianity had a problem. The early Christians had teachings about and a belief in the coming of a transforming new era. This could be the coming of the kingdom Jesus proclaimed ("Truly I tell you, there are some standing here who will not taste death until they see that the kingdom of God has come with power," Mark 9:1) and/or the appearance of Jesus on "the day of the Lord Jesus Christ" (see above on 1 Cor. 1:1-9) or as, in this Gospel reading, the Son of Man coming in clouds with great power and glory. None of this, however, had happened, and the longer it did not happen, the greater the problem. The Fourth Gospel may be thought to have *solved* the problem by understanding the return of Jesus as the coming of the Spirit he had promised. With different nuances, the other Gospels hold on to the expectation of the kingdom coming and/or Jesus' return (here in Mark 13:30 Jesus even insists that "this generation will not pass away until all these things have taken place"), while suggesting that the time may be somewhat lengthened. One is to be ready and alert, while undue speculation is discouraged (see Mark 13:5-8, 21-22). The timing cannot be known from a human perspective. Even the Son did not know (v. 32) or predict. Matthew begins to suggest that this extended period is a time for the mission of the church, and Luke suggests that it is a time for endurance and testing. Mark's Gospel outlines various historical, natural, and cosmic events that must first take place, but disciples need to keep alert and awake (repeated three times in vv. 33, 35, and 37). Moreover, one can be sure that the words of Jesus (not least in this regard), though "heaven and earth will pass away," "will not pass away" (v. 31).

How much of this teaching and language go back to the historical Jesus can be debated. There is good reason to believe that Jesus did expect a dramatic coming of God's "kingdom," and we know that before, during, and after his time various forms of apocalyptic speculation existed. It would seem Jesus may also have told other parables about the need to be prepared (e.g., Matt. 22:11-13; 25:1-12). More important for our purposes, however, is how the churches found themselves compelled to use and develop the expectation they inherited.

Mark (or his tradition) has put together (into this "little apocalypse") a number of sayings and stories. A comparison with their placement in Matthew and Luke suggests that they come from a variety of places in the traditions. The story about the doorkeeper who is to stay watchful (13:34-36) has been fit into this context, beginning much as does Matthew's and Luke's parable of the talents (Matt. 25:14-30; Luke 19:12-27). "On a journey" could have been added in Mark as a reference to Jesus' having gone away. The servants, each with their own work, may allude to other disciples in Mark's audience. In any case, the admonition is clear, as it is in the earlier "lesson" of the fig tree (Mark 13:28-29). Although in the latter case the leafing of the tree provides indication of the approaching time, one never knows when the master of the house is about to return. Be alert! Be prepared.

The depiction of "those days" in the first verses (13:24-27) of the longer version of the Gospel reading is like language that can be found in descriptions of the "day of the Lord" in the Hebrew scriptures and later apocalyptic literature (e.g., see particularly Isa. 13:10). It is a way of saying that what is to happen will affect the whole creation and be cosmic in its significance. To this picture is added, under the influence of the book of Daniel, the "Son of Man coming in clouds" (Mark 13:26). Behind Daniel's vision there stands a myth of the younger god (in appearance like a human) coming to join (replace?) in glory and kingship the "Ancient of Days" (Dan. 7:13-14). Jesus or the early churches adapted this language to describe the appearance in glory and judgment of Jesus as this Son of Man. In the book of Enoch (1 Enoch—there also coupled with the Son of Man), and in other Jewish and Christian sources (see particularly Matt. 13:41; 24:30; 25:31; Mark 8:38), are found the accompanying angels. Here they gather the "elect from the four winds" (Mark 13:27; see Rev. 7:1) as the divine judgment and protection are vindicated.

With this dramatic picture of cosmic closure, and with his collection of stories and sayings about what is imminent, Mark seeks to ensure that disciples will wait and watch, continuing to trust in Jesus' words and, above all, staying awake and alert. At least as much in Mark's time as our own, hearers would have known the function of story to describe "it is like" (see 13:34) and of poetic language to describe the indescribable. All this

> MARK SEEKS TO ENSURE THAT DISCIPLES WILL WAIT AND WATCH, CONTINUING TO TRUST IN JESUS' WORDS AND, ABOVE ALL, STAYING AWAKE AND ALERT.

was and is not to be taken literally, but the essential message is so intended: "Beware! Keep alert." Something important is about to happen!

Responding to the Texts

The philosopher and theologian Paul Tillich, so the story goes, was once taken to a Yankees' game. For the most part he seemed inattentive to the game, not really understanding the ins and outs of baseball and more interested in talking about philosophical and theological matters. In the first half of the ninth inning, with the Yanks leading by a run, the visiting team loaded the bases with only one out. Much of the crowd was on the edge of its seat. Even Tillich grew quiet. The batter slapped a hot ground ball that looked like it was going into center field. But ranging far to his left, Kubeck was able to glove the ball. He flipped it to Richardson, who fired it to Collins at first just in time for the game-ending double play. Tillich leapt to his feet and, waving his hat in the air, shouted, *"Kairos, kairos, kairos!"*

The Greek word he was shouting in that cheering stadium is sometimes translated "opportunity time" and stands in contrast to clock and calendar time or linear time. While one might be accused of employing *kairos* time as a way of psychologizing or demythologizing biblical language about the day of the Lord and the *end* of time, it is arguably a way of digging deeper into these texts and asking about what is really being pointed to here. Clearly a great deal is said to be at stake—nothing less than a culmination of the meaning of life when what is of holy and lasting value will be revealed and preserved, and all else, particularly the wrong and the evil, will be put to an end.

When does that time come? Throughout history the people of God have longed for it. They have lived through fears and terror and many a disappointment. One sympathizes with the psalmist who commented, "My eyes grow dim with waiting for my God" (Ps. 69:3). Many early Christians thought the new age was near. So did groups of later Christians who sold their goods (they might have been more convincing had they given them away!) in preparation for a predicted day of the Lord. But it did not come as they expected, and it is in many ways amazing that Christianity has continued and grown when it posits such a seeming mistake at the heart of its Good News.

Still the disciples are told to keep on waiting, watching, longing, hoping, staying alert. Indeed, there is a great deal of such waiting in the Bible—for exodus from slavery in Egypt, return from exile, the rebuilding of Jerusalem, the return of the prophet, the coming of the Messiah, the coming of the kingdom and the new age, and the return of Jesus. The people hope for salvation, and it becomes part of their story and its interpretation to try to understand why God often does not seem to hear—why evil and suffering often appear dominant. Is God angry? Is it our sin? And yet we are told God is faithful. The evil will be judged and the suffering redeemed. "Be alert! Watch!"

Perhaps in some way it is the waiting that is important. Maybe it is in looking for the kingdom of God and trying to live by its ways that disciples are to become the people God hopes for—those who will "put first the kingdom of God" and its ways of mercy, peace, and hungering and thirsting for righteousness. The hungering and thirsting help make a people more just and fair. In desiring the time when all can be loved, they begin to love their neighbors as themselves.

> MAYBE IT IS IN LOOKING FOR THE KINGDOM OF GOD AND TRYING TO LIVE BY ITS WAYS THAT DISCIPLES ARE TO BECOME THE PEOPLE GOD HOPES FOR.

One could compare it to bird-watching. What makes bird watchers the kind of people they are is not just spotting birds. It is also the preparation—getting the right clothes and equipment, being in good shape, trekking out into the woods, developing keen sight, watching, staying awake and alert, being ready. And when the moment comes, it makes sense of all the preparation and waiting, the conversations about birds, reading the books, getting up early, being bit by mosquitoes, sitting in the rain.

Christians have been told that they don't know the exact time of Christ's return. Not even the Son knows. What they are to believe is that God's ways are coming. Justness will be made known. God "will also strengthen you to the end" (1 Cor. 1:8)—to this end and goal. In the meantime they are to be God's alert people, for Jesus said the kingdom had drawn near. In some ways it is already among us. Often Jesus spoke of those beginnings—the leaven and mustard seed, the discovery of the treasure and the pearl. Do not miss that! *Kairos* time! It brings hope. It is the beginning in which disciples may now participate. R. S. Thomas told of it in his poem "The Bright Field."

I have seen the sun break through
to illuminate a small field
for a while, and gone my way
and forgotten it. But that was the pearl
of great price, the one field that had
the treasure hid in it. I realize now
that I must give all that I have
to possess it. Life is not hurrying

on to a receding future, nor hankering after
an imagined past. It is the turning
aside like Moses to the miracle
of the lit bush, to a brightness
that seemed as transitory as your youth
once, but is the eternity that awaits you.

SECOND SUNDAY IN ADVENT

DECEMBER 8, 2002

REVISED COMMON	EPISCOPAL (BCP)	ROMAN CATHOLIC
Isa. 40:1-11	Isa. 40:1-11	Isa. 40:1-5, 9-11
Ps. 85:1-2, 8-13	Psalm 85 or 85:7-13	Ps. 85:9-10, 11-12, 13-14
2 Pet. 3:8-15a	2 Pet. 3:8-15a, 18	2 Pet. 3:8-14
Mark 1:1-8	Mark 1:1-8	Mark 1:1-8

FIRST READING

ISAIAH 40:1-11 (RCL, BCP);
ISAIAH 40:1-5, 9-11 (RC)

Interpreting the Text

In hymnic tones, at once majestic and tender, the prophet tells of God's coming in might and in mercy. The time of exile is soon to end. The people's iniquity was the cause of exile, but now the penalty has been paid—even doubly paid, and the term of service is over. The double imperative "Comfort, Comfort" (stylistic for this section of Isaiah; see 51:9, 17; 52:1; 57:14; 62:10) may suggest a corresponding doubling of Jerusalem's comfort. Jerusalem is used here and in subsequent chapters for all God's people—the particular for the whole.

The voice that calls out the prophet's mission is God's voice from the council of heaven. The vivid picture of the way being prepared in the wilderness may derive from ancient Middle Eastern scenes of a king approaching his city and temple while servants sought to smooth out the mounds and gullies. But now the royal and divine road comes from Babylon to Jerusalem, with echoes also of the people's exodus path through the wilderness from Egypt. The message the prophet is to proclaim contrasts the transitory condition of human life ("the grass withers, the flower fades") with the promise of God's word, which "will stand forever" (v. 7).

"The glory of the LORD shall be revealed" (v. 5). God comes "with might," and his ruling "arm" (God's power for victory; see Isa. 59:16) will enable him to deliver both reward and recompense. These are both "good tidings" and tender words from a God who will be like a shepherd with the lambs and other sheep. At once is heard a message of dependence on God and confidence in God's promise and power to save. The prophet's picture words remind of the justness of divine judgment while offering a declaration of God's mercy and might, not only to God's own people but to the world.

Responsive Reading

PSALM 85:1-2, 8-13 (RCL);
PSALM 85 OR 85:7-13 (BCP);
PSALM 85:9-10, 11-12, 13-14 (RC)

Heaven and earth meet in this psalm of petition and assurance. It could well come, as does this Sunday's first reading, from the era of the ending of exile. But psalms were used over and again. The words may also allude to other times of challenge and of hope. (Some suggest the psalm may contain a petition for rain; see v. 12.) It begins, as does Isa. 40:1-11, with a reminder of sin and God's anger and of forgiveness and pardon. Restoration is still a plea (v. 4) and a hope (v. 12), but that hope relies on God's steadfast love *(chesed)* both appealed to (v. 7) and assured (v. 10).

In vv. 8-13 a priest or prophet is called upon to deliver this assurance in moving and dramatic words. In ordinary human life it is hard to reconcile the demands of righteousness and justice and the longing for the fullness of peace. Only God can enable them to kiss each other. God speaks this peace to the faithful who turn *(shuv)* their hearts (their reasoned emotions) to God. God's steadfast love and the people's faithfulness (v. 10a) will come together as friends. This loyalty will "spring up from the ground" as the righteousness of God looks down from the sky (v. 11). Then is salvation near at hand, and God's glory (majestic presence; see Isa. 40:5) "may *dwell* in our land" (v. 9).

Second Reading

2 PETER 3:8-15a (RCL);
2 PETER 3:8-15a, 18 (BCP);
2 PETER 3:8-14 (RC)

Interpreting the Text

From the perspective of the writer of 2 Peter, at least a generation has passed since the first churches were founded (see 3:4), quite possibly several more generations (an inference from 3:15-16a). The letter has been dated as late as the early second century of the Christian era. Its author, who sees himself as a follower of Peter, felt inspired to say what Peter would say in this time. Among the issues to be addressed was the "day of the Lord." (Regarding this "day" see the interpretation of 1 Cor. 1:1-9 for the First Sunday of Advent.) Evidently scoffers (3:3-6) were questioning the hope of the return of the Lord and seemingly also maintaining that this world was destined to go on without an end.

In response the author urges expectant waiting. Disciples should understand that from the divine perspective time can appear quite differently. God may also be showing forbearance (v. 9), giving time to come to repentance (on the significance of this, see the Gospel reading commentary below), for the sake of salvation (v. 15). But (and this is a big *but* echoed in other places in the New Testament, particularly the Gospel of Matthew, e.g., Matt. 13:24-30, 36-43) the end and judgment will come. Using an analogy from the Gospels (Matt. 24:43; Luke 12:39), the author of 2 Peter maintains that the Lord's day will come like a thief; in other words, without warning and likely when one least expects it.

Disciples are to wait, then (3:12, 13, 14), but with a hastening desire for "the coming of the day of God" (v. 12). They are to use the time to be at peace and so to be found "without spot or blemish" (v. 14). The latter phrase reflects Levitical cultic language and suggests a distancing and separation from all worldly ways. The depiction of the end of this world in fire, before the creation of new heavens and a new earth, also encourages a distancing from the ways of the world. Such fiery imagery, familiar in some Jewish apocalyptic writings of the time, runs the danger of encouraging Christians to treat the whole of God's creation as disposable—as a hotel rather than home for humanity. It seems better, as in Revelation 21, to imagine the transformation of the world. Yet what is most important in this author's understanding is that Christians know that God's purposes will be fulfilled. This will happen in God's time while disciples are to wait in expectation, using the time for repentance and ethical living.

THE GOSPEL
MARK 1:1-8

Interpreting the Text

Mark's proclamation begins urgently. If this evangelist knew at least bits of the birth narratives (why wouldn't he?), they are not important to his story. This "beginning" (of the first part of the Gospel, or of the whole of Christianity?) is the good news *of* Jesus Christ (what Jesus taught) or, more likely Mark intends, *about* Jesus, or it is both. Enough time has passed by since Jesus' death and resurrection that the designation "the anointed one" or "the Messiah" (Christ) has virtually become part of Jesus' name. The additional title "Son of God" may have been added later, making Mark's original beginning even more abrupt.

The first actor on stage is John the baptizer, whose ministry helped prepare for and pointed the way to Jesus. In historical perspective this of course is early Christian interpretation of what was likely a more complex human relationship. In their lifetimes it would appear that John was better known. Certainly the evidence of Josephus suggests this as does Mark's "all the country of Judea, and all the people of Jerusalem," even if an exaggeration. John's disciples and his form of baptism (see Acts 19:1-5) may have continued for a while in a sort of parallel with the Jesus movement (see also John 3:23). We do not, however, know about John's message and activity with any precision. His baptism, like those of the Dead Sea group(s), may have had a more ritual, cleansing aspect and could have been repeated. He may have believed he was the one preparing the way for the Lord God, or for the prophet Elijah, or that he was Elijah (as in Mal. 3:1; 4:5).

No matter now! Combining prophetic words from Mal. 3:1 (and Exod. 23:20) and "good tidings" (see Isa. 40:9) from our first reading (Isa. 40:1-11), Mark effectively links the story of Jesus Christ to the hopes and longings of the prophets of Israel. The promised time is come! Such combinations of biblical prophecies are found often enough in the Dead Sea Scrolls or other writings of the time. Mark, having taken this one over from earlier tradition, attributes the whole to Isaiah. He also, because of John's desert locale, has the voice "crying in the wilderness" rather than (per Isaiah) depicting the way being prepared in the wilderness.

> WHAT JESUS BRINGS, ACCORDING TO JOHN, IS A NEW KIND OF BAPTISM—INVOLVING MORE THAN THE FORGIVENESS OF SINS.

John certainly appears to have been a wilderness figure and an outsider. His clothing was reminiscent of Elijah (see 2 Kings 1:8). His diet of locusts and wild honey may have been for ritual purity or asceticism, or it may have been the food of a rather poor Bedouin. His message may have been as stark as it sounds. Repentance (Greek *metanoia,* "a changing of heart and mind"; in Hebrew *shuv,* "a turning of life") was required for forgiveness of sins. This was necessary for preparing the way of the Lord. Mark 1:7-8 then links this preparation directly to the coming of "the one who is more powerful" (which once may have referred to a figure yet to appear but here clearly refers to Jesus) to whose ministry John completely subordinates his own.

Did Jesus also baptize with water? The slim evidence from John's Gospel (3:22; 4:1-2) about Jesus doing baptisms points both ways. More importantly, what Jesus brings, according to John, is a new kind of baptism—involving more than the forgiveness of sins. Both Matthew (3:11) and Luke (3:16) say it will be a baptism "with the Holy Spirit and with fire" (perhaps in earlier tradition "with wind and fire"). A new power is here with Jesus.

Good news evidently begins in the wilderness. The repetition of biblical typology drives this awareness home. To reach the promised land the people must go by way of the wilderness. To return home from exile the people must pass through the wilderness. John lives and preaches in the wilderness. He calls those who would submit to his baptism for the remissions of sins into the wilderness. Jesus, too, will come to John by the Jordan and then be driven farther into the wilderness for his time of temptation. The wilderness, away from the settled and easier ways of life, was frequently seen as a place for purification, for getting away from worldly ways and distractions. It was a place of preparation, of struggle, of waiting and expectation. Here one prepares the way of the Lord. The wilderness seems to be full of hope. But sooner or later one asks, don't we get tired of all the expectation and straightening of paths and then waiting some more?

> TO REACH THE PROMISED LAND THE PEOPLE MUST GO BY WAY OF THE WILDERNESS.

God's sense of time must come from a different perspective than ours. Indeed, Einstein helped us to see that, in very large perspective, time is relative to position and speed in relation to the cosmic speed limit of light. Were one to approach the speed of light, time, as we think of it, would virtually come to a standstill. As the fourth dimension, time is so joined to space's three dimensions it is better to talk of *spacetime.* Moreover, some mathematical scientists reasonably posit a series of yet other dimensions, at least one of which could be another kind of time. And, just in psychological terms, I can tell you that my summers seem to go a lot faster than when I was a kid. Given God's age, it is no wonder that a thousand years could go by like a day (see again 2 Pet. 3:9).

So I understand why it is important to think in other ways than the clock's and calendar's linear time. There are, for example, crucial moments of decision in life. There are times when true character is revealed and times that would be sad to just let pass by. There is R. S. Thomas's "bright field" (see above, p. 9) that is "the eternity that awaits you."

Still, however, my life and the life of the people of God seem to involve considerable waiting for God's purposes to be more fully known. There is a lot of waiting for evil to be shown up and the ways of God to grow. Reinhold Niebuhr held that "the meaning of history is, but it is not yet." Okay, that may give some confidence, but when? Outside my lifetime? Outside of human time?

Nor am I sure that I want to go into the wilderness. I have grown to like, or at least need as part of my coping with life, a lot of the big city's worldly entertainment and distractions. A couple of friends once noted to me that while they thought they could be appreciative of John the Baptist's ministry, they were glad they didn't have him for a next-door neighbor. Do we really need hair shirts and locusts (it sounds like one of those TV *Survivor* programs) and all that much repentance? And, again, how long are we supposed to wait?

I suppose that the answer to that question depends, at least in large measure, on what one really wants. There is a French saying that speaks of a kind of coiling up or being willing to store up energy in order to be better able to move or jump forward: *reculer pour mieux sauter.* There is at least a time in life to go on retreat—to pull back, to save energy, to live—even if for a few days, with life less cluttered and wearing our badge of "Have I told you how busy I am?" Perhaps one may become more attentive—better able to see what all the busyness may be trying to cover up, and what might be worth moving forward toward—perhaps what may be already here. "Seek first God's kingdom . . ." (see Matt. 6:33; Luke 12:31). Quite possibly one can only see that way or ways of God from some kind of wilderness—with a kind of single-mindedness of purity of heart that demands a lot of attentive waiting.

C. S. Lewis once observed that, when we really think about it, what we long for is not so much to possess beauty but to participate in it. We long to become a part of God's ways. "What must I do to inherit eternal life?" asked the scribe (Luke 10:25). The question was not about life that just goes on and on but life that truly matters. This would mean loving God with heart, mind, soul, and strength and one's neighbor as oneself—or at least wanting to, which may be enough. That would mean beginning to participate in the love and compassion of God. For an individual and for a people that would mean getting a lot of things straight and repairing much that is crooked.

It would mean a changing of heart and mind *(metanoia),* the turning *(shuv)* of one's attention, and a new sense of God's presence or Spirit in life. It would also mean, though not without struggle, "while you are waiting for these things . . . to be found by [God] at peace" (2 Pet. 3:14). Paul tells of "the peace of God, which surpasses all understanding" (Phil. 4:7), and sometimes I think truer words were never spoken. I surely do not understand, much less often experience, such peace. But there are also at least some other times when I think I may just begin to get what I cannot understand—how "steadfast love and faithfulness" might "meet" and the longing for "righteousness and peace [to] kiss each other" (Ps. 85:10) find its consummation in the love of God.

In his poem "Ash Wednesday," T. S. Eliot included what must be one of the shortest of prayers: "Teach us to care and not to care." It is not that we are sometimes to care and other times not. Rather, the poet intimates, there can be a careless caring and a caring carelessness. There is a trust in the promise of God that enables one at the same time to go on caring with something of God's love and compassion while believing that, as Dame Julian envisioned, "All will be well." Eliot incorporated this vision into his conclusion of the "Four Quartets." He was trying to find words to intimate how time and eternity might intersect. That too is beyond our understanding but is surely worth waiting for. I may at times grow tired in the waiting and seek my distractions. There surely is a lot we still do not understand—not least the evil in our times. But then our longing grows again, and with it our hope and expectation.

THIRD SUNDAY IN ADVENT

DECEMBER 15, 2002

REVISED COMMON	EPISCOPAL (BCP)	ROMAN CATHOLIC
Isa. 61:1-4, 8-11	Isa. 65:17-25	Isa. 61:1-2a, 10-11
Psalm 126 or	Psalm 126 or	Luke 1:46-48, 49-50,
Luke 1:47-55	Canticle 3 or 15	53-54
1 Thess. 5:16-24	1 Thess. 5:(12-15),	1 Thess. 5:16-24
	16-28	
John 1:6-8, 19-28	John 1:6-8, 19-28	John 1:6-8, 19-28
	or John 3:23-30	

FIRST READING
ISAIAH 61:1-4, 8-11 (RCL);
ISAIAH 61:1-2a, 10-11 (RC)

Interpreting the Text

The enlivening Spirit *(ruach)* of Yahweh God anoints (chooses and blesses) this servant prophet to bring "good news." The good news resounds in the Bible because of the use of Isa. 61:1-2 by Jesus in Luke 4:18-19. (See also Matt. 11:5; Luke 7:22.) A new day has begun. This is a day of "vengeance of our God," but far more in terms of comfort, liberty and new life—of rescue and vindication—than of getting even. The Spirit, as a sure indication of God's presence and activity, inspires this servant and God's people in other parts of the latter portions of Isaiah (42:1, 5; 59:21). Here the time of renewal and restoration, to which this and other of the Isaiah songs refer, is that of return from exile and the rebuilt city and life of Jerusalem. From that time on, as Jesus' use shows, the joyous language could be used in other times of hope and longing.

There are, of course, echoes in the themes of *release* and *liberty* of the exodus and probably of the release of slaves after six years (Exod. 21:1-6), and perhaps of sabbatical and jubilee years (Leviticus 25) as well. Much of the power and beauty of the language comes from the specificity of its imagery: "a garland instead of ashes," "the oil of gladness, "the mantle of praise," and "the ancient ruins," which will be built up (vv. 3-4). As the Lord of justice (hating robbery and wrongdoing) makes an everlasting covenant (see 54:9-10; 55:3; 59:21) with the people, the servant who exults (with "my whole being") on behalf of God's people is clothed with "the garments of salvation" and "the robe of righteousness" like a bridegroom decked with a garland and a bride with her jewels (vv. 10-11). Then, as surely as the earth and a garden bring forth what is sown, so Yahweh God causes the righteousness (of vindication) and praise to spring up, not just for Israel's benefit but for all the nations (see vv. 5-6) to see.

ISAIAH 65:17-25 (BCP)

Although Isaiah 66 concludes the latter sections of Isaiah with final verses of demand and vindication, chap. 65 and especially vv. 17-25 might be a more fitting culmination and perhaps at one time filled that role. The new Jerusalem will be the centerpiece of a new creation. In lyric language that makes one think of the ending of the entire Bible in Revelation 21–22, there will be new heavens and earth. No more will there be weeping or distress. In this paradise of utter fairness, no one will die an untimely death or labor in vain. Even the fierce competitiveness of the animal world will cease (see also Isa. 11:6-7), and there will be no hurting or destroying in "my holy mountain" (i.e., Zion and the place of paradise near to the heavens; see Isa. 25:6-10; Ezek. 20:40; and the same language as Isa. 65:25 in Isa. 11:9).

RESPONSIVE READING
LUKE 1:47-55 (RCL);
LUKE 1:46-48, 49-50, 53-54 (RC)

The use of Mary's hymn of servanthood, of blessing, and of confidence in the justness and rightness of God carries forward and responds to the visions of Isaiah. The psalm-like passage (which once may have been ascribed to Elizabeth) derives from Hannah's song (1 Sam. 2:1-10) and can be seen as a culmination of all birth promises in the scriptures. It repeats and brings to fruition two other great and related biblical themes: that God works through the lowly and insignificant (Abraham and Sarah, Moses, Ruth, David, Amos, et al, and Israel itself) and turns things upside down. It is not the proud, the powerful, and the rich who ultimately prosper, but the lowly and the hungry. (The past tense of the verbs makes this an even more certain prophecy.) The words anticipate Jesus' blessings and woes in Luke 6:20-26 (see the blessings in Matt. 5:1-12) and Jesus' parables of reversal (the prodigal and elder brothers; the all-day and one-hour workers; the dinner party, etc.), along with repeated words of warning and promise about the first being last and the last first.

PSALM 126 (RCL, BCP)

Psalm 126 is a fitting antiphon to the readings from Isaiah. The psalmist remembers the laughter and joy of the return from exile when great things were done for Zion and then prays for a new time similar to that. Water (always a precious commodity in that part of the world) will flow in places dry throughout most of the year. (The Negeb is the arid region in southern Palestine.) The parallelism in vv. 5 and 6 emphasizes the hope and promise. Fortunes will be reversed as those who sow in tears will renew the shouts of joy of v. 2.

SECOND READING

1 THESSALONIANS 5:16-24 (RCL, RC);
1 THESSALONIANS 5:(12-15), 16-28 (BCP)

Interpreting the Text

Verses 12-15, which form part of the context for the following verses (and may be used in the BCP reading), call for a community of peace, encouragement, and cooperation. Those in leadership roles are to be respected—more, they are to be esteemed in love. The idlers, fainthearted, and weak (probably general descriptions rather than specific groups) are, in turn, to be admonished, encouraged, and helped. All are to be shown patience.

The larger context is one of some uncertainty and even worry about the coming of the Lord. When will this be? What will happen to those who have already died? Paul encourages the Thessalonians (4:15-18) with a dramatic picture of the end and follows this by urging them to remember that "the day of the Lord will come like a thief in the night" (5:2). Then in this reading he prays that "the God of peace" will sanctify them "wholly" *(holotelēs)* in spirit, soul, and body (only used here by Paul and probably three aspects rather than parts of a person, though not without reference to the fullness of resurrection). So may they be kept *holoklēros* (complete, wholly sound, undamaged) at the coming *(parousia)* of the Lord Jesus Christ. Paul then assures them that the God who is faithful "will do this" (5:24).

It is in this context that the Thessalonians are to "rejoice always, pray without ceasing, give thanks in all circumstances" (5:16-17). (Notice the repeated phrasings in twos, threes, and fours throughout the passage, giving a rhetorical structure and strength.) The linkage of prayer and thanksgiving, along with joy, is very Pauline (see Phil. 4:4-6; Col. 3:15-17; 1 Thess. 3:9-10).

The admonitions not to quench the Spirit nor despise prophecies and to test everything (5:20-21) cause anyone familiar with Paul's letters to think of his advice to the Corinthians (see 1 Corinthians 12–14) with regard to spiritual gifts. More than a few of these communities must have had a lively sense of the Spirit's presence among them. Paul wants to encourage this spirituality, but he also wants to be sure it is tested. Here he is not specific about the form of testing, but it will be done in the light of making sure they "hold fast to what is good" and "abstain from every form of evil" (5:21-22).

THE GOSPEL
JOHN 1:6-8, 19-28

Interpreting the Text

All four authors of the canonical Gospels, along with the traditions they drew upon, found it important to establish the relationship between John (known in the Synoptics as the Baptist) and Jesus. The Fourth Gospel does this by inserting into a kind of prose poem (perhaps originally composed for the figure of the Wisdom of God but then adapted for Jesus as the incarnate Word) a passage (1:6-8) in a yet more prose form that tells how John "came witnessing in order to witness" (using two forms of the Greek word from which the English word *martyr* derives). The Gospel takes up John's witness again in 1:19-28, and the two passages are joined to form this Sunday's Gospel reading.

It would be interesting to know whether the fourth evangelist knew one or more of the other Gospels. My best guess is that he did not but that he did know some of the same and similar traditions that he, probably along with a previous community or communities of faith, adapted to his own perspective. The perspective on John the Baptist took what was likely a more complex human story (see above, p. 13, on John, Jesus, baptism, and the possibility of a continuing John the Baptist group) and made it very clear that John was Jesus' precursor. On this precursor role the Fourth and the Synoptic Gospels agree, but the Fourth Gospel makes explicit the denial of any possibility that John could legitimately have been considered as the Messiah or the destined great prophet like Moses (see Deut. 18:15). These roles are for Jesus. Nor, unlike in Matthew and Mark, is John to be regarded as Elijah, the prophet who, in the last words of the canonical prophecies (Mal. 4:5), is to be sent "before the great and terrible day of the Lord comes." Moreover, the Fourth Gospel leaves out the story of Jesus' baptism by John, probably in order to avoid any suggestion that Jesus was at one time subordinate to John's ministry.

Parallel to the Synoptic Gospels one does find (John 1:23) the use in slightly different words (from Isa. 40:3) of the voice crying out in the wilderness to "make straight the way of the Lord." This ministry, John maintains, is what he does have to testify about himself. Also, as in the Synoptic Gospels, he subordinates himself by saying he is not worthy (*axios;* compare the Synoptics' *hikanos* = able or fit) to untie the thong (a slave's role) of Jesus' sandal.

This highly structured scene (across the Jordan in a now unknown town of Bethany) seems almost like a courtroom in which John gives his testimony of denial about himself while pointing to Jesus: "one whom you do not know, the one who is coming after me" (1:26-27). "The one you do not know" echoes 1:10-11 and adumbrates all the trouble "the Jews" will have knowing and believing in Jesus in this Gospel. "The Jews" (1:19) for this evangelist are a kind of generalized way of referring to religious officialdom and others who did not accept Jesus. The fact that the Gospel could use the term in this way likely suggests a locale and a time when there were few, if any, in this community who still regarded themselves as Jewish-Christians and after there had been some history of argument about Jesus. In this sense the usage belongs to a particular context in history, and note of that should be taken in any contemporary use of the tradition. In all this, what is most important from the Gospel's perspective is that John came as a witness to the one who is the true light that comes from God into the world (1:7-9).

> WHAT IS MOST IMPORTANT FROM THE GOSPEL'S PERSPECTIVE IS THAT JOHN CAME AS A WITNESS TO THE ONE WHO IS THE TRUE LIGHT THAT COMES FROM GOD INTO THE WORLD.

JOHN 3:23-30 (BCP, alt.)

This reading tells of a time that seems quite realistic in historical and human terms when some, at least, may have seen competition between John and Jesus, possibly between their disciples as well. This Gospel uses the scene to make clear again, through his own words, John's subordinate role. The passage is curious in that parts of it are awkwardly stated and others not as clear as they might be, almost as though it has not been completely worked into the Gospel. John 3:23-24 is awkwardly expressed; 4:2 corrects the impression (3:26) that Jesus himself was baptizing. It is not clear whether the aphorism of 3:27 refers to John or Jesus. John 3:28 must be interpreted in order to understand that Israel is the bride and Jesus the bridegroom (see Mark 2:18-19). Nor is it certain whether the quotation from John ends with v. 30 or continues through v. 36, although similar confusions are found elsewhere and are perhaps deliberate in this Gospel. Yet the main thrust of the passage does stand clear. John, as a friend of the bridegroom, has listened and rejoiced to hear the bridegroom's voice. His role is now fulfilled and over. Jesus must increase while John decreases, which was, of course, historically true and no doubt even more evident by the time the Gospel was written.

More than a few preachers (and I count myself among them) have given over portions of their Advent sermons to cautions about too much Christmas holiday spirit and too much Christmas joy too soon. Look, we point out, how at the mall Christmas trees and decorations are up before Thanksgiving. Listen to all the Christmas music and concerts in the first weeks of December. Think of all the people worn out by Christmas shopping and holiday parties before the twenty-fifth rolls around. Yes, we know the economy needs a boost and that Christmas sales account for nearly half of some stores' and businesses' profits, but, for heaven's sake (with a stress on that), whose birthday is it anyway? And how can one celebrate Christmas when the trees go down and the music stops the day after? It seems like the fast food and "I'll have it now" generation(s) don't have much waiting in their bones. And the instant gratification of having Christmas joy before Christmas surely misses the true spirit of Christmas.

What, then, are we to do with the joy—the Good News, liberty, comfort, and gladness—that sounds throughout these lessons? "I will greatly rejoice in the LORD, my whole being shall exult" (Isa. 61:10). "But be glad and rejoice forever . . . Jerusalem as a joy . . . I will rejoice" (Isa. 65:18-19). "My spirit rejoices in God my Savior" (Luke 1:47). "Then our mouth was filled with laughter, and our tongue with shouts of joy" (Ps. 126:2). In response to the Thessalonians' concerns and worries, Paul tells them to "Rejoice always" (1 Thess. 5:16). Even, at least in an alternative Gospel reading, John the Baptist speaks of himself as one who "rejoices greatly at the bridegroom's voice. For this reason my joy has been fulfilled" (John 3:29). Some of that joy has to be heard between the lines of the Fourth Gospel's earlier testimony of John who has come to bear witness to the one whose sandal thong "I am not worthy to untie" (John 1:27), the light coming into the world (1:7-9). I suppose we could call all this *anticipatory* joy. But it seems more than that—more like a secret about what God is up to that believers cannot keep to themselves. It is bursting out.

> I SUPPOSE WE COULD CALL IT ANTICIPATORY JOY. BUT IT SEEMS MORE THAN THAT—MORE LIKE A SECRET ABOUT WHAT GOD IS UP TO THAT BELIEVERS CANNOT KEEP TO THEMSELVES. IT IS BURSTING OUT.

I remember once being told that in Advent ours was *solemn* joy. I think I understood something of what was intended, but I had trouble knowing how I was to hold my face after that. What does solemn joy look like? And how does one do it while saying, "Our mouth was filled with laughter, and our tongues with shouts of joy"?

One of my favorite Christians is Desmond Tutu. He has had, of course, to be brave and persevering and has suffered much with his people. But even during the worst of the struggles with apartheid, Desmond could be counted on to find something humorous in life to smile about. No, maybe not all the time, but regularly when I met him, he seemed to be mirthful. It was as though he knew a secret about God that kept him trusting in God. It was also, if you will, a subversive joy. His opponents didn't know what to do with it or him. He could seem like a prankster who wouldn't let up. His friends and colleagues found it a contagious joy. It kept them going too.

When I went to El Salvador in a time of civil war, friends told me that I would discover God's presence "thick" there. I wasn't sure what they meant until I found myself with people in some tough and even tragic places. They often were praying and singing. God, they believed, was near to them. I said to myself that, with all their strife and poverty, it must seem like Christmas will never come into their lives. It will, at best, always seem like Advent. But, if so, they know Advent joy.

FOURTH SUNDAY IN ADVENT

DECEMBER 22, 2002

REVISED COMMON	EPISCOPAL (BCP)	ROMAN CATHOLIC
2 Sam. 7:1-11, 16	2 Sam. 7:4, 8-16	2 Sam. 7:1-5, 8b-12, 14a, 16
Luke 1:47-55 or Ps. 89:1-4, 19-26	Psalm 132 or 132:8-15	Ps. 89:2-3, 4-5, 27, 29
Rom. 16:25-27	Rom. 16:25-27	Rom. 16:25-27
Luke 1:26-38	Luke 1:26-38	Luke 1:26-38

FIRST READING
2 SAMUEL 7:1-11, 16 (RCL);
2 SAMUEL 7:4, 8-16 (BCP);
2 SAMUEL 7:1-5, 8b-12, 14a, 16 (RC)

Interpreting the Text

This composite passage combines several perspectives and themes. The older story is taken up in the first nine or so verses and, among other things, explains why the temple was not built in David's time. Through the prophet Nathan the Lord tells David that God has no need or particular desire for a house in which to dwell. In v. 8 the Lord of hosts reminds David how God took an obscure lad from the pasture and made him a prince, cutting off his enemies before him. David does not need to build a temple like other kings do (partly to establish their own greatness); God will make for David a great name. Verses 10-11a tell how God is more interested in providing a "place" and security "for my people Israel," while vv. 11b-16 then develop the theme that the "house" God covenants with David to establish will be the dynasty of David through his son Solomon. Into this promise has been supplied in v. 13 the recognition that Solomon did, indeed, build a temple/house for God's name and more than an inference that it was God's will to have this house. The lectionary readings that omit v. 13 avoid the need to take up this complexity on Advent's Fourth Sunday and, instead, allow hearers to concentrate on the promise of God to fulfill the covenant with David—not with a temple, but by establishing his house, kingdom, and throne forever (v. 16).

The entire passage presents us with some of the rich complexities of trying to interpret history and God's will along with the mixed character of human motivation as this is done. At first (v. 3) Nathan tells David the Lord is with him in his plan to build a house for God. David wants to do this to house the Ark of God that he brought to Jerusalem (chap. 6; see also Ps. 132:5 where David vows not to sleep until he has done this), but this is also a way of building his own reputation and influence. Nathan then gets a different slant on God's will. God has no need to be tied down to one place. God is instead on the move and is fully capable of raising up David from the sheepfold, winning a name for him, and making a place for God's people without a temple.

The reading then elaborates on this plan and promise in terms of the Davidic house and dynasty, first, with reference to Solomon to whom God will be like a father. This sonship, however, can also mean chastisement if there is not a son's obedience to God. There is recognition here that things did not finally work out for Solomon or the dynasty. Indeed, later Jesus and then Christians were left wondering just how the covenant and promise were to be fulfilled. How was and is God faithful to the promise?

> GOD IS FULLY CAPABLE OF RAISING UP DAVID FROM THE SHEEPFOLD, WINNING A NAME FOR HIM, AND MAKING A PLACE FOR GOD'S PEOPLE WITHOUT A TEMPLE.

RESPONSIVE READING
LUKE 1:47-55 (RCL)

The Magnificat tells of another of God's servants, chosen from obscurity, for whom God will do great things (v. 49) in God's way. The promise of God "made to our ancestors" (in this case, first to Abraham) "and his descendants forever" is already being fulfilled by filling the hungry and lifting up the lowly. It is being fulfilled in what God is now doing through Mary's pregnancy. Further on in Luke 1:47-55, see the readings for the Third Sunday of Advent.

PSALM 89:1-4, 19-26 (RCL, alt.); PSALM 89:2-3, 4-5, 27, 29 (RC)

Verses 1-2 respond to the reading from Samuel with a song and declaration of God's steadfast love and faithfulness that are to all generations and forever. Verses 3-4 focus this love and faithfulness in the Davidic covenant: "descendants forever," "your throne for all generations." Verses 19-26 elaborate on this vision by telling of how God has chosen and is with David and how the enemies have been crushed (see the enemies having been cut off in 2 Sam. 7:9).

Verses 26–27 are a kind of coronation oracle (cf. Ps. 2:7 and 2 Sam. 7:14). The anointed one is the firstborn to whom God is Father. Verse 29 repeats the theme of v. 4. Although the whole of Psalm 89 is a mixture of praise and lament ("How long, O LORD. . . ," v. 46), foreshadowing what will happen in the crucifixion of the new chosen one, the verses of this lectionary response concentrate on the promise.

PSALM 132 OR 132:8-15 (BCP)

This ceremonial psalm quite possibly had a liturgical setting in a procession commemorating the finding of the Ark in Jaar (v. 6, or Kiriath Jearim where the Philistines had returned it; see 2 Sam. 6:13—7:2) and its then being brought to Jerusalem. Thus in v. 8 the Lord and the Ark of the Lord rise up and go to their resting place. The covenant with David is then remembered and rehearsed and specifically interpreted in terms of God's choosing of Zion and God's residence there and blessing, especially (v. 15) on the poor and needy (as in the Magnificat). Obviously this reading also looks forward to the new chosen one and God dwelling with God's people in Jesus.

SECOND READING
ROMANS 16:25-27

Interpreting the Text

This doxology was added to Paul's long and complex Letter to the Romans by a later disciple who wanted to make reference to several of the great themes of the letter while doing so in language reflective of passages in the probably deutero-Pauline correspondence (Eph. 3:1-13; Col. 1:24-29; 2:2-3). The "mystery that was kept secret ['in silence'] for long ages" is the Christ event in its fullness, including "the proclamation of Jesus Christ . . . made known to all the Gentiles." First, it was "in silence," because God's purposes in Jesus (in "the prophetic writings") could only acquire their true meaning through Jesus and the gospel given to Paul about him along with its proclamation.

All this, Christians now know, was part of the plan and wisdom of the eternal and wise God and of God's purpose and command "to bring about the obedience of faith." This last phrase is interesting in that it exactly repeats Rom. 1:5 (see also 6:16) where, as here, it is explicitly related to the Gentiles, and inevitably brings up the question of how Paul understands faith; that is, whether it is primarily God's faithfulness in Jesus, our response of faith, or some combination of both. One could, for instance, here understand this obedience to be the response of faith or, more probably, the obedience that responds to the faith that the faithful God has made known, especially in Jesus' own faith (fullness). In any event, the verses end in praise, summing up the letter and anticipating the praise and glory of Christmas with a nice Christological flourish. The word(s) (one letter in Greek) "to whom" were probably added and offer the glory more directly to Jesus. But, however that part of the doxology is read, glory is now offered "through Jesus Christ." He is the one in whom and through whom God is best glorified and God's purposes are best made known.

THE GOSPEL
LUKE 1:26-38

Interpreting the Text

"Nothing will be impossible with God" (v. 37), the angel Gabriel tells Mary, reminding of another messenger of the Lord and the words to Abraham (Gen. 18:14) after aged and barren Sarah laughed to think she might yet have a child. The words are also a further link between Gabriel's two annunciations—the first to Zechariah, who wonders how his wife, Elizabeth, can bear a child since they are both getting old. But if having a child at an older age seems like a miracle, how about a virgin conceiving a child?

After noting that various fabulous figures from antiquity were said to have had miraculous births, a number of theologians have attempted to interpret the story of Jesus' birth mythologically or in terms of some more naturalistic understanding. Early Christians, it is suggested, may have misunderstood that Isa. 7:14, used as a prophecy of Jesus' birth, referred initially to a young woman. Later "young woman" came to be translated with a word that meant virgin—*parthenos;* v. 27, a status Mary is said to make explicit in Luke 1:34: "How can this be, since I am a virgin?" In those times, however, to have been betrothed to a man meant that Mary and Joseph could have been living together. Mary then, it is maintained, could have conceived quite naturally. Moreover, it is further argued, wouldn't it be at least as fitting for Jesus to have been conceived as well as born in fully human circumstances? If Joseph were physically Jesus' father, the linking of Jesus' lineage to David through Joseph would make better sense (v. 27; see 2:4).

But that kind of fittingness and sensibility is not Luke's story. He models this annunciation (and the one to Zechariah) after well-known earlier annunciations presaging the births of Isaac, Sampson, and Saul. Here and there one finds patterns of angelic appearance, surprise (fear), reassurance, the announcement of a birth and naming of a child, predictions of the child's future, further objection or concern, more reassurance by word or sign, and a final acceptance. In this case, the miracle of what is to happen is a vital part of the story both for Mary and its hearers. Luke does not tell us, as does Matthew repeatedly, that "this took place to fulfill what had been spoken through the prophet," but the message is clear that this is the culmination of scriptural typologies and prophecies. This is *the* child, and the activity of the Holy Spirit (often with Jesus in Luke's Gospel; see 4:1-2, 14, 18; 10:21) is with Jesus from conception. Jesus, in other words, is to be unique. He will be holy (*hagios;* v. 35). Something new and surprising is happening. The transcendent has entered into human life and history. This message about God's purposefulness is more important to Luke's Gospel than any explanations of how the conception could have happened.

SOMETHING NEW AND SURPRISING IS HAPPENING. THE TRANSCENDENT HAS ENTERED INTO HUMAN LIFE AND HISTORY.

If there were earlier traditions linking the infant Jesus both to the obscure little village of Nazareth (hence "Jesus of Nazareth" or, in some traditions, with other possible implications, "the Nazarene") and to David's home of Bethlehem, Luke responds to them by having the annunciation take place in Nazareth and the birth in Joseph's ancestral home of Bethlehem. The child's name will be Jesus (*Iēsous,* from the ancient Hebrew name Joshua), which means "the Lord saves." He will be great, the Son of the Most High (here not so much a divine title as a designation of relationship; see again 2 Sam. 7:14; Pss. 2:7; 89:26-27), and will inherit the throne of David and fulfill all that earlier hope and promise.

Responding to the Texts

The tension is tangible on the Fourth Sunday of Advent. The expectation has shifted from earlier prophecies and visions of God's coming and hopes for a second coming of Jesus (along with judgment and a new age) to how and when Jesus first came in human life and what this coming tells us of God and God's love and faithfulness. With the prophecies and longings of old to guide us, we sing, "O come, O come, Emmanuel, and ransom captive Israel"; "O come, thou Branch of Jesse's tree . . . thou Key of David . . . Desire of nations . . . bid thou our sad divisions cease, and be thyself our king of peace."

In the year 2002 this Sunday falls on December 22. Tuesday is Christmas Eve. Even the preachers' minds may be more on how we will get the church decorated, and on Christmas homilies, and on all manner of other preparations than this Sunday's message. Should we again tell people to wait—to be expectant? What should that waiting and expectation now be like? Perhaps the examples of David and Mary and of Paul's words to us from Romans give a clue. God's purpose in Jesus, Paul's letter tells us, is "to bring about the obedience of faith" (Rom. 16:26). Whether we understand this as *our* faith (as belief and/or faithfulness) or, more likely intended, obedience to the faith that God has shown us in Jesus, or some combination, we are to be obedient. That obedience involves being willing to pay attention, to will and seek what we believe God wants, to be at the ready. "Here am I, the servant of the Lord," says Mary. "Let it be with me according to your word" (Luke 1:38). Obedience is being in the Lord's service and the service of others for God even if we do not know what this all means or what is to be asked of us.

David tries to offer such obedience even if he has trouble understanding. He wants to build a temple for the presence of God. Why does God not have this as a priority? How will God rather "appoint a place for my people Israel" (2 Sam. 7:10) and keep his covenant promise with David?

We too have trouble understanding. "O come, O come. . . ." But how does God come? When does God come? A son has been promised for a long time. So has a prince of peace. What do we expect to realize again in less than three days?

Bonaventure held that God's center is everywhere and God's circumference nowhere. We cannot define or confine God—certainly not with our religions or temples or, for that matter, our calendars. Yet, as Paul also is reported to have said, God "is not far from each one of us" (Acts 17:27). And sometimes, we are told, God chooses especially to make the divine nearness and presence palpable in human life. Since "nothing will be impossible with God," the manifestation of God's presence will probably next be in a way we are not expecting. What kind of king? What kind of son? What kind of coming?

We must wait expectantly in obedience—attentive to God's ways. Such obedience and attentiveness shapes our expectations. It shapes us to be the kind of people God hopes we are becoming—a servant people ready for God's ways of presence. "O come, O come, Emmanuel."

THE SEASON OF CHRISTMAS

FREDERICK HOUK BORSCH

Introduction

At a meeting of English and German theologians between the two world wars, the English grew restive. One of them finally blurted out, "All you Germans ever talk about is the cross." "And all you English talk about," retorted the Germans, "is the incarnation." We, in our turn, might respond that it is good we have both the cross and the crib. Without the crucifixion and resurrection, the incarnation of God in Jesus would lose its full significance. Unless God were incarnate in Jesus, the

crucifixion and resurrection would lose their saving meaning. Christmas tells us something very important about God's willingness to draw so near to human life as to share in it and to understand from our side, as it were—from the inside, its color and beauty and pageantry, and also its heartbreaks and passions.

William Temple, English theologian and later the Archbishop of Canterbury, maintained that Christianity was the most materialistic of all religions. Every religion can slip into its world-denying mode, separating the spiritual from the material, the soul from the body. But in the incarnation—at the heart of its faith—Christianity tells this story of God embodied, feeling, tasting, breathing, seeing, smelling, fearing, hoping, hearing, and loving with us. This Son, who "is the reflection of God's glory and the exact imprint of God's very being," has "become," as the Letter to the Hebrews puts it, "like his brothers and sisters in every respect, so that he might be a merciful and faithful high priest in the service of God. . . . For we do not have a high priest who is unable to sympathize with our weaknesses, but we have one who in every respect has been tested as we are, yet without sin" (Heb. 1:3; 2:17; 4:15).

Jesus' life began as a baby. In one of my all-time favorite "religious" cartoons, the viewer first notices the beaming face of Mary as she is approached by one of

31

the three wise men. In the wise man's hands is a box of disposable diapers. The anachronism makes us laugh, but we also laugh to think how much Mary would have appreciated such a practical gift, helping her deal with bodily functions as well as all the other parts of life with a new baby.

Christmas gives us much to celebrate, but its story should always come as a surprise: a baby! We thought God might send a mighty one to conquer evil and to save, not a vulnerable infant, one who needed our love and care. The story of Christmas offers much to celebrate with its message of Emmanuel—God with us. But it is also challenging. In the tradition of my church, the day after Christmas is the saint's day for Stephen, the first Christian martyr, stoned to death for his faith. Two days later is called Holy Innocents, the commemoration of all the little ones King Herod was said to have slaughtered when he was trying to kill the baby Jesus. We remember as well all the children killed by war or human indifference. I also know that some people feel lonely and depressed at Christmastime—let down afterward. I recall as a child having fights with my cousins on Christmas afternoon when I was worn out with all the excitement and there were no more presents. Jesus was born into a real world where only our response of love to God's love in us can bring peace and true Christmas joy and love to others.

THE NATIVITY OF OUR LORD I / CHRISTMAS EVE

DECEMBER 24, 2002

REVISED COMMON	EPISCOPAL (BCP)	ROMAN CATHOLIC
Isa. 9:2-7	Isa. 9:2-4, 6-7	Isa. 9:1-6
Psalm 96	Psalm 96	Ps. 96:1-2, 2-3, 11-12, 13
	or 96:1-4, 11-12	
Titus 2:11-14	Titus 2:11-14	Titus 2:11-14
Luke 2:1-14, (15-20)	Luke 2:1-14, (15-20)	Luke 2:1-14

FIRST READING

ISAIAH 9:2-7 (RCL);
ISAIAH 9:2-4, 6-7 (BCP);
ISAIAH 9:1-6 (RC)

Interpreting the Text

This poem of hope and exultation (familiar through Handel's *Messiah,* especially v. 6, and seen by Christians as a prophecy about Jesus) was first composed in a complex historical period when Assyrian armies were invading parts of Israel, and Israel and Judah were falling in and out of alliance and struggling with one another, particularly over the efforts of Judah to stay neutral in relation to Assyria. In Judah, in other words, there were reasons for both hope and fear. At some point in this saga (possibly, although then somewhat out of context with what precedes and follows, at the time of the accession of Hezekiah to the throne in 715 B.C.E. and after the fall of Samaria and the Northern Kingdom), the prophet envisions an ideal king and an "endless peace" (v. 7) that includes justice and righteousness—full fairness and right living. Fulfilling prophecy of old (see above on 2 Sam. 7:1-16 in Fourth Sunday in Advent), this will be the rule and kingdom of David. This rule will be established not by human power but by the "zeal' (jealous love) of the Lord of hosts (as Yahweh also won the victory in the time of Midian, v. 4; see Judg. 7:15-25).

The new reign is the light (v. 2) that now shines in what is otherwise a time and land of darkness. The idealized language may well refer to the hopes for a real king but also goes beyond historical realism in envisioning the perfect king of the future, a messiah. As in 7:14 the prophet may be thinking first of an actual birth, in this case of one who is to be the wondrous king. But this praise is more likely part of a coronation oracle—perhaps with its stylized language (paralleled elsewhere in the region for kings) used at an actual enthronement. The royal one is God's Son (see 2 Sam. 7:14; Ps. 2:7) and is given great names and titles. The new king is not God, strictly speaking, but, because he is related to God in his sonship, he bears titles and has attributes of wisdom (this "wonderful counselor") and of might that are God-like. He is in this sense, "Father for all time" (or perhaps "for a wide realm"). In this new age of a just and righteous peace, "the yoke," "the bar," and the "rod of the oppressor" are all broken, and the trampling boots and bloody garments of war burned up. Then there will be joy as at the time of harvest and victory in battle (v. 3). In the midst of difficulties and continuing political uncertainty, what a vision the prophet offers!

RESPONSIVE READING

PSALM 96 (RCL);
PSALM 96 OR 96:1-4, 11-12 (BCP);
PSALM 96:1-2, 2-3, 11-12, 13 (RC)

The origin of this hymn of praise may have been in a festival that annually celebrated the creation of the world as re-creation and the new enthronement of the Lord as king and creator and judge of all. With a somewhat different verse order, the hymn is also found in 2 Chron. 16:23-33, used there in connection with the procession of the Ark of the Covenant to Jerusalem. One can imagine the call for gift bearing, obeisance, and dancing being acted out liturgically. The cry "The LORD is king" (see Pss. 93:1; 97:1; 99:1) could well have had the force, "The Lord has become king."

The psalm describes, in other words, a new world era. This is why it is "a new song" (v. 1) and is so suitably sung at Christmas and in response to Isa. 9:2-7. Particularly to be noted is the monotheistic (or at least henotheistic) insistence (vv. 4-5) that the Lord is the creator who is more to be feared than the gods of all other people, gods that are but idols. All the families of the peoples are to ascribe glory to him (vv. 7-8), and even all of nature (vv. 11-12) is to rejoice and exult. Here is praise for what God has done, is doing, and will do. Creator and judge, God—in the language of the book of Revelation (1:8)—is "the Alpha and the Omega," the one who has become king for all, "who is and who was and who is to come."

Interpreting the Text

Three themes should be particularly noted in this passage. Hearers of the reading live between the two advents—the two epiphanies (vv. 11–13; note also 1 Tim. 6:14; 2 Tim. 1:10; 4:1). The grace of God has appeared (epiphanied); Jesus has come to "redeem" ("ransom"; Greek *lutromai;* see Mark 10:45; 1 Tim. 2:6). Now disciples, living "in the present age" (v. 12), "wait for the blessed hope and the manifestation [epiphany] of the glory of our great God and Savior, Jesus Christ." The incarnation and ministry of Jesus are here set in the broader context of the whole salvation story.

Echoing the prophecy of Isa. 9:6 (particularly with its title of "Mighty God" for the wonderful ruler), Jesus is here called "our great God and Savior." Although it is rare in the New Testament to refer to Jesus directly as God (see John 1:1; Rom. 9:5; Heb. 1:8), and it is possible here to translate "of the glory *(doxa)* of the great God and our Savior, Jesus Christ," the author probably has named Jesus God, although without all the implications of later Christological reflection.

Titus was a follower and companion of Paul, who, this letter tells us, was left behind to continue his ministry in Crete. The pastoral epistles of Timothy and Titus, whether written in their lifetimes or by later disciples teaching what they believed Paul would teach were he still alive, are concerned with right Christian living and good deeds "in the present age." The grace of God, which has appeared (i.e., the gracious act of God in Jesus rather than Paul's more dynamic use of grace) has brought salvation (from the same root as the word *savior*) to all (see 1 Tim. 2:6; 4:10). This grace *trains* (we might say *forms*) disciples "to renounce impiety and worldly passions and to live lives that are self-controlled, upright and godly." The themes of redemption from iniquity and of purification, along with being zealous for good works, are set out again in Titus 2:14 and presented as what God does to make a people of God's own. The language reminds one of 1 Pet. 2:1-5, 9-10, and there as here may have been associated with baptism. The virtues named may not seem as heroic as those involved in the giving away of all one's possessions or martyrdom, but they are the solid and lasting virtues that are to inform Christian living between the two epiphanies.

THE GOSPEL

LUKE 2:1-14, (15-20) (RCL, BCP);
LUKE 2:1-14 (RC)

Interpreting the Text

Simple glory! In three richly textured scenes, Luke presents the story of how, in history seen in both secular and divine perspective, a child was born in humble circumstances while the glory of the Lord shone round and a multitude of the heavenly hosts sang. Verses 1-7 tell of the birth. The second scene (vv. 8-14) describes the annunciation (following the earlier angelic annunciations to Zechariah and Mary) by the angels. In scene three (vv. 15-20) the shepherds come to see the sign of the child lying in a manger and to tell what they had heard and seen. It is a birth, as Luke has already told us it would be, both natural and supernatural—happening on earth, while heaven draws near. The action and purpose of God intersect human history. (Note how this intersection is presented in Luke 3:1-6 as well.) While the births of other great figures of this era were also accompanied by supernatural signs, Luke presents the birth of Jesus as unique.

> IT IS A BIRTH, AS LUKE HAS ALREADY TOLD US IT WOULD BE, BOTH NATURAL AND SUPER-NATURAL—HAPPENING ON EARTH, WHILE HEAVEN DRAWS NEAR.

Although interesting attempts have been made to reconcile the problem created by these first verses regarding the date of Jesus' birth, the evangelist was far more concerned with the theological and symbolic significance of his narrative than our understanding of historical accuracy. Both Matthew and Luke (1:5) indicate that these events took place during the lifetime of King Herod, who died in 4 B.C.E., while Quirinius did not become the Roman legate, or governor, of Syria until A.D. 6. Josephus also knew about some form of enrollment about this time (note also Acts 5:37). While it is possible that Luke is referring to some other unknown or little known registration for a census, his primary interest, after noting the secular time period, is to give the reason for bringing the couple to Bethlehem, the city of David, in which it had been prophesied the Davidic king would be born. Although Mic. 5:2 is not quoted by Luke, its echo would have been in the ears of the hearers of the time: "But you, O Bethlehem of Ephrathah, who are one of the little clans of Judah, from you shall come forth for me one who is to rule in Israel, whose origin is from of old, from ancient days."

The contract of betrothal (Luke 2:5) was in many ways more important than marriage itself. Luke understands that Mary conceived as a virgin (1:34; and see above in Fourth Sunday in Advent in this regard), but Joseph, who represents the Davidic lineage, is the father in every other way. The term *firstborn (prototokos),* which would come to have later Christian significance for Jesus as the divine Son (cf. Col. 1:15, 18; Heb. 1:6; Rev. 1:5), has a rich Jewish background for one who is the heir and favored child and the child especially devoted to God who must be redeemed (Exod. 13:1-2, 12-13; see also its use in Luke 2:23).

Because there was no room for the family "in the guest room," the birth took place where the animals were kept. This circumstance, together with the awareness that shepherds were often poor and looked down upon because their outdoor and regularly nomadic work meant they could not fulfill many religious observances, has led to interpretations of Luke's narrative that stress the poverty surrounding Jesus' birth in the spirit of 2 Cor. 8:9: "for your sake he became poor." Luke has a special concern for the poor (see 4:18; 14:13, 21). It could also be, however, that Luke's primary interest is in describing the peculiarity of the nativity's location as it was dictated by circumstances, and that several of the details are meant to show how well the baby was cared for despite these circumstances.

Shepherds, in any event, would not have been the first people one would think of as witnesses of this glory and sign. The angel's words ("Do not be afraid . . . I am bringing good news of great joy") recall similar words to Zechariah and Elizabeth, especially in the manner in which initial awe and fear must be overcome with joy (a significant Lucan motif). The glory *(doxa)* shining about the shepherds is reminiscent of the salvation glory in Exod. 16:7, 10; 24:17.

There is a textual variant and several possible translations to deal with in v. 14. The peace on earth "among those whom [God] favors" is almost surely Luke's intent rather than a suggestion that it is the goodwill of humans that helps bring this peace about. Further on vv. 15-20, see the Nativity of Our Lord II, Christmas Dawn.

Responding to the Texts

Simple glory! The seeming oxymoron captures the spirit of Christmas: "Silent night" and "Hark! the herald angels sing"; "O little town of Bethlehem" and "Angels from the realms of glory"; "Once in royal David's city stood a lowly cattle shed," and "Joy to the world! . . . repeat, repeat the sounding joy." Joy sounds throughout our readings: "You have increased [the nation's] joy; they rejoice before you as with joy at the harvest" (Isa. 9:3). "Worship the LORD in holy splendor. . . . Let the heavens be glad . . . let the field exult, and everything in it. Then shall all the trees of the forest sing for joy" (Ps. 96:9, 11-12). "I am bringing you good news of great joy" (Luke 2:10).

Joy comes because "the grace of God has appeared," enabling disciples to "wait for the blessed hope and the manifestation of the glory of our great God and Savior, Jesus Christ" (Titus 2:11, 13). This is the "Wonderful Counselor, Mighty God, Everlasting Father, Prince of Peace" (Isa. 9:6) foreseen from long ago.

"Declare his glory among the nations. . . . Ascribe to the LORD glory and strength. Ascribe to the LORD the glory due his name" (Ps. 96:3, 7-8). "The glory of the Lord shone around them," and the heavenly hosts sing, "Glory to God in the highest heaven" (Luke 2:9, 13-14).

Yet the glory comes to the shepherds in the night. The light that shines is seen by a "people who walked in darkness." It shines on "those who lived in a land of deep darkness" (Isa. 9:2) and, as the hymn would have it, "how silently, how silently, the wondrous gift is given!" An exclamation point follows the *silentlies!* The message is heard out in a field by shepherds. Light shines in darkness. Emmanuel lies in a manger.

There is still darkness in our world, and the retelling of the story of the birth of Jesus—sandwiched between the tinsel and toys and the ongoing terrors and tragedies of life—may come to seem like just a sweet story from the past. Preachers might, in turn, want to tell their stories of how the spirit of the one born to be the crucified and loving Lord (the lowly one who brings great hope while glory shines in the night) will cause us to sing in hope and adoration and still be "zealous for good deeds" (Titus 2:14). I love to remember some of my first Christmases. We would drive the ninety miles south from Chicago to the town of 650 people where my mother was born. With some other cousins and aunts and uncles, we would stay in my grandparents' large house that was also a funeral home. My grandfather was an undertaker, and upstairs, just off the hallway where I sometimes slept on a cot, empty coffins were on display. Downstairs in the middle parlor, or in the back parlor behind, even at Christmastime, there could be a body in the coffin that had been chosen for it. In the days after Christmas, families would then come for the viewing. The service might be held in that middle parlor. I could sometimes hear them whispering and sobbing.

> PREACHERS MIGHT WANT TO TELL THEIR STORIES OF HOW THE SPIRIT OF THE ONE BORN TO BE THE CRUCIFIED AND LOVING LORD (THE LOWLY ONE WHO BRINGS GREAT HOPE WHILE GLORY SHINES IN THE NIGHT) WILL CAUSE US TO SING IN HOPE AND ADORATION AND STILL BE "ZEALOUS FOR GOOD DEEDS."

I yet remember those Christmases with happiness. One thing I think I began to understand is that good things—even important things—can happen in small ways. We sang "O Little Town of Bethlehem" and retold the story of the tiny baby in the manger. There were also angels singing from on high and wise men coming from afar, but one could not miss the point of the apparent insignificance of it all in that stable in out-of-the-way Bethlehem or, for that matter, that little town in central Illinois.

There was something solemn about those Christmases too. The sliding doors to the rear parlor might be shut because a body was "at rest" there. One Christmas night, after all the children were finally in bed, I heard my grandfather back the hearse down the driveway to go out into the darkness on one of those necessary errands of his. I was already beginning to understand that Christmas does not come apart from tears. The deepest meaning of the joy and glory of "God is with us"—of Emmanuel—would have to happen in that home with its caskets and presents, all my relatives and the bodies at rest, the hymns and the hugs, the feasting and love and sobbing.

THE NATIVITY OF OUR LORD II / CHRISTMAS DAWN

DECEMBER 25, 2002

REVISED COMMON	EPISCOPAL (BCP)	ROMAN CATHOLIC
Isa. 62:6-12	Isa. 62:6-7, 10-12	Isa. 62:11-12
Psalm 97	Psalm 97 or	Ps. 97:1, 6, 11-12
	Ps. 96:1-4, 11-12	
Titus 3:4-7	Titus 3:4-7	Titus 3:4-7
Luke 2:(1-7), 8-20	Luke 2:(1-14), 15-20	Luke 2:15-20

FIRST READING

ISAIAH 62:6-12 (RCL);
ISAIAH 62:6-7, 10-12 (BCP);
ISAIAH 62:11-12 (RC)

Interpreting the Text

Jerusalem's approaching vindication is so near that it seems already begun. Not infrequently in these portions of Isaiah it is difficult to tell whether the voice of the prophet or the Lord through the prophet is speaking. The opening of v. 6 might seem to be the Lord's words, commissioning the ever vigilant and never silent watchmen. Then the second part of v. 6, and more certainly v. 7, sounds like the prophet telling the watchmen to keep the people in remembrance of the Lord. They are to take no rest in doing this and give the Lord no rest until God fulfills the promise to establish Jerusalem and make it a city of universal praise. The admonishment to give God no rest may sound rather daring, but it is not unlike the sometimes hectoring and pestering voice of the psalmist (e.g., "Rouse yourself! Why do you sleep, O LORD?" Ps. 44:23). Watchmen were obviously important figures for the security and defense of a city, and one hears of them elsewhere in Isaiah (21:6-7; 52:8; see 40:9) and in some of the other prophets (e.g., Ezek. 3:16-21; 33:1-9; Hab. 2:1), where they often are surrogates for the mission of the prophets.

Verse 8a then reminds of the Lord's oath by means of God's right hand and mighty arm (see Exod. 6:6; Deut. 4:34; Isa. 51:5, 9). God's response is found in vv. 8-9. Foreigners (foreign armies and the like) will not eat the people's grain or drink their wine. These will be for the people who have grown them and labored for them. The reference to the drinking of wine "in my holy courts" has led to the reasonable suggestion that the Feast of Tabernacles is in mind.

Verses 10-12 are a culmination of the whole chapter and much of this portion of Isaiah. Verse 10 could refer to the processional entrance of the Ark (note the liturgical force and excitement of the double imperatives) and is also reminiscent of Isa. 40:3-4: "Make straight in the desert a highway for our God" and of the people's return from exile. The salvation/victory coming to them will again be known throughout the world. God brings both reward and recompense (repayment for past suffering; see 40:10), and the people's new status is established with new names. As in 62:4, when "Forsaken" and "Desolate" become "My Delight Is in Her" and "Married" (recall Abram becoming Abraham and Jacob becoming Israel in Gen. 17:5 and 32:28, and Simon becoming Peter in Matt. 16:18), the four new names in v. 12 ("Sought Out" seeming to be the most tender) not only describe the new situation but are full of promise and of new relationship with God.

RESPONSIVE READING
PSALM 97 (RCL, BCP);
PSALM 97:1, 6, 11-12 (RC)

As is true of Psalm 96, this is a hymn to the kingship of God. The opening shout, especially if the psalm was once used liturgically (perhaps in an annual renewal festival), could well have the force, "The Lord has become king!" The very earth is to rejoice in response. In language familiar from other psalms (see 18:7-15; 29:3-9; 50:3) the approach of God is like the coming of a great thunderstorm—lightning flashing all around and the earth trembling. But it is *chesed* and *emunah,* God's righteousness and justice, that are the foundation—the basis— of God's throne, God's rule and right to rule. The greatness of God puts down all worship of other gods (mere idols; see Ps. 96:5). The worshipers of other gods are ashamed, and all other gods bow down (v. 7), perhaps also acted out liturgically. In v. 8 it is Jerusalem's turn to respond with joy because of God's righteousness and judgment. The towns of Judah around Jerusalem join in. Verse 10 promises that the lives of those who hate evil and are faithful will be protected. They have nothing to fear from the wicked. Now light appears and there is joy for the righteous. It is a new day and a new time. As Christmas day dawns, Christian worshipers also join in with their joy and thanks.

NOW LIGHT APPEARS AND THERE IS JOY FOR THE RIGHTEOUS. IT IS A NEW DAY AND A NEW TIME. AS CHRISTMAS DAY DAWNS, CHRISTIAN WORSHIPERS ALSO JOIN IN WITH THEIR JOY AND THANKS.

SECOND READING

TITUS 3:4-7

Interpreting the Text

The reading should begin with v. 3. This provides the start of the before/now pattern (see Eph. 2:1-10 and cf. Rom. 6:17-18; 1 Cor. 6:9-11; Col. 3:7-8). Once we were foolish, disobedient, deceived, and enslaved by all kinds of passions (v. 3), but now that God's love and kindness have saved us, all is changed. The stress on the power of God's love, "not because of any works of righteousness that we had done" (v. 5) but "having been justified by his grace" (v. 7), is Pauline. While the letter is almost surely written by a later disciple, the author may be incorporating earlier materials or at least ideas. "The saying is sure" in v. 8 (used elsewhere in 1 and 2 Timothy) may indicate that parts or all of vv. 3-7 are being quoted, possibly coming from a baptismal formula. Certainly the "water of rebirth" (one could translate "the washing of regeneration") refers to the washing away of sin and the new life of baptism as does the "renewal by the Holy Spirit" that is "poured out on us richly through Jesus Christ our Savior." Indeed, the passage has a more than incipient trinitarian character. While what "appears" (the *epiphany* of v. 4) is God's love and kindness, the whole of what God has manifested is made known in the rebirth and renewal by the Holy Spirit and through Jesus Christ. This not only brings about a new kind of life but makes disciples "heirs according to the hope of eternal life" (v. 7).

From a trinitarian and Christological perspective, it is also interesting to notice on Christmas morning how both God and Jesus Christ are "our Savior." While the designation "Savior" is certainly known in the Hebrew scriptures, it also came to be an important title for Hellenistic gods and emperors. In the Pastoral Epistles, where it is used of God (here and in 1 Tim. 1:1; 2:3; 4:10; Titus 1:3; 2:10) and also of Jesus (here and in 2 Tim. 1:10; Titus 1:4; 2:13), one might sense a kind of confessional insistence, that is, "not Caesar, not other gods, but our Savior God and our Savior Jesus Christ."

CHRISTMAS, WITH ITS MESSAGE OF THE BIRTH OF THE INCARNATE ONE, IS THE FOUNDATION AND REASON FOR OUR REBIRTH AND OUR HOPE.

The Letter to Titus is concerned with sound and proper living—the doing of good and avoidance of evil. It is, the passage reminds us, God's goodness and loving-kindness through Jesus that makes such renewal and our hope in eternal life possible. Christmas, with its message of the birth of the incarnate one, is the foundation and reason for our rebirth and our hope.

LUKE 2:(1-7), 8-20 (RCL);
LUKE 2:(1-14), 15-20 (BCP);
LUKE 2:15-20 (RC)

Interpreting the Text

Most liturgists and preachers are more likely to use the whole of Luke 2:1-20, or at least vv. 8-20, rather than just vv. 15-20 at this service. For a commentary on vv. 1-14, see the interpretation above for Christmas Eve I.

Luke 2:1-20 is a story, or more like a play (a Christmas pageant!), told in three scenes. In the middle scene the klieg lights of glory shine on the shepherds in the field. Now the shepherds return to that part of the set where wait Mary and Joseph and the baby wrapped with bands of cloth in an animal's manger for a crib.

The shepherds, who were at first terror-stricken, go eagerly ("with haste") into Bethlehem to see this "sign" (v. 12) signaling "good news of great joy" (v. 10). The klieg lights are off now. It will take eyes of faith to see that this humble scene of the little family without a home is the center of divine activity and that the baby is the promised sign. The shepherds become witnesses of what they have seen and heard. The "all" of v. 18 suggests that at least a small group were now gathered around the family. One can imagine that they would have been amazed, perhaps not knowing how to take in what the shepherds were telling them, while the shepherds, after returning to their fields and work, cannot do other than continue to echo the heavenly host of v. 14 by praising and glorifying God.

> IT WILL TAKE EYES OF FAITH TO SEE THAT THIS HUMBLE SCENE OF THE LITTLE FAMILY WITHOUT A HOME IS THE CENTER OF DIVINE ACTIVITY AND THAT THE BABY IS THE PROMISED SIGN.

Then there is Mary, left with the baby to protect and care for. She remembers the angel who had come to her. She treasures the words of the shepherds' angels (in a sermon one might compare the treasures brought by the Magi) and ponders them. Indeed! What will all this mean for her child and for her? What is God up to? Again in Luke 2:51, after the twelve-year-old Jesus explains his absence from his parents while he was three days in the temple, Mary "treasured all these things in her heart." What is the meaning of Gabriel's assurance to her that she had "found favor with God" (Luke 1:30), and what will the angels' song of glory and peace portend? What manner of glory?

Responding to the Texts

Many a good sermon puts members of the congregation in the shoes of the figures in the biblical story. Instead of sitting in the pew, one is invited to go out into the chilly, nighttime fields and enter into the stable. Indeed, many of us remember dressing up as children to do just that in some church chancel. We put on our shepherd's bathrobes, or angel-wings were fastened to us by Mrs. Humphries. Maybe when we were older, we were lucky enough to be Mary or the silent, solemn Joseph. We were nearly blinded by the bright lights while the choir and congregation sang "Hark! the Herald Angels Sing." Later we peered into the manger-like crib with its doll baby Jesus, perhaps wondering what swaddling clothes were and, in our own way, amazed and pondering the meaning of it all.

Mary becomes a kind of model disciple, treasuring the shepherds' words and seeking to grow in her faith and understanding, which will be severely tested in the years to come. The shepherds are model believers who, despite their initial terror and awe, respond with haste to go see Jesus. They then leave praising and glorifying God. How do we react and respond to what we have seen and heard?

Our major way of responding to the appearance of "the goodness and loving kindness of God our Savior," the Letter to Titus reminds us, is through our baptism: "the water of rebirth and renewal by the Holy Spirit." "According to God's mercy," we have "been justified by God's grace" and "become heirs according to the hope of eternal life" (i.e., the life that truly matters and endures). In thanksgiving for this mercy and graciousness, we promise to turn from evil ways (proscribed several times in this letter). In the baptismal covenant of the *Book of Common Prayer,* disciples promise "to renounce the evil powers of this world which corrupt and destroy the creatures of God" and "all sinful desires that draw you from the love of God." Followers of Jesus will be "zealous for good deeds" (Titus 2:14), "seeking to serve Christ in all persons, loving your neighbor as yourself," and striving "for justice and peace among all people" while respecting "the dignity of every human being" (BCP, p. 305). These surely are the Christmas gifts that most offer praise and glory to God and are the further signs of God's peace.

In many cultures at the rebirth of baptism, and on other occasions of renewal, a person may take on a new name to signify new life and sense of purpose. At birth Jesus can be thought of as receiving many new names and titles. The name Jesus itself means "God saves," and he is also "a Savior, who is the Messiah, the Lord" (Luke 2:11). He is to be called "Emmanuel," which means "God is with us" (Matt 1:23). In the prophetic words of Isa. 9:6, he is "Wonderful Counselor, Mighty God, Everlasting Father, Prince of Peace." And in this morning's first reading, the people of God are also given new names to celebrate God's graciousness. They are now "The Holy People, The Redeemed of the LORD, Sought Out, A City Not Forsaken" (v. 12). Perhaps the preacher could ask the people what new name they would like today—for themselves individually and/or as a congregation to tell of their joy and sense of renewal. I would like to be called "Sought Out." I hear the Christmas story; I sing its hymns and know again how "the goodness and loving-kindness of God our Savior [has] appeared" to be "God is with us," to be "Prince of Peace," in God's surprising way as a baby, as one who would give himself for me and for us. No wonder the angels are singing!

THE NATIVITY OF OUR LORD III / CHRISTMAS DAY

DECEMBER 25, 2002

REVISED COMMON	EPISCOPAL (BCP)	ROMAN CATHOLIC
Isa. 52:7-10	Isa. 52:7-10	Isa. 52:7-10
Psalm 98	Psalm 98 or 98:1-6	Ps. 98:1, 2-3, 3-4, 5-6
Heb. 1:1-4, (5-12)	Heb. 1:1-12	Heb. 1:1-6
John 1:1-14	John 1:1-14	John 1:1-18 or 1:1-5, 9-14

FIRST READING

ISAIAH 52:7-10

Interpreting the Text

In the opening scene (v. 7) one sees the messenger coming over the mountains (high hills) to Jerusalem to bring the message of Good News (see Isa. 40:9) and peace. He announces the salvation of God's victory, saying, "Your God reigns." Because of this message, and perhaps because he is splendidly fleet of foot, the very feet of the messenger (see also Nah. 1:15) are "beautiful" (quoted by Paul in Rom. 10:15).

In the next scene (v. 8) one is to imagine the sentinels or watchmen on the ruined walls of the city. (On the important role of watchmen in the prophetic writings and as surrogates for the prophets, see above on Isa. 62:6-12 in Christmas I). The message of God's victory is that the people are coming home from exile and their victorious God with them. God has brought salvation with his "holy arm" (v. 10—often synecdoche for God's might; see, e.g., the commentary on Ps. 98:1 below; Deut. 26:8). Now with their own eyes the sentinels see what is taking place, and together they sing. (On "comfort" for God's people, see also the announcement of Isa. 40:1.) In v. 9 Jerusalem itself—even its very ruins—joins in the singing, for in v. 10 it is affirmed that all this is being done before the whole world—"The ends of the earth shall see the salvation of our God." Anticipating the responsorial psalm, all are singing for joy because of God's kingship and salvation. With a kind of double vision Christians make this end of exile and homecoming of God part of their own Emmanuel—"God is with us"—music.

PSALM 98 (RCL);
PSALM 98 or 98:1-6 (BCP);
PSALM 98:1, 2-3, 3-4, 5-6 (RC)

The language of Psalm 98 is not only a fitting response to Isa. 52:7-10, but it repeats themes and images found there and at other places in Isaiah 40–55. As in Isa. 52:7-10, it is God's arm that has won the victory of salvation, and "all the ends of the earth have seen the victory of our God" (Ps. 98:3). God's marvelous deeds go all the way back to Exodus and the salvation from slavery in Egypt, but certainly the return from exile is very much in mind as well. In all this God's *chesed* ("steadfast love") and *emunah* ("faithfulness") toward God's people are especially to be remembered.

As in Ps. 96:1 the song is new because of the new circumstances in which it is sung—the new hope it brings. Verses 1-3 recall God's acts and offer praise. Verses 4-6 call the people to join in with instruments, no doubt during some period in the use of the psalm, in actual temple worship. Verses 7-9 remind us that this is also a God who comes to judge in righteousness and with equity, and all of nature and "all who live in it" are bid to join in song. As the floods are invited to clap their hands and the hills sing for joy, Christmas churchgoers are themselves well prepared to break into "Joy to the world! The Lord is come . . . while fields and floods, rocks, hills, and plains repeat the sounding joy."

SECOND READING
HEBREWS 1:1-4, (5-12) (RCL);
HEBREWS 1:1-12 (BCP);
HEBREWS 1:1-6 (RC)

Interpreting the Text

Whether only the first several verses or the whole of this passage is read in the liturgy, it would be wise to find the congregation's best reader for this well-structured and eloquent declaration of Christ's sonship (vv. 1-4) and demonstration of his supremacy over angels (vv. 4-14). Verses 1-4, nicely broken up into three sentences by the NRSV, are one long, sonorous sentence in the Greek. As with vv. 5-14, it has been suggested that vv. 2-4, or parts thereof, come from an earlier hymn or formulary, perhaps once in praise of Wisdom (cf. Wisd. of Sol. 7:22-30; Prov. 8:30) or the Word (*logos;* see the commentary on John 1:1-4 below) as semi-personified attributes of God. If this be so (and there are at the last strong parallels with the thought and language of the Jewish philosopher-exegete Philo of Alexandria), it only furthers the author's argument that in Jesus God has brought to fruition all past anticipatory revelation. In his reference to "many and various ways," the author is suggesting that, although valuable, there is an incomplete and varied character in God's revelation through the prophets. Now, in the final stage of history, "he has spoken to us by a Son . . . [who] is the reflection [probably better than a more active translation like "effulgence"] of God's glory and the exact imprint of God's very being" (Greek *hypostasis,* adumbrating later Christological debate). This imprint (Greek *character,* a word used by Philo of the *logos*) would be the exact stamp made by a signet in a clay impression. One thinks of the "image" *(eikon)* of God in Col. 1:15-20 where there is also (as in John 1:1-4) a developed Christology regarding Jesus' role in creation. Hebrews 1:3 emphasizes, as well, that the Son has a continuing role in creation as he "sustains [or "bears along"] all things." He does this "by his powerful word" (or "speech," not *logos,* but clearly alluding to Genesis 1; cf. Ps. 33:6, 9).

In these remarkable verses, in which nearly every word is packed with significance, we also learn of the Son's role in redemption through the purification of sins. This more cultic language will be developed throughout the epistle in terms of Jesus' role as the superior high priest "forever." After he had completed this purification, he was given his place "at the right hand of the Majesty on high" (v. 3; see also v. 13, used frequently in early Christian acclamations of Jesus' ascension; cf. Ps. 110:1).

The author next turns to the demonstration, by means of a catena of seven quotations from the Hebrew scriptures, that this Son is superior to all angels. One has to assume that there were contemporaries of the author who were giving exalted roles to angels and perhaps viewing Jesus as one of them or like them (cf. the "rulers and authorities" of Col. 2:15). No, the author argues through the words of scripture and sometimes the very voice of God in them, angels, who are not everlasting and who are not called Son but who are to worship the one who is Son, are inferior in every way. The thrust of the argument is to exalt the role and status of the Son (not actually named as Jesus until 2:9).

THE GOSPEL
JOHN 1:1-14 (RCL, BCP);
JOHN 1:1-18 OR 1:1-5, 9-14 (RC)

Interpreting the Text

This sometimes lyric passage is potent with significant themes and phrases that, except for the word "Word" *(logos)* itself, will echo and be developed throughout John's Gospel: light, darkness, life, true, truth, world, born, blood, flesh. The passage is also tough and demanding, forged not just in the head of a poet and theologian but among people with different understandings and beliefs. Light struggles with darkness, acceptance with nonacceptance. There are questions about who John is and who Jesus is. Believers are not born of the will of the flesh, but believe in the Word who became flesh. The world does not know him, but he has made known in the world the unseen God. And throughout, hearers are being asked what they believe about this witness.

Much of the structure and wording of the passage, apart from the obvious prose insertions of vv. 6-8 and v. 15 regarding the ministry of John the Baptist (on which see the interpretation of the Gospel reading for the Third Sunday in Advent), are thought to have come from an earlier poem about the *logos* of God—a poem that may have had Hellenistic as well as Jewish influences. *Logos* played an important role in both Greek philosophy (as the mind or intelligence of God become immanent in the rationality, order, and harmony of the universe) and in Jewish thought and speculative reflection on the creative Word of God (see again Genesis 1; Ps. 33:6-9). Jewish and Hellenistic ideas are married in the writings of Philo of Alexandria (see the commentary above on Heb. 1:1-14). If this evangelist made use of such a poem, he, probably along with his tradition, has infiltrated and adapted it for the story of and teaching about Jesus.

Despite its apparent simplicity and because it is poetic language, the passage presents ideas that are often not easy to pin down, especially in a Gospel that will use double meanings and deliberate misunderstandings of words to advance its themes. *En archē* = "In the beginning" is an obvious allusion to Gen. 1:1, but *archē* can also have the sense of first cause and can mean "ruler," "authority," and "domain" as well. In gnostic lore, and even in New Testament times, it came to refer to angelic and demonic powers. This *logos* was "with *(pros)* God" and "was in the beginning with *(pros)* God." The Greek word *pros* can mean "with" in a rather stationary sense or imply something more dynamic like "toward" God. In any case, what does it mean to be *with* God? This might seem to be cleared up when we read the evidently unambiguous "and the Word was God," but it is possible that here the inference is something more like "divine" than complete identity with God. And then see the several alternative translations in vv. 3-4, 9, and 14 in the marginal readings.

Perhaps on Christmas Day there seems little point in the preacher worrying about any of these nuances and variant translations, but it is a reminder of what the evangelist knew well: just as the Word is powerful, words are powerful. They have nuances and figurative as well as more literal meanings. They are even worth fighting over, especially if one wants to convey theological meaning. Care needs to be taken in how they are heard and used.

The life of this Word was light for all people, but, although he came into the world as the Word become flesh, among his own he was not known or accepted. Only to those who believed (the evangelist knows these were for the most part Gentiles rather than Jewish people) did he give power to become children of God. But this was by the will of God and not human activity.

The Fourth Gospel does not have a birth narrative. Likely the evangelist did not wish to think in terms of a particular moment when the Word became incarnate, especially as a baby, but the basic theological fact is still central to this Gospel: The Word that was with God, through whom all things came into being, "became flesh and lived among us." This is John's Christmas story, and this is why we read the prologue to this Gospel on this morning.

THE WORD THAT WAS WITH GOD, THROUGH WHOM ALL THINGS CAME INTO BEING, "BECAME FLESH AND LIVED AMONG US." THIS IS JOHN'S CHRISTMAS STORY, AND THIS IS WHY WE READ THE PROLOGUE TO THIS GOSPEL ON THIS MORNING.

Evidently there were some among the early Christians who had their doubts and objections (see 1 John 4:2). How could the Word who was and is of God, and who is the life principle of the universe, become flesh? Why would the Word want to? What would this do to the Word to become part of human frailty and transience? Perhaps, for our sakes, the Word only appeared to do this.

"The Word became *sarx*," the evangelist insists, "and lived among us, and we have seen [in this flesh] his glory, the glory as of a father's only son, full of grace and truth" (v. 14). "From his fullness *(pleroma)* we have all received, grace upon grace" (v. 15). The grace that came through the law of Moses has been fulfilled, and he has added his new grace and truth. It is the only Son, the unique one of God, who in human flesh has made known the unseen God.

Responding to the Texts

The wonder and mystery of Christmas can be presented as a story about a child's lowly birth or in more theological terms. This morning's readings from the opening chapters of the Gospel of John and the Letter to the Hebrews invite us to think in theological language: the Word who was with God, through whom all things come into being, became flesh, making known the unseen God. He is God's Son, "the reflection of God's glory and the exact imprint of God's very being" (Heb. 1:3), "through whom he also created the worlds" (1:2), and who, we are later told, became "like his brothers and sisters in every respect" (2:17).

The advantage of story is that it can be remembered and catch the heart and imagination in a way that more reflective language may not. Hearers are invited into the narrative to make something of its significance for themselves. As Emily Dickinson put it: "Tell all the truth, but tell it slant / Success in circuit lies." The danger, however, is that Christmas churchgoers might feel merely sentimental about the manger, shepherds, and angels and miss much of what is being said. This is where John and Hebrews can come in. In the same way that a Savior, who is the Messiah, the Lord (Luke 2:11), came in the obscurity of a baby's birth, so the life and light of all people was *hidden* in flesh. This is scandalous! This is amazing. This is, in flesh, the Word of God, the exact imprint of God's very being, become flesh for us. How does that grab you? What does that tell you about God, our world, and your life?

When the message of the incarnate God as "God with us" is believed and affirmed, there then is reason to take up the joyful language of Isa. 52:7-10, Psalm 98, and the Christmas hymns: "O sing to the Lord a new song." "Make a joyful noise to the Lord, all the earth." "Joy to the world . . . let heaven and nature sing." "How beautiful upon the mountains are the feet of the messenger who announces peace, who brings good news, who announces salvation." "Go tell it on the mountain, over the hills and everywhere; go tell it on the mountain, that Jesus Christ is born!" And is this not the preacher's deepest hope—that people will go forth from the Christmas liturgy with joy and good news that they want to share with others?

THIS IS, IN FLESH, THE WORD OF GOD, THE EXACT IMPRINT OF GOD'S VERY BEING, BECOME FLESH FOR US. HOW DOES THAT GRAB YOU? WHAT DOES THAT TELL YOU ABOUT GOD, OUR WORLD, AND YOUR LIFE?

Maybe these churchgoers will want to tell others the story or offer their reflections on it. Perhaps they will struggle with words, as these lessons do, to find the images that point to the wonder and mystery of God among us. Perhaps they will do so with familiar hymns as new songs. Perhaps, after hearing of the glory light that shone around the shepherds, and of the one who is the Light of the world and the reflection of God's glory, and having seen all the Christmas lights, they will go home and want to light candles for the one who is the light that shines in the darkness, the true light, which enlightens everyone. In some classroom they may have learned that light, which scientists still struggle to understand, is silent and itself invisible. It becomes known when it shines on something. It first began to shine after the creation of the world. That creation light is still reaching out in the universe. It is the light of life. And now it has shined among us and in our hearts and minds—enlightening our lives. "I want to walk as a child of the light. . . . Shine in my heart, Lord Jesus."

FIRST SUNDAY AFTER CHRISTMAS / HOLY FAMILY

DECEMBER 29, 2002

REVISED COMMON	EPISCOPAL (BCP)	ROMAN CATHOLIC
Isa. 61:10—62:3	Isa. 61:10—62:3	Sir. 3:2-7; 12–14 or Gen. 15:1-6; 21:1-3
Psalm 148	Psalm 147 or 147:13-21	Ps. 128:1-2, 3, 4-5 or Ps. 105:1-2, 3-4, 6-7, 8-9
Gal. 4:4-7	Gal. 3:23-25; 4:4-7	Col. 3:12-21 or 3:12-17 or Heb. 11:8, 11-12, 17-19
Luke 2:22-40	John 1:1-18	Luke 2:22-40 or 2:22, 39-40

The First Sunday after Christmas, which is observed as the festival day of the Holy Family of Jesus, Mary, and Joseph in the Roman Catholic Church, might seem a bit of a letdown after all the celebration of Christmas—something like the Second Sunday of Easter. But it can be not only a wonderful day to continue singing the Christmas hymns and to enjoy the Christmas decorations, but also a time to be more reflective about the meaning of Christmas and its significance for our lives.

FIRST READING
ISAIAH 61:10—62:3 (RCL, BCP)

Interpreting the Text

Isaiah 61:10-11 is also read on the Third Sunday in Advent. There these verses sound more expectant, while in the Christmas season they are heard with a sense of what God has done. They are words of joy proclaimed by the prophet speaking for the whole community of Jerusalem. Verse 10 likens the imagery of being clothed with the splendid garments of salvation and righteousness to the wedding finery of a bridegroom and bride. (The wedding language is picked up again in 62:4-5.) Verse 11 adds the imagery of plants shooting up from a field and garden. The imagery offers the certainty that righteousness and praise will spring up for Jerusalem: "As the earth brings forth its shoots . . . so the Lord GOD will cause righteousness and praise to spring up before all the nations." All the nations will see the restoration of Jerusalem. This is to be a sign for all peoples.

In 62:1-3 we hear the prophet speak on his own for Zion's and Jerusalem's sake. He intercedes for Jerusalem so that her vindication (deliverance) and salvation will shine like a bright burning torch (perhaps as at the brightly lit Feast of Tabernacles). Again, the nations will see the light of this triumph of Zion's salvation. And from the Lord's own lips a new name will be given (in v. 4 "My Delight Is in Her" and "Married"; see also 62:12). The new name (as often in Israelite lore; see the commentary on Isa. 62:6-12 for Christmas I) signifies a new status and relationship with God. Jerusalem will be like a crown in God's hands, perhaps suggestive of an ancient tradition when gods wore a crown that was made to look like the city's walls. The people's new day is surely dawning.

SIRACH 3:2-7, 12-14 (RC)

This is *wisdom* from one known as Jesus, Son of Sirach (the book is otherwise known as Ecclesiasticus), an author and likely compiler who lived in Jerusalem nearly two centuries before Jesus' birth. The reading offers counsel to children to observe the fifth commandment by honoring one's father and mother. Viewing the holy family as a kind of model family, one could use the passage to reflect on the virtues of family life on this Sunday.

RESPONSIVE READING
PSALM 148 (RCL)

Psalms 146–150 all begin and end with the call, "Praise the LORD!" which in Hebrew is "Hallelujah." Psalm 148 begins (vv. 1-6) with this praise "from the heavens." Verses 7-12 then respond with praise "from the earth," involving all manner of creatures and features of the natural world, ending (vv. 11-12) with the praise of every human—rulers and people, men and women, old and young. The praise is offered to God as the creator (vv. 5-6), while v. 14 recalls the raising up of the Messiah and the special reason for praise on the part of Israel.

Every creature of heaven (beginning with angels, recalling to us those of the Christmas story) and of earth praises God in an idyllic harmony. All the universe is in tune, and the psalm must have influenced "The Canticle of the Sun," attributed to St. Francis, which in the translated hymn begins, "Most High, omnipotent, good Lord, to thee be ceaseless praise outpoured, and blessing without measure." The hymn and the psalm can be heard as a response of praise and thanksgiving for the incarnation—God's presence within and God's love of the creation.

PSALM 147 OR 147:13-21 (BCP)

The first eleven verses begin with praise and thanksgiving to God for the divine might and wisdom in rebuilding Jerusalem and in lifting up all the downtrodden. This, we then hear, is the same Lord who is the creator of the heavens and the sustainer of nature. Verses 12-20 offer praise for God's special care of Jerusalem and the people Israel. The whole psalm is a hymn praising God for universal power and providential care.

PSALM 128:1-2, 3, 4-5 (RC)

The psalm is known as one of the wisdom psalms, taking up the frequent teaching that those who live in fear (awe) of the Lord and do God's will will be rewarded with a devoted and prosperous family life. The picture is idyllic (although respect for God and God's will can certainly lead to a well-ordered life) and is meant to respond to the lesson from Sirach and to continue the theme of reflection on the good family life.

SECOND READING
GALATIANS 4:4-7 (RCL);
GALATIANS 3:23-25; 4:4-7 (BCP)

Interpreting the Text

Paul has been admonishing the Galatians for coming to think that at least a partial observance of the law of Moses (circumcision, a ritual calendar) was necessary for justification and being made right with God. That justification, as Paul tells them in sometimes exasperated and no uncertain terms, comes only by faith. The law had a role as a kind of tutor to us when we were like minors, but now, with the coming of Christ and of faith, the tutor's discipline is no longer needed. Nor are we subject to it. For we are now made the true children of God by adoption. Furthermore (Paul's argument is a bit convoluted), we are like heirs who, when little, were treated similarly to the slaves of the household. But now we are no longer minors.

Therefore (4:4-7), "when the fullness of time had come [and the term of minority was over], God sent his Son, born of a woman" (a strong statement of the incarnation), subject to the law in order to (a) redeem those under the law and (b) grant them adoption as children. *Redemption* (literally that they might be bought back; on the theme for Paul see Gal. 3:13; Rom. 3:24; 8:23; 1 Cor. 6:20; 7:23) means being paid for so that one is no longer a slave and can be adopted. Because of this adoption and as its sign, the Spirit ("the Spirit of his Son") has been sent into our hearts enabling the adopted ones to cry, "Abba! Father!" (Gal. 4:6). *Abba* is the Aramaic word for father, and its use here and in Rom. 8:15 (also with reference to adoption) and Mark 14:36, together with the Greek word for father, may suggest a fixed liturgical formula. Our redemption and adoption all begin with Jesus "being born of a woman." It all begins with Christmas.

> OUR REDEMPTION AND ADOPTION ALL BEGIN WITH JESUS "BEING BORN OF A WOMAN." IT ALL BEGINS WITH CHRISTMAS.

COLOSSIANS 3:12-21 OR 3:12-17 (RC)

The first part of the reading (vv. 12-17) continues an address to the baptismal community. They had earlier been told to put to death two lists of five vices. Now, as God's chosen and beloved ones, they are to put on (as with a baptismal garment) "compassion, kindness, humility, meekness, and patience"—all virtues of gentleness and caring that, along with forgiveness and the love that chains everything together into a complete whole, make for a harmonious community. This is the one body in which the "peace of Christ" (the fullness of love and mutuality) rules in believers' hearts. "The word of Christ" (here probably more the teaching about Christ than the teaching of Christ or Christ as the Word) is to dwell in them so that they may teach and admonish wisely, singing psalms, hymns, and songs with thankfulness, and doing all in the name of the Lord Jesus.

In the context of such a loving, compassionate, and humble baptismal community, the author presents a "household code" of conduct, similar to those offered by Hellenistic philosophers and found also in several other New Testament letters (Eph. 5:21—6:9; Titus 2:1-10; 1 Pet. 2:13—3:12; cf. 1 Tim. 2:8-15; 6:1-2). The pattern in vv. 18-21 is for wives and children to "be subject" and "obey," followed by the responsibility of husbands and fathers. While these are to be relationships of love in the baptismal community, a greater mutuality in Christ between husbands and wives would today be the ideal in most contemporary societies and in the church.

The Gospel

LUKE 2:22-40 (RCL);
LUKE 2:22-40 OR 2:22, 39-40 (RC)

One would love to know where these stories came from. Later apocryphal gospels relate tales of Jesus' infancy, trying to fill in the blank years. Even today one can find guesswork and historical fiction about Jesus' early life. Many of these stories are less edifying than Luke's.

It seems probable that Luke inherited a collection of stories about Jesus' birth and infancy. The collection may well have included the poems spoken by Mary, Zechariah, and Simeon, which we know from their first Latin words as the Magnificat, Benedictus, and Nunc Dimittis. Much of this material is heavily influenced by the Hebrew scriptures and may well derive from meditations on them. In particular the stories in 1 Samuel 1–2 of the birth of Samuel, Hannah's prayer, Samuel's dedication to the Lord, Samuel's early years in the temple (Eli may have been a model for Simeon), and the manner in which Samuel "continued to grow both in stature and in favor with the LORD and with the people" (2:26; so of Jesus in Luke 2:40, 52; cf. Luke 1:80 in reference to John the Baptist) seem to have been seminal. The material may then have been knit together by Luke, the historian and evangelist, who strongly flavored the narrative with his own emphases—among them that the gospel of and about Jesus was for all peoples, the important role of women (here Anna is "paired" with Simeon in a pattern found often in Luke in addition to other stories involving women), and the frequent and decisive activity of the Holy Spirit, stressed both in the Gospel and Acts.

Another important theme for Luke is that of the law-abiding character of Christianity. Throughout Luke-Acts one of his major concerns is to show that Christianity does not merit persecution or calumny from the Roman officials or, for that matter, from the Jews themselves. The early Christians, as Luke understood them, were still in many ways an observant offshoot of Judaism that believed Jesus to be God's chosen one. This Gospel mentions five times (2:22, 23, 24, 26, 39) that in the early days of Jesus' infancy, the proper duties were performed "according to the law" ("of Moses" or "of the Lord"). In Jesus' circumcision and naming (v. 21), in the dedication of the firstborn, and in the purification (it would seem of the whole family rather than just Mary; Luke has the spirit of the law right rather than all the details), everything was done fittingly.

While it would not have been necessary to have the purificatory and dedicatory rites performed in the temple or its precincts, Luke suggestively has the child Jesus come to the city and the temple (and back again every year, notably when he was twelve; 2:41-42) since they will be so important at the end of his ministry. Later in Luke's Gospel we do not even hear the false testimony at Jesus' trial that he said something about destroying the temple. Jesus was a true Jewish boy, brought up in a proper Jewish family. Moreover, there is never any question throughout Luke 2 (and unlike some of the apocryphal gospels where the boy Jesus works some rather strange miracles) that he was a fully human baby and lad, even if he was "filled with wisdom" and some extraordinary things were predicated of him—not least Simeon's prediction of troubles to come (2:34-35).

JOHN 1:1-18 (BCP)

See the commentary on this Gospel reading for Christmas III.

Responding to the Texts

It still seems insignificant. Yes, some interesting things have been predicted about Jesus by an old man and an old woman. They seem full of hope but also full of years, perhaps having hung around the temple too long. It is nice that all the proper rituals were observed and the lad is evidently growing up well. But for us it is now four days after Christmas and precious little has changed. Have you had a look at the newspapers? Same old. Same old stuff about wars and rumors of wars, economic problems, and deaths on the highway. The environment may be going down the tubes too while people continue to put their vague hopes in new technologies rather than God.

I tried going back and rereading the lesson from Isaiah and the psalm. They seemed joyful and so full of hope and promise, but then I think of what eventually happened to Jerusalem and of modern Jerusalem still being fought over rather than a city of peace. I do, however, keep hearing the prophet's words:

For as the earth brings forth its shoots,
    and as a garden causes what is sown in it to spring up,
so the Lord GOD will cause righteousness and praise
    to spring up before all the nations. (Isa. 61:11)

The people of God have had to live so long with promise. But these words still insist it is going to happen—righteousness and praise will spring up just as surely as seeds spring up. This could happen in some unexpected ways. I know that from being a gardener. I also remember what Jesus said about little seeds and insignificant beginnings. The kingdom of God is "like a mustard seed, which, when sown upon the ground, is the smallest of all the seeds on earth" (Mark 4:31).

THE PEOPLE OF GOD HAVE HAD TO LIVE SO LONG WITH PROMISE. BUT THESE WORDS STILL INSIST IT IS GOING TO HAPPEN—RIGHTEOUSNESS AND PRAISE WILL SPRING UP JUST AS SURELY AS SEEDS SPRING UP.

He also told a story about someone who scatters seed on the ground that grows up all by itself even though the planter does not know how (Mark 4:26-29). There is truth in that, for even though one might know a lot about botany, there is yet a kind of mystery to the principle of life and growth.

Jesus claimed that the kingdom, that is, God's ways, have drawn near. The disciples claimed that in Jesus God's ways were already begun, that one could follow him and start living by the ways of love and peace, of righteousness and justice. Paul says this when, in his always interesting way, he claims that we can now have a relationship with God as grown-up sons and daughters and call upon the God of all creation with the intimacy of "Abba, Father." He insists this all is begun with Jesus "born of a woman" (Gal. 4:4). That is a lot to believe, and there is a lot I don't yet understand, especially about why the Jesus movement still seems so small and its ways not very powerful compared to the power of worldly values—not to speak of evil, suffering, and death.

Yet I realize the drawing near of God's kingdom does make a difference. I sometimes call this difference "the problem of the good." We all know about "the problem of evil"—why there is so much wrong and tragedy. But why is there any goodness at all? Why don't people just live for themselves and take up as much space as they can? Why do we care for those on whom life is especially hard and try to love and respect others? Such love and caring may often seem pretty small, but thank God it is in our world. A lot of my faith and hope begins with this small boy. The problem of the good may not yet be huge, but it has begun.

THE NAME OF JESUS / HOLY NAME / MARY, MOTHER OF GOD

JANUARY 1, 2003

REVISED COMMON	EPISCOPAL (BCP)	ROMAN CATHOLIC
Num. 6:22-27	Exod. 34:1-8	Num. 6:22-27
Psalm 8	Psalm 8	Ps. 67:2-3, 5, 6, 8
Gal. 4:4-7 or Phil. 2:5-11	Rom. 1:1-7	Gal. 4:4-7
Luke 2:15-21	Luke 2:15-21	Luke 2:16-21

Much is happening on this day. We are ringing in the new year, and some are also celebrating the Feast of the Holy Name while others are thinking especially of Mary, Mother of God. We also have a variety of readings to reflect on, some of which we have commented on for previous liturgies during this Christmas season. Let us first read and reflect on these lections, many of them briefly and by referring back to earlier commentary, and then see where it all might take us for our homilies and sermons.

FIRST READING
NUMBERS 6:22-27 (RCL, RC)

Interpreting the Text

Today the emphasis falls especially on the last verse, 27. The Lord's *name* pronounced over them in blessing makes the Israelites God's people. They are identified with and by God (see also Deut. 12:5 and esp. Isa. 43:1, "I have called you by my name, you are mine"). This makes them responsible to live as a people who honor God and show forth God's righteousness and mercy in the world. It also makes God responsible for a people who are God's own. The name is identity. It is character. It is powerful. Nor is there any "may" about this blessing (a word sometimes used in contemporary versions of the blessing with the effect of softening the impact). This is what the Lord will do and does.

The right to give blessing was not always restricted to Aaron and his line, but here in v. 22, in what likely is a postexilic development (though the prayer is surely earlier), the authority of Moses gives this responsibility especially to "Aaron and his sons." Thus the words have become known as "the Aaronic blessing." The prayer is artfully constructed in three sentences, each sentence (in the Hebrew) about a third longer than the one preceding, building in a kind of crescendo and ending with the word *shalom*—the peace that is the fullness of well-being, wholeness, harmony, and integrity. Because the blessing is offered in the second person singular, it is suitable for individual as well as corporate use. To each person and to the community it gives the Lord's protection, graciousness, and peace.

The word picture of the shining face and lifted countenance of the Lord had special significance in Israel. If an individual was not allowed into the presence of a king or superior, if one could not see his face, or if the countenance was not benign toward one or was cast down, that person was in trouble. In Deut. 31:18 and Pss. 13:1; 30:7; 44:24; 51:11; and 104:29, the Lord hides his face and people respond in dismay. When the Lord looks favorably upon the people, when the Lord's face shines (smiles, looks graciously), then people respond with gladness (see Pss. 4:6; 31:16; 33:18; 34:15; 80:3, 7, 19). Note the opening of Psalm 67 (see the commentary below), which can be used in response to this reading.

EXODUS 34:1-8 (BCP)

The setting of this theophony (anticipated in 33:17-23) is Mount Sinai. The context is the renewal of the covenant through the rewriting of the commandments on two new stone tablets like the ones Moses earlier had shattered. The heart of the passage, especially for this day's liturgy, is the pronouncement of the divine name, which in Hebrew traditionally is unnamable (cf. Exod. 3:13-15), its four letters YHWH sometimes being translated as Yahweh. (On the significance of God's name for God's identity and the identification of God's people, see the commentary above on Num. 6:22-27.)

As kings of that time would do, the name of the one making the treaty or covenant is given. This is God's self-manifestation and not only the name but God's character is now made known in words from what was likely an ancient cultic confession echoed in Num. 14:18; Neh. 9:17, 31; Ps. 103:8; Jer. 32:18; and Jonah 4:2. God's people will forever struggle to experience the Lord who is at once merciful and righteous, stern in judgment while full of forgiveness and steadfast love. Moses can only bow down and worship.

RESPONSIVE READING
PSALM 8 (RCL, BCP)

A major reason for the use of this psalm in today's liturgy is the reference to the majesty of God's name in the refrain of vv. 1 and 9. The predominant feature of the name here is God's glory, which is wondrous in the creation and is shared with humanity. The first two verses and the last verse were probably spoken or sung in a chorus. Verses 3 through 8 were then delivered by an individual, a mortal (a "son of man"), perhaps the king as representative of all the people. (The use of "son of man," which became a title of Jesus, could be seen as another reason for the choice of this psalm today. Jesus as our "forerunner" (Heb. 6:20) can be regarded as the model of humanity, become lowly (see the commentary on Phil. 2:6-7 below) but fulfilling God's hope for us.

One pictures the psalmist gazing up at the night sky like Gerard Manley Hopkins: "O look at all the fire-folk sitting in the air! The bright boroughs, the circle citadels there!" We now look up and know that there are more than 100 billion galaxies! What is human life in this scheme? Yet here we are with intelligence and awareness and a stewardship of dominion (as a gift from God) over other creatures. (The psalmist remembers, and so do we, the opening chapter of Genesis.) The creation is awesome and full of wonder, and the people respond in worship: "O Lord, our Sovereign [YHWH, our God], how majestic is your name in all the earth."

PSALM 67:2-3, 5, 6, 8 (RC)

The first verse of the psalm responds with very similar words to the Aaronic blessing of Num. 6:24-26. This is a hymn of thanksgiving and praise at harvest time (see the last two verses) and a prayer that these blessings may continue.

SECOND READING
GALATIANS 4:4-7 (RCL, RC)

Interpreting the Text

This reading is also used on the First Sunday after Christmas. See its interpretation there. Today several themes can be emphasized. "Born of a woman, born under the law" (v. 4) helps us remember that Jesus was both human and Jewish. On the day when his circumcision and naming are commemorated, it is fitting to hear these words almost like a creedal confession, which role it might have played in very early Christianity.

Although neither Jesus nor Mary is named in the passage, both are vital to it. One thinks of Mary as she is presented in today's Gospel reading, treasuring and pondering what the shepherds told her and then, eight days later, having Jesus circumcised according to the law and giving to him the name the angel Gabriel had revealed to her (Luke 1:31).

Along with all the earlier readings for this day that reflect on the significance of God's name, one will also note (in v. 6) how those who are now God's children and heirs by adoption are enabled by the Spirit of God's Son, sent into their hearts, to cry out "Abba! Father!" The great and holy God, whose name in so many other ways is unknowable or unutterable, is called upon as Abba. This is the new relationship with God won for us by Jesus born of Mary.

PHILIPPIANS 2:5-11 (RCL, alt.)

This rich hymn was probably already in use in the early churches (perhaps especially at Philippi) before Paul incorporated it into his letter. It may have derived from a still earlier hymn about one who was first with God in heaven or about one who was "in the form of God" (v. 6) as was Adam but did not misuse that status. In the latter case, one might find here some parallel with Psalm 8—with a mortal "son of man" made little lower than God, and now, in Jesus' case, through his humbling and death, exalted.

The hymn culminates in the giving of the name that is above every name. The rhetorical force of the hymn leads to the title Lord. Jesus Christ is now to be called Lord. God is known as Lord in the Hebrew scriptures, as we have noted particularly today in the earlier readings. Now Jesus is Lord, a phrase that would also ring out challengingly in the political realm where "Caesar is Lord." On another hearing, however, one might understand that the name above all names, the name at which "every knee should bend," is Jesus (v. 10). Early Christians used a number of designations to try to describe their faith in Jesus. He was Son of God, Son of Man, Teacher, the Prophet, Savior, Messiah, Lord. The designations Christ and Lord were so identified with him that they virtually became parts of his name—the Lord Jesus Christ. All these designations were needed, because none alone was sufficient to tell about who he was and is. The titles become his so that, along with saying, "Jesus is Lord," we might acclaim, "The Lord is Jesus." The name of the Lord and the name above all names is the name given to the baby on this day of commemoration—Jesus.

THE NAME OF THE LORD AND THE NAME ABOVE ALL NAMES IS THE NAME GIVEN TO THE BABY ON THIS DAY OF COMMEMORATION—JESUS.

ROMANS 1:1-7 (BCP)

In vv. 2-6 Paul may well be using an early Christian form of creed. The phrase "spirit of holiness" (v. 4, almost surely referring to the Holy Sprit) is not found elsewhere in Paul's writings and could come from that earlier formulary. One might also discern here a rather early form of adoptionistic Christology—

that is, the human Jesus "descended from David according to the flesh" was "appointed" or "installed" "Son of God with power according to the Spirit of holiness by resurrection from the dead." There are, however, different ways of translating several of the words in the latter half of this statement, and it more likely is intended that Jesus' being the Son of God was made known by his resurrection from the dead.

Particular attention should be given today to the words "for the sake of his name" (v. 5). That name could be the designation "Son of God," although it also could be understood that the name foremost in Paul's mind was that of Jesus Christ, to whom the new Roman Christians were now called to belong. Of David according to the flesh, Jesus Christ is now known as the Son of God in power through resurrection from the dead.

THE GOSPEL
LUKE 2:15-21 (RCL, BCP);
LUKE 2:16-21 (RC)

Interpreting the Text

Luke 2:15-20 was heard as the Gospel reading for the Christmas II liturgy and may also have been used in Christmas I (see the commentaries there). Verse 21 brings the first part of the story of Jesus' birth to its completion. It began with the visitation to Mary by the angel Gabriel who announced the name of the child Mary would conceive (1:31). We next heard of Mary's visit with Elizabeth, the birth of John the Baptist, the birth of Jesus, the angels' announcement to the shepherds, and (in the first five verses of this reading) of the shepherds coming to find Mary, Joseph, and the baby and to tell all they had seen and heard. As John was circumcised on the eighth day and given his name (1:59-63), so now was Jesus according to Jewish custom and law. One is reminded again of the basic human circumstances, understandings, and limitations into which Jesus was born. His name, not uncommon at the time but special and full of significance for him and hearers of the gospel, means "the Lord saves" or "salvation from God," an etymology that Matthew makes clear (1:21) and Luke may allude to (2:11) when the angels declare that there "is born this day in the city of David a *Savior.* . . ."

In many ways this is Mary's story, too. Today we may think of her as she treasures and ponders the shepherds' words (Luke 2:18), but we also may imagine her life in all that comes before and afterward, not least later in this chapter when Jesus is presented in the temple and Mary hears the words of Simeon and Anna. Then there is the visit to Jerusalem when Jesus is twelve, after which Mary "treasured all these things in her heart" (2:51). Nor can one help but think of what is still to come and especially of Simeon's fateful words to Mary, "A sword will pierce your own soul too" (2:35).

One could say that Mary had little choice in all this. What does one do after the visit of an angel? What could this faithful woman do after conceiving? What could she do but care for the baby? Luke presents Mary to us as a real woman, young, at times fearful and troubled, burdened by pregnancy and then the child's care, but who calls herself "the servant of the Lord" (1:38, 48), seeking to do what is to her God's mysterious will. This is her duty, her pain and sorrow, and her blessing (1:48). She has, indeed, much to treasure and much to ponder.

Responding to the Texts

A number of thoughtful homilies and sermons can flow from these texts. The occasion and liturgy for the day will in large measure suggest the theme. If one were preaching about Mary, one might further reflect on the Savior Jesus "born of a woman, born under the law" (see the commentary above on Gal. 4:4-7). And the homilist might ponder with Mary as she "treasured all these words and pondered them in her heart" (Luke 2:19). The heart in that era was regarded as the locus of understanding more than just feelings. What is in our hearts and minds as we treasure and ponder? What does it mean to treasure and ponder words and a message such as this?

Another sermon, or part of a sermon, could help hearers ponder these texts at the beginning of a new year. One could focus on Psalm 8 and the human condition. Although we are seemingly insignificant parts of a vast universe, yet we are, with our intelligence and awareness, a kind of crown of creation. Yet, given all our potential for love and responsibility, look at the ways we often end up trying just to serve ourselves and sometimes, with all our coping habits, not very well at that. The theme need not be new year's resolutions, but more the kind of people we would like to become—the character we would like to be known for and what we believe God wants for us. It is a time for forgiveness and new life. The author of "The Cloud of Unknowing" wrote that "God, with God's all merciful eyes, sees not only who we are and who we have been, but who we will be."

Into a liturgy for this day one might want to incorporate the Aaronic blessing from Num. 6:22-27 and perhaps reflect on it in the sermon. What a blessing for the new year with the Lord's face beaming upon us and giving us peace. What, we may ask, is the peace we are longing for this new year?

And then one remembers that this blessing puts God's name on us. We bear God's name. I know others had the experience I did as a teenager when I was told that, wherever I went and whatever I did, I should remember that I bore with me my family's name. I had something to live up to. Believers, blessed by God, bear God's name and, in this sense, God's reputation with them. Nor is this God, the God of the 100 billion galaxies, whose name is in so many ways unknown to us, a God who does not also draw near. Indeed, through the Spirit in our hearts we are encouraged to call out "Abba! Father!" (Gal. 4:6).

We who are Christians know God by a special name: "The Lord Is Salvation," "The Lord Saves," Jesus. On this day in the history of our salvation, we remember the baby given the name Jesus. We think of him who for our sakes "humbled himself," even to "death on a cross," that "every tongue should confess that Jesus Christ is Lord" and "at the name of Jesus every knee should bend" (Phil. 2:6-11). At baptism we hear, "You are sealed by the Holy Spirit in Baptism and marked as Christ's own forever" (BCP, p. 308). In addition to our own name, we go by Jesus' name. As Desmond Tutu often reminded many of us, we who are Christians carry

IN ADDITION TO OUR OWN NAME, WE GO BY JESUS' NAME.

Jesus' reputation with us in our hands wherever we go. Christians, as Paul said of us, are "ambassadors for Christ" (2 Cor. 5:20). That is surely an appealing and challenging way for us to begin the new year.

SECOND SUNDAY AFTER CHRISTMAS

JANUARY 5, 2003

REVISED COMMON	EPISCOPAL (BCP)	ROMAN CATHOLIC
Jer. 31:7–14	Jer. 31:7–14	Sir. 24:1–2, 8–12
or Sir. 24:1–12		
Ps.147:12–20	Psalm 84 or 84:1–8	Ps. 147:12–13, 14–15,
or Wisd. of Sol.		19–20
10:15–21		
Eph. 1:3–14	Eph. 1:3–6, 15–19a	Eph. 1:3–6, 15–18
John 1:(1–9), 10–18	Matt. 2:13–15, 19–23	John 1:1–18
	or Luke 2:41–52	
	or Matt. 2:1–12	

FIRST READING
JEREMIAH 31:7-14 (RCL, BCP)

Interpreting the Text

Jeremiah 31:7-9 is a prophecy and picture of the exiles' return. Verses 10-14 describe their restored life in idyllic terms. There are parallels with the language of Isaiah 40–55, but Jeremiah is here evidently thinking of the return of those taken into exile from the Northern Kingdom nearly a century earlier. The promise is to Jacob and Israel. Ephraim is singled out as the firstborn to indicate God's special care. In the larger perspective, however, Jeremiah looks forward to the restoration of the united kingdom. In v. 12 even Israel can worship again in Zion, and there will be a normal and happy life for all. Above all, the prophet is seeking to offer hope to a people much in need of it. Throughout there is a comfort (cf. Isa. 40:1) and much singing and rejoicing. Even the weakest who might otherwise be left behind (the lame, the blind, pregnant women, and newborn children) will return. They will weep as they come (in joy, or v. 9 may refer to the weeping as they went forth). God will lead them back. Their new life is compared to a watered garden. Mourning will be turned to joy as there will be dancing and merriment by young women and men with the old joining in. Even the priests will know abundance! This is a happy and consoling vision in Jeremiah's time or for any new year.

Again we have a lesson drawn from this wisdom book (see Christmas I) compiled and written by a Jerusalem resident, Jesus ben (son of) Sirach, almost two centuries before the birth of Jesus. These verses are the first part of a hymn of praise to personified Wisdom (Greek *sophia*) that begins the second major section of the book. Much of it is modeled on Prov. 8:22-36.

Wisdom (v. 3) comes forth from the mouth of God. God speaks forth Wisdom, who then has a vital role in the world's creation and a special calling to dwell with and bless God's people. Wisdom is everywhere in creation but has a home in Israel among the people God has chosen, particularly in beloved Jerusalem (v. 11). One can see how Wisdom, both natural and supernatural, cosmic yet dwelling with God's people, was seen as a prefigurement for Jesus as Wisdom (cf. Col. 1:15-20) and Word (as in John 1:1-18, one of today's readings).

RESPONSIVE READING

PSALM 147:12-20 (RCL);
PSALM 147:12-13, 14-15, 19-20 (RC)

These verses form a separate section of Psalm 147. In the Greek translation of the Hebrew scriptures (the Septuagint), they are treated as a separate psalm. Praise is sung to God for peace and blessings. This makes the psalm a fitting response and continuation for the themes of Jer. 31:7-14. The blessings are enumerated in everything from securing the safety of the city, to providing food, to sending snow and sleet and then melting them, and finally to providing the law, God's "statutes and ordinances to Israel" (v. 19).

In vv. 15-20 we hear of the work of God's creative word both in the natural world and as the revealed word to Israel, for God "has not dealt thus with any other nation" (v. 20; cf. Deut. 4:8; 7:6-7). The psalm thus becomes a helpful response to Sir. 24:1-12 and an anticipation of John 1:1-18.

WISDOM OF SOLOMON 10:15-21 (RCL, alt.)

Written in Alexandria, probably no more than a generation before Jesus' birth, this book praises the role of Wisdom in creation and in human life and history, especially among God's people Israel. In the last part of a section illustrating how Wisdom did God's work through a series of figures from Adam to Moses, vv. 15-21 tell how Wisdom, having entered into the soul of "a servant of the

Lord" (i.e., Moses), led the holy people on their exodus from Egypt through the
Red Sea's "deep waters." It was Wisdom that opened the mouths even of the
mute and of children so that they could join in singing hymns to the Lord. In this
way the response carries on the praise of Wisdom in Sir. 24:1-12 and also helps
prepare for John 1:1-18.

PSALM 84 or 84:1-8 (bcp)

The psalm may well have been intended to be sung by pilgrims coming
to the temple on a festival day. Verses 1-2 offer praise for the temple itself, and vv.
3-4 tell of the happiness of those who are privileged to serve in the temple and
even of the birds who nest there (one pictures them flitting around the precincts
and sometimes within the temple). Verses 5-7 describe the journey. This psalm
would fit best with the alternative Gospel reading, Luke 2:41-52.

Second Reading

EPHESIANS 1:3-14 (rcl);
EPHESIANS 1:3-6, 15-19a (bcp);
EPHESIANS 1:3-6, 15-18 (rc)

Interpreting the Text

Traditionally this letter is viewed as written by Paul during a time of
imprisonment, perhaps in Rome in the early 60s. More probably the letter
was composed by a disciple a generation or more later. It was then intended as a
form of recapitulation of Paul's overall understanding of God's plan of salvation,
setting forth what Paul would have said for that time were he still living. After
the salutation, the letter opens with a lengthy hymn of praise and thanksgiving
(vv. 3-14) that then takes on a tone of intercession along with gratitude for the
Ephesians' faith and love and what God has done in them (vv. 15-23). The whole
is an outpouring of praise that may well derive from liturgical language used in
association with baptism. The major themes of spiritual blessing, election, sonship, and dedication would belong in such a setting, and in this connection it is
interesting to note the praise to the Father (v. 3), and for the work of Jesus Christ
(vv. 4-13) and the Holy Spirit (vv. 13-14). The Spirit is spoken of frequently
throughout the epistle.

The major interest of Ephesians is to place the salvation that God has accomplished in Christ in the context of a universal salvation history—"a plan for the
fullness of time, to gather up all things in him" (v. 10). The Christ event is no
accident of history but part of God's design from the beginning to bring about

both a new cosmic unity and the unity of Jews and Gentiles in a saved humanity. This "mystery" of God's will (v. 9) is now set forth in Christ. The phrase "in
Christ" (or "in him" or equivalent) is found frequently throughout these verses
and then in the following chapters. "In Christ" God has accomplished this universal plan of salvation. "In Christ" is the unity of humanity. "In Christ" were
the Ephesians "marked with the seal of the promised Holy Spirit" (v. 13).

"Every spiritual blessing" (v.3) is given its meaning throughout the passage.
The blessings are "in heavenly places" in the sense that they originate from a realm
above all human uncertainties and vicissitudes.
The intent in vv. 4–5 ("chose us in Christ before
the foundation of the world" and "destined us
for adoption") is to confirm the certainty of
God's eternal purpose rather than the predesti-
nation of individuals. The words "holy and
blameless" (v. 4; cf. 1 Pet. 1:18-19; 2:1-10, lan-

> THE CHRIST EVENT IS NO ACCIDENT OF HISTORY
> BUT PART OF GOD'S DESIGN FROM THE BEGIN-
> NING TO BRING ABOUT BOTH A NEW COSMIC
> UNITY AND THE UNITY OF JEWS AND GENTILES
> IN A SAVED HUMANITY.

guage that may also relate to baptismal liturgy) recall the requirements of sacrifice in the Hebrew scriptures. "Adoption" stresses God's initiative. The references
to God's "pleasure" (v. 5) and to Christ as "the Beloved" (v. 6) call to mind Jesus'
own baptism (see Mark 1:11).

Verse 15 does sound a bit odd if Paul himself is actually writing the letter, since
he lived among the Ephesians for nearly three years. Whoever the author may
have been, unceasing prayer is now offered that these Christians may have the gifts
of wisdom and vision befitting their having been chosen by God (cf. Col. 1:9;
2 Thess. 1:11). In a lovely phrase the wisdom and revelation that are given enable
deep insight into the hope and rich inheritance of God's saints with "the eyes of
your heart" (v. 18), that is, in the deep inner knowing of experience and faith.

THE GOSPEL
JOHN 1:(1-9), 10-18 (RCL);
JOHN 1:1-18 (RC)

Interpreting the Text

This Gospel lesson was read for Christmas III (see the commentary
there) and is also used on the First Sunday after Christmas (BCP). On this Sunday all of the prologue to John's Gospel, or otherwise its last nine verses, follows
particularly well what we heard in Sir. 24:1-12 about the Wisdom that is everywhere in creation and comes to dwell with God's people. This same Wisdom (in
the Wisd. of Sol. 10:15-21) was present to guide the people of God out of Egypt
through the Red Sea waters. As the *Logos,* Jesus assumes this ministry of Wisdom,

now become flesh, making this Gospel reading a fitting capstone to these earlier readings and to the season of Christmas. John 1:1-18, in its own way, tells the story of salvation history that is lifted up in today's reading from Ephesians. It is the will of God that has enabled those who have received the Word made flesh to become children of God (John 1:12). They have seen his glory, the glory that is God's as only a father's only son could make it known. The grace of the law "was given through Moses," but "grace [here God's work of grace with all that is implied in becoming flesh, self-offering, forgiveness, and God's favor] and truth came through Jesus Christ" (v. 17). This truth is greater than any previous revelation, for this Word is "the only Son, who is close to the Father's heart [bosom, a picture of intimacy], who has made him known" (v. 18). Jesus is the true bread and wine in this Gospel, "the way, and the truth, and the life" (14:6).

MATTHEW 2:13-15, 19-23 (BCP)

Matthew carries on the story of Jesus' nativity with his account of the family's withdrawal into Egypt and their later return. The narrative is presented with remarkable economy. Its major function is typological, that is, to help hearers understand how Jesus' early life paralleled that of the Israelites going down to Egypt and returning. It also recalls the story of Moses. Moreover, all this is "to fulfill what had been spoken by the Lord through the prophet, 'Out of Egypt I have called my son' " (v. 15; see also Hos. 11:1). Jesus is to be the true Israel, the chosen one of God, and the new Moses. Moses also had been persecuted by a king as a baby. He also had been hidden in order to be saved. The measure of the evangelist's consciousness of this parallelism is shown in v. 20, where the similarity with Exod. 4:19 is striking. Moses could return to his ministry because "those who were seeking your life are dead." The plural in Exodus accounts for the plural in Matthew's phrasing.

Matthew stretches his method to account for the fact that Jesus was raised in the Galilean hamlet of Nazareth (a town unknown in the Jewish scriptures or later Jewish writings) and that Jesus came to be referred to as Jesus of Nazareth, or the Nazarene or Nazorean. There is no obvious reference to support the prediction that he should be called a Nazorean. Perhaps this is the reason Matthew refers to "the prophets" rather generally in the plural. One possibility is that the derivation is from *nazir* and the ancient Nazirite vow through which a child was dedicated to God and an ascetic lifestyle (see Num. 6:1-21; Judg. 13:2-7; 1 Sam. 1:11; and of John the Baptist, Luke 1:15). Alternatively, it is suggested that the evangelist had in mind the similarity of sound with *netzer* in Isa. 11:1. Jesus was the "branch" from the root of Jesse, David's father. Whatever the derivation of Nazorean, the overall thrust of Matthew's story is clear. In Jesus the scriptures are fulfilled. He is the total fulfillment of scriptural hope—the true Israel, the new Moses.

LUKE 2:41–52 (BCP, alt.)

Luke concludes his nativity narratives with the story of the family's pilgrimage to Jerusalem when Jesus was twelve. (Psalm 84 is particularly apt in connection with this Gospel reading.) To his amazed and concerned parents, who had returned to Jerusalem after missing him on their journey homeward, Jesus responds, "Did you not know that I must be in my Father's house?" (v. 49). Throughout his nativity stories Luke stresses the Jewish piety and law-abiding character of Jesus and his family. (Note also that in v. 51 Jesus is obedient to his parents: "Honor your father and mother.") The story also emphasizes Jesus' wisdom (v. 52) and comprehension of his Jewish heritage and points to his future role as a teacher whose authority will be greater than that of all the teachers of Judaism. When Jesus returns to the temple late in his ministry, it will be to cleanse it before his rejection and death. On his growing in wisdom and stature (v. 52), compare 1 Sam. 2:26; and Luke 1:80; 2:40.

Responding to the Texts

Again on this Sunday we have several texts as options, and no doubt on January 5, 2003, there will also be a number of churches anticipating the Feast of the Epiphany. Such a variety of opportunities may seem like a burden or blessing to the preacher. Let us see today's options as a blessing.

There are certainly a number of sermons here about Jesus as Word and Wisdom who, in becoming flesh, fulfills God's wise but surprising plan for salvation by bringing grace and truth to believers. Jesus becomes known as the *Logos,* who was with God from the beginning, because he not only spoke God's word but enacted it in his life and ministry. One recalls Origen's observation that Jesus, who proclaimed the kingdom *(basileia)* of God, had come to embody it; Jesus was *auto-basileia,* the kingdom himself. In today's vernacular, we might say that Jesus walked the talk. He did as he said. In this embodied Word of God, which God, as it were, first spoke and through whom all things were made, and who then entered into the very flesh of life, the Christmas story is complete.

The reading from Ephesians, with its praise and thanksgiving for the mystery of God's work of salvation "in Christ," is also a summary of the significance of the incarnation. Given the rich baptismal language in this reading, one might consider fashioning a liturgy in which all present could remember their baptism and renew their baptismal vows, giving the opportunity also to preach about "spiritual blessing," "forgiveness," and "the riches of his grace that Jesus lavished on us." It is still near enough to New Year's Day (and the first day after January 1 that many people will be in church) to talk about renewal and new life in Christ in relation to the secular beginning of the year. One might reflect also on what it means to be "marked with the seal of the promised Holy Spirit" and what it means in relationship with others to have this mark of the Spirit of Jesus on our brow as "the pledge of our inheritance."

Someday I would like to make a whole sermon out of that lovely phrase "the eyes of your heart": "So that, with the eyes of your heart enlightened, you may know what is the hope to which he has called you, what are the riches of his glorious inheritance among the saints" (Eph. 1:18). I am reminded of Jesus' saying about the eye being the lamp of the body. "So, if your eye is healthy, your whole body will be full of light" (Matt. 6:22; Luke 11:34). I greatly desire to be enlightened with the light of God's wisdom so that I might see the things that matter most, the things God would have me see. I greatly long to look out through the eyes of my heart with something of God's wisdom and compassion so that my spirit, in the Spirit of Jesus, might see God's love in others and the face of that love in Jesus Christ our Lord.

I GREATLY LONG TO LOOK OUT THROUGH THE EYES OF MY HEART WITH SOMETHING OF GOD'S WISDOM AND COMPASSION SO THAT MY SPIRIT, IN THE SPIRIT OF JESUS, MIGHT SEE GOD'S LOVE IN OTHERS AND THE FACE OF THAT LOVE IN JESUS CHRIST OUR LORD.

THE SEASON OF EPIPHANY

JAMES M. CHILDS JR.

Introduction

Vision, mission, and anticipation are three thematic words that summarize much of what we experience in the Epiphany season. First of all, this is a season of revelatory splendor. As the events of these weeks march on, we get a clearer picture of who this Jesus is, this babe of Bethlehem born under a star. That bright star sets the tone. This is a season of light, brightness, and transfigured glory. In Jesus we see that, as prophets foretold, those who were in darkness were to see the light of God's gracious embrace of all peoples from all nations. In this Jesus we see that the darkness of human sin is penetrated and dispelled by the inexhaustible forgiveness of God's steadfast love. Indeed, as the light of Epiphany shines on Jesus, it illumines the fullest meaning of God's covenant love for Israel and all humankind. Epiphany light leads us to the truth of Jesus as the promised Messiah and, what is more, the Son of God, in transfigured glory. In all these ways our vision is sharpened.

As the Christ is revealed for us to see, so also is our *mission*. The Epiphany season is a missional season. The star of Bethlehem, which draws the Magi to the Christ child, is an outreach star, beckoning those from outside the covenant into a ever expanded covenant, a home for all who will come and adore him. In the Epiphany season we see the groundwork laid for Paul's mission to the Gentiles, and we see revealed the groundwork for our mission to keep the light shining on the Christ.

> THIS IS A SEASON OF LIGHT, BRIGHTNESS, AND TRANSFIGURED GLORY. IN JESUS WE SEE THAT, AS PROPHETS FORETOLD, THOSE WHO WERE IN DARKNESS WERE TO SEE THE LIGHT OF GOD'S GRACIOUS EMBRACE OF ALL PEOPLES FROM ALL NATIONS.

We can say even more. The Epiphany readings help us see that the promise of God in Christ at the heart of our mission is a promise for the whole person and the whole world. Healing goes together with forgiveness.

Justice is companion to love in God's purposes. The flourishing of the whole earth complements the flourishing of human life under God's blessing. The combined witness of God's people on earth tends to all these spiritual and material concerns for the promise of God's salvation is as comprehensive as God's creation.

In the Epiphany season our eschatological sensitivities are heightened. We are made aware of the manifold ways in which God's actions in history constitute an unfolding plan of salvation. Things are happening. Long held and even forgotten hopes are being rekindled. God has a future for our tired world after all. In the lessons of Epiphany we begin to see that in the little town of Bethlehem, as the hymn puts it, "the hopes and fears of all the years are met in thee tonight." Fulfillment is in the air. In the Epiphany season what we discover about Jesus as Messiah and Son of God anticipates and enables us to more fully understand the culmination of that revelation in the cross and resurrection.

We are being schooled in our role as a people of *anticipation*. We have seen the revelation of the future God has for our world in the bright light of the star, in the bright light of the transfiguration mountain, and in the bright light of the open tomb. We now await the final epiphany, the arrival of God's future. Our eschatological sensitivities are heightened. In our worship we reach out to that future in the fellowship of the heavenly banquet anticipated in the Eucharist. In our mission to the world we seek to bring the light of God's future into the darkness of the present that others might anticipate with us the fulfillment of the promises God has kept in the Christ.

THE EPIPHANY
OF OUR LORD

JANUARY 5, 2003

REVISED COMMON	EPISCOPAL (BCP)	ROMAN CATHOLIC
Isa. 60:1-6	Isa. 60:1-6, 9	Isa. 60:1-6
Ps. 72:1-7, 10-14	Psalm 72 or 72:1-2, 10-17	Ps. 72:1-2, 7-8, 10-11, 12-13
Eph. 3:1-12	Eph. 3:1-12	Eph. 3:2-3a, 5-6
Matt. 2:1-12	Matt. 2:1-12	Matt. 2:1-12

FIRST READING
ISAIAH 60:1-6 (RCL, RC);
ISAIAH 60:1-6, 9 (BCP)

Interpreting the Text

A little historical background is useful to start our interpretive work with this text. It will also serve as background for other readings from the book of Isaiah that will follow. Isaiah of Jerusalem is considered to be the author of chapters 1–39. An anonymous author, designated Second Isaiah, is responsible for chapters 40–55. Chapters 56–66, Third Isaiah, then, is considered by many to be the work of a disciple or disciples of the author of Second Isaiah. The question of authorship itself, however, does not need to detain us. What is important is that one prominent reason for distinguishing the three distinct segments of the book is that each reflects a different historical situation. Knowing this is a helpful key to the meaning of the text. For our immediate purposes it is sufficient to note that Second Isaiah reflects the period of exile in Babylon, and in Third Isaiah, or at least in chapters 56-66, it seems clear that the people have returned to Jerusalem.

There is certainly continuity between Second and Third Isaiah in the substance of God's promise to do great and decisive things for the people of Israel and for all people through Israel. The prophet of Second Isaiah comforts an exiled and downtrodden people with the promise that "the glory of the LORD shall be revealed, and all people shall see it" (40:5). Now, back in Jerusalem, the promise is coming to fulfillment: "The glory of the LORD has risen upon you" (60:1). God is with Israel, the chosen ones, whom God has kept through thick and thin. The glory of God is the *presence* of God in the Hebrew scriptures. There are echoes here of the exodus, the signature saving event of Israel's history, not only in the theme of return from exile, but also in the glory of God, the empowering presence of God among the people (e.g., Exod. 40:34). This deliverance is God's doing. The events of history are in God's hands, a proclamation punctuated by the theme of light and the response of the nations.

The prophet of Second Isaiah tells us that God has called Israel to be "a light to the nations" (42:6). Now the promise of this calling has become a call to action: "Arise, shine; for your light has come," and "Nations shall come to your light, and kings to the brightness of your dawn" (60:1, 3). This is epiphany. God is with Israel; God's glory is upon them, and the light of God's presence, the revealing of God's saving love for the entire world, shows through them in their deliverance and penetrates the darkness that covers the nations. The nations are drawn to the light and bring their tributes of wealth, a symbolic act not of fealty to Israel, but in praise of God who is with them (60:5-6).

The call to be a light to the nations blends salvation and vocation. The light is there, but it must still face the darkness. One day there will be no darkness, only the perpetual day of God's completed reign (60:19-20), but in the present there is work to do. In the difficult days of rebuilding Jerusalem, the people must confront their heritage of denying God, a heritage of falsehood and injustice (59:12-15). Succeeding chapters make clear that God's rehabilitation of Israel for their role as a witness to the nations will be a comprehensive one. The scope of God's saving work in their midst includes both spiritual renewal and the triumph of justice. God is determined to make a new heaven and a new earth (65:17).

Responding to the Text

God is with Israel. God is moving in history to save Israel, to restore them to their promised land and through them to show all people the salvation that is theirs. The light of God's glory has shone upon the people, and they in turn become a light to all the nations that languish in darkness. These are themes of God's self-revelation, themes of Epiphany. They certainly point to our calling as God's people to continue that epiphany through our witness in the world: "But you are a chosen race, a royal priesthood, a holy nation, God's own people, in order that you may proclaim the mighty acts of him who has called you out of darkness into his marvelous light" (1 Pet. 2:9).

The larger context of our text tells us that ours is a manifold witness to God's love, even as God's saving work for Israel reaches into all facets of their life. God's love includes the establishment of justice, peace, prosperity, and the renewal of all creation along with the renewal of our spirits.

How has God been with us to lead us out of the darkness of our own exiles into the light of new beginnings? Perhaps at the personal level it has been recovery from a broken family life that had us longing for reconciliation, healing, and a new birth of love. For others the return to our homeland in joy is a return from the exile of disease or addiction, a time to rebuild our lives on the rubble of our past defeats. Still others return from the exile of mourning into the light of Easter when God brought us out of death to new life.

In our society many are captive to idols even as Israel was captive to Babylon. The idols are familiar ones: success, material wealth, popularity, acclaim, and power. Israel returning to the ruins of its former glory is promised wealth and power among the nations of the world, to be sure. But these signs of God's favor are blessings to be held in justice and lifted up as signs of God's mercy to all. If we as a society lift up the marks of success, wealth, and power as ends in themselves to the neglect of justice, peace, and mercy, they become idols that captivate us.

> IF WE AS A SOCIETY LIFT UP THE MARKS OF SUCCESS, WEALTH, AND POWER AS ENDS IN THEMSELVES TO THE NEGLECT OF JUSTICE, PEACE, AND MERCY, THEY BECOME IDOLS THAT CAPTIVATE US.

Whether we are struggling to return from our personal exiles or working to lead our society out of captivity to its idols, we know the task of returning home and rebuilding will be an arduous one. There will be a great deal of rubble to clear away. We are not yet at the ultimate homeland, the new heaven and new earth that God has prepared for us. Still, God has brought us this far and will be with us all the way. Moreover, God has called us and empowered us as children of the light to help one another along the way. "Arise, shine; for your light has come."

RESPONSIVE READING

PSALM 72:1-7, 10-14 (RCL);
PSALM 72 OR 72:1-2, 10-17 (BCP);
PSALM 72:1-2, 7-8, 10-11, 12-13 (RC)

As the opening verse makes clear, this is a prayer of blessing for the king, which may well have been used at a coronation or other official observance. What is noteworthy is the emphasis on the virtues the king should possess. He is to be a defender of justice, one who cares for the poor and the needy, and one who fights oppression and rules in peace. The power of the king is consolidated not in military might or great wealth, but in the traits of divine mercy. To such a one the kings bring tribute and the nations give service (vv. 11-14). Indeed, the king, in delivering the oppressed, mirrors the saving work of God even as he is called upon to embody the traits of God's compassion. He, as Israel in our Isaiah text, is to be a blessing to the nations. So it is that the prayer concludes in v. 17 with an echo of the ancient promise to Abraham that all nations be blessed in him (see Gen. 12:2).

SECOND READING
EPHESIANS 3:1-12 (RCL, BCP);
EPHESIANS 3:2-3a, 5-6 (RC)

Interpreting the Text

The theme of light in Isaiah is succeeded here by the theme of *revelation* (vv. 3, 5). The idea is the same, however, the showing forth of God's "eternal purpose" in history (v. 11), now seen to culminate in Jesus the Christ. What is envisioned in Isaiah (and intimated in Psalm 72) concerning the nations being drawn to the light of God is now made explicit in the missionary work of the apostle Paul.

In our text Paul's life and work are defined by his outreach to the Gentiles. The Greek word that we translate "Gentiles" is also the word for "peoples" or "nations." This linguistic connection with Isaiah gives us a further point of contact with the words of the prophet and their ultimate fulfillment in Christ Jesus. Yet we have even more to think on.

The translation of the Greek as "Gentiles" rather than peoples or nations reflects the nuancing of the Greek word in Jewish culture to connote religious outsiders. It is all the more remarkable, then, that these Gentiles have become "fellow heirs, members of the same body" (v. 6). This is a mystery only now revealed to all of humanity. God has done a radically new thing and a radically inclusive thing. As befits the notion of a "mystery" in Pauline literature and here in Ephesians, what is revealed is far more profound and wonderful than any product of human imagining. The promise we have in the gospel of Jesus Christ overrides all boundaries and barriers to make one people of God from all the peoples of the world. No longer are there religious outsiders. Paul, "the very least of all the saints" (v. 8), has been given grace to bring this glorious message of the gospel to the Gentiles in accordance with God's plan. Now in his succession, the church, which God has created by grace, will be the agent of that revelation, even to the angels themselves.

Responding to the Text

The missionary impulses that are discernable in Isa. 60:1ff. stand out in bold relief in this discussion of the mission of Paul to the Gentiles. The mystery now revealed to all humankind that all are heirs to the gracious promise of the gospel of Jesus Christ is the "epiphany" of this reading. Moreover, this mystery of God's unfathomable wisdom is now to be made known through the church (v. 10) that is created by that gospel grace.

As an epiphany church or a mission church, the church is global in its scope. As a global church in mission, the church locally embraces the full diversity of the communities it serves. There are to be no religious outsiders or barriers of ethnicity, gender, or class. The familiar words of Gal. 3:28 come immediately to mind: "There is no longer Jew or Greek, there is no longer slave or free, there is no longer male and female; for all of you are one in Christ Jesus."

God's unconditional acceptance of all people is but another expression of the radical and unconditional love and forgiveness shown forth in Jesus Christ. This boundless grace in the face of human sin is the key to the unity of all in Christ. We celebrate it also as it is embodied in the Eucharistic meal. Paul reminds us as he did the factious Corinthians, "Because there is one bread, we who are many are one body, for we all partake of the one bread" (1 Cor. 10:17). The church's inclusion and embrace of all kinds of folk from all kinds of cultural and social backgrounds is itself a proclamation of the gospel and a response to our epiphany calling.

> THE CHURCH'S INCLUSION AND EMBRACE OF ALL KINDS OF FOLK FROM ALL KINDS OF CULTURAL AND SOCIAL BACKGROUNDS IS ITSELF A PROCLAMATION OF THE GOSPEL AND A RESPONSE TO OUR EPIPHANY CALLING.

Fulfilling this calling is often difficult. Our congregations frequently reflect the demographic and geographic divisions that characterize our communities, and effectively crossing those boundaries is hard. Living as we do in cultural separation from one another, prejudicial attitudes seep into our minds without our even noticing them, and ignorance of one another makes communication difficult. Furthermore, we are not without our fears that diversity within the church will bring changes that shake our sense of security and intrude on our comfort zone. We can adopt a variety of strategies and partnerships to deal with our limits of opportunity and understanding. The key, however, is to confront the limitations of sin that frustrate genuine openness to all our neighbors.

For Paul, who calls himself "the very least of all the saints," the power for his incredible change from a zealous anti-Christian Jew to a Jew who embraced the Gentiles in the name of Jesus was, of course, Jesus. The grace of God in Jesus Christ is our power too, and it works. An African American pastor of my acquaintance tells of moving to a new city and immediately seeking out the nearest Lutheran church. When his family went to worship there, they discovered it was a Swedish congregation with the service in Swedish. Within a few days the pastor came to their home to welcome them to the congregation. He told them that there would now also be services in English so that they could feel included. They did feel included, and they stayed.

THE GOSPEL
MATTHEW 2:1-12

Interpreting the Text

Matthew is chief among the Gospels in its attention to the fulfillment of the Hebrew scriptures as seen in the events of Jesus' life and work. This is evident throughout our text.

The light of God that had risen upon Israel, drawing the nations in darkness to that light (Isa. 60:1-3), is now sharply focused in the singular star of Bethlehem. All the events of God's self-revelation in history are coming together in the one place to which the star points, the babe in the manger. This is the birth of the Messiah, destined to happen in Bethlehem according to the prophet Micah (Matt. 2:6; see also Mic. 5:2). He is the definitive Word of God's Word.

The appearance of the Magi, then, opening their treasures and paying homage, connects us with Isa. 60:3, 5-6 and Ps. 72:10-11. What must have seemed at the time a hyperbolic promise of Israel's glory, given the ragtag band of exiles returning to rebuild Jerusalem, is now taking on a new and fuller meaning.

The presence of the Magi adds more to the unfolding drama of the text than just another instance of prophetic fulfillment typical of Matthew. Their presence serves as a means through which we receive further revelation of the sort of redeemer God has sent and the sort of God who sent him. The references to kings coming to pay tribute in both Isaiah 60 and Psalm 72 has helped form the popular tradition that these visitors from the East were kings. Certainly that is not the meaning of the term *Magi*. Closer to the truth of that term might be the other prominent idea that these men were "wise men." Does this mean learned men or, as some have suggested, astrologers, who might have been expected to be alert to the star? Another possibility that has been suggested is that they were servants of kings. Whatever their precise identity, they stand in stark contrast to the character of the one earthly king in the piece, Herod, and the religious authorities he consulted. They symbolize something very different from the often distressing manifestations of kingly power.

The Magi had as their sole concern to find and worship this newborn king of the Jews, and when they found him they were "overwhelmed with joy" (v. 10). They knelt down and emptied their treasure chests (v. 11), seemingly oblivious to the lack of royal trappings in the humble surroundings of Jesus' birth and the unprepossessing young woman, Mary, who was his mother. Herod had as his sole concern hanging on to his kingly power, a concern evidently shared by the scribes and the chief priests. To this end Herod was ready to employ any deceit and any brutality.

Whatever the Messiah was to be, he was not to be a king after the manner of this world.

Responding to the Text

This is *the* Epiphany text and the focal point for the themes in all the other readings for the day. Certainly we should stress the ineluctable progression of God's purposes being revealed in history and coming to the beginning of their surprising fulfillment in Bethlehem. God is relentless in love. God's purposes will not be thwarted by our faithlessness or the treachery of the powerful. This is a gospel message of great comfort in a world that often seems to be careening out of control as the lust for power in all quarters turns people against one another and leads us into hostility, violence, and disdain for one another's needs.

It is also a gospel message that points the way to what sort of people we are to be as God's people in this world. It strikes one that the attitude of humility and adoration we detect in the conduct of the Magi blends nicely with the simple and humble circumstances of the Christ child and foreshadows the way in which Jesus would lead his followers. The way of Christ is the way of service rather than power and privilege (Matt. 20:25-28). The way of Christ is the way of concern for the poor and the outcast (recall Psalm 72!). Paul admonishes us to have the mind of Christ, who emptied himself of his divine power and became a servant even to the point of death on the cross (Phil. 2:4ff.).

> THE WAY OF THE CHRIST IS THE WAY OF SERVICE RATHER THAN POWER AND PRIVILEGE. THE WAY OF CHRIST IS THE WAY OF CONCERN FOR THE POOR AND THE OUTCAST.

The well-known Epiphany hymn "Brightest and Best of the Stars of the Morning" has a stanza that fits.

Vainly we offer each ample oblation,
Vainly with gifts would his favor secure;
Richer by far is the heart's adoration,
Dearer to God are the prayers of the poor.

We lay our earthly treasures before the Christ child in devotion to his ongoing Epiphany of love and salvation. However, the greatest of these gifts is to present ourselves in service to the Christ, embracing the "poverty of spirit" that Jesus has taught us (Matt. 5:3) and that his grace in our lives makes possible.

THE BAPTISM OF OUR LORD / FIRST SUNDAY AFTER THE EPIPHANY

JANUARY 12, 2003

REVISED COMMON	EPISCOPAL (BCP)	ROMAN CATHOLIC
Gen. 1:1-5	Isa. 42:1-9	Isa. 42:1-4, 6-7
		or Isa. 55:1-11
Psalm 29	Ps. 89:1-29 or 89:20-29	Ps. 29:1-2, 3-4, 3, 9-10
		or Isa. 12:2-3, 4bcd, 5-6
Acts 19:1-7	Acts 10:34-38	Acts 10:34-38
		or 1 John 5:1-9
Mark 1:4-11	Mark 1:7-11	Mark 1:7-11

FIRST READING
GENESIS 1:1-5 (RCL)

Interpreting the Text

These familiar words begin the creation account ascribed to the Priestly writer. This is later than the Yahwist narrative of creation in Gen. 2:4ff. Indeed, scholars date the Priestly document after the exodus. Therefore, since the story of creation is written after the deliverance of Israel from slavery in Egypt, the central saving event of the Hebrew scriptures, it is plausible to infer some points of contact between the creating work of God and God's saving work.

The vision of God in this text is one that stresses transcendent power. God is able to create with a word. God overcomes the disordered reality of chaos and darkness by creating light. In the separation of light from darkness, we have the start of an ordered world. We also know, however, that, in the Bible, darkness has connotations related to the human condition of sin and estrangement from God. Thus, as we have seen in other readings for this season, light is also associated with God's saving work that brings people out of their darkness. As in the creation, only the transcendent power of God can bring an ordered world out of the nothingness of chaos and darkness. So only God's power can bring us out of the nothingness of sin and death to light and life.

Out of the nothingness of the dark void, God brought forth the light and began the world of days, the dawn of time, and the intricate and wonderful world of living things that was to follow. Out of the dark void of our sin God has brought us into the light of salvation and made of us a new creation in Christ (2 Cor. 5:17). Indeed, the Christ in whom we are a new creation is the very Word who was in the beginning with God and through whom all things were created (John 1:1-3). He is the light of life that shines in the darkness of the world and the world did not overcome that light (John 1:5).

This Word of creative and saving light speaks to a disordered world divided by hostilities rooted in greed, religious intolerance, and racial and cultural prejudices erupting in terrorism, war, and cruel forms of competition. Divided in this way among ourselves, we are also divided within ourselves by the contradictory impulses that signal the lingering of sin. As God's creation of light brought order for a harmonious world, so the light of God's redemption can lead us into the ways that make for harmony among us and peace within.

ISAIAH 42:1-9 (BCP);
ISAIAH 42:1-4, 6-7 OR ISAIAH 55:1-11 (RC)

Interpreting the Texts

The theme of Israel as a light to the nations that we met in Isa. 60:3 is with us now in the antecedent prophecy of Second Isaiah (42:6). Again, it is an integral part of the promise of God's deliverance of Israel and of Israel's call to refract that light of God's glory to the world (Isa. 55:5).

Now, however, we also have in vv. 1-4 the first of the Servant Songs. Whether the Servant was understood as Israel or an individual or both, Christians have seen the fullest meaning of these texts in the person and work of the Christ. In any case, the prophet sees the establishment of justice as central to the work of the Servant. The Hebrew word for "justice" *(mishpat)* has several nuances of meaning. In this context, as in Psalm 72, it means "righteousness" or a society ordered in concert with God's norms for a "right" or just world. In Isa. 59:9 we are led to understand that where there is justice, there is light, and in its absence there is darkness!

The *ruach* of God, "spirit" or "breath," is upon the Servant, the same *ruach* that is there in the creation giving life and breath (42:5) and overcoming the chaos and darkness (Gen. 1: 2). The divine creating spirit that empowers the Servant is the same spirit that makes Israel a beacon to the peoples (42:6). This one and only God will now do new things (42:9), offering words of pardon and mercy, words that transcend our own thoughts and with the transcendent power to accomplish God's purposes (Isa. 55:7-11).

Responding to the Texts

It seems fair to pull some things together in this way: to be a servant after the Servant is to be light. It is to bear witness to and serve the Word of God's justice and mercy in word and in deed. This can be a very discouraging vocation, however, one that requires a durability of spirit.

The Israelites in exile, without power or prospect, must have wondered some at the prophet's grasp on reality as he uttered those lofty words of God's promises for the people. God's thoughts, as the prophet spoke them, were indeed higher than theirs in all likelihood. For many who were relatively comfortable in Babylon, these eloquent visions of their future may have been unwelcome as well as seemingly unrealistic. So also we, the people of God, exiles in today's secular world, may find that our witness falls on the ears of those whose thoughts are not God's thoughts. We speak of peace and hear calls for revenge. We strive for reconciliation among people after the manner of Christ's love but in response hear a call for retribution and an attitude of rejection. We advocate for justice in our land, but inequality, prejudice, and unmet basic needs are too often what we find. We lift up the generosity of Christlike love but in the face of what seems to be a culture of selfishness. We offer forgiveness and enjoin mercy, but we encounter instead voices of judgment and condemnation.

Yet, through it all, we have the Spirit to sustain our faith against the gainsayers. We have the Spirit, the energy of the creator God, who gives life and breath to our humblest efforts. After all, Jesus said, "You *are* the light of the world" (Matt. 5:14). And that is an indicative!

RESPONSIVE READING
PSALM 29 (RCL);
PSALM 89:1-29 OR 89:20-29 (BCP);
PSALM 29:1-2, 3-4, 3, 9-10 (RC);
ISAIAH 12:2-3, 4bcd, 5-6 (RC, alt.)

In Psalm 29 the prayer for blessing of the people that comes at the end of this hymn rests its hope in the majestic power of God who is king of the whole creation and worthy of both our praise and our trust. Only a God of such might can truly bless and protect the people.

In Ps. 89:1-29 we have yet another song, extolling now both God's almighty power over the creation and the steadfast love of God for the people. Central to this song is the celebration of God's faithfulness to the covenant with David. All three of these songs offer fitting hymns of worship in the light of the themes involved in the readings for this day.

In Isaiah 12 we have a song or perhaps two songs of praise and thanksgiving for God's deliverance of Zion. God's power is certainly lurking there, but it is divine mercy that takes center stage.

SECOND READING
ACTS 19:1-7 (RCL);
ACTS 10:34-38 (BCP);
ACTS 10:34-38 (RC);
1 JOHN 5:1-9 (RC, alt.)

Interpreting the Texts

Two things stand out in Acts 19:1-7. First, the dialogue between Paul and the Ephesian Christians confirms once more the difference between the baptism of John and that of Jesus. The baptism of Jesus bestows the Holy Spirit and with it the gifts of the Spirit. John's baptism was one of repentance in anticipation of Jesus. Second, the comment that there were about twelve in the group (v. 7) invites us to see a connection with the original twelve and infer that there is a new round of ordination to apostolic office through baptism and the laying on of hands made present in the missionary ministry of Paul.

In Acts 10:34-38 the emphasis is back on what happened to Jesus in his baptism by John. In the verses that follow, Peter's speech concerning Jesus highlights this event when Jesus was anointed by the Spirit, received power, and began his public ministry. As we read this we should not be tempted to draw an adoptionist conclusion that Peter is placing this as the time at which Jesus became the Son of God and the Messiah. Peter's speech in 3:12-26, as some commentators have noted, is a clear picture of Jesus as the Messiah of God's eternal plan and the Author of life (v. 15). Thus, we can see the baptism of Jesus as the affirmation of, not the beginning of, divine sonship and messianic identity. Moreover, this recognition of God's everlasting plan coming to fruition in Jesus is punctuated by Peter's realization that God "shows no partiality," that the promise of the Messiah is for all nations (10:34-35) even as the prophets had proclaimed concerning God's deliverance.

First John 5:1-9 begins by expanding upon the theme of love so prominent in that epistle. The love by which we "conquer the world" is rooted in faith in Jesus as the Son of God. His claim on our faith and his authority are confirmed by the Spirit at his baptism, the water, and by his saving sacrifice on the cross, the blood.

Responding to the Texts

These texts speak powerfully to our lives as Christians. Baptism into Christ bestows the Spirit and ordains us to the ministry of the whole people of God. It is the start of a lifelong calling and eternal membership in the communion of saints. We can renew the connection we previously made with 1 Pet. 2:9 by underscoring now the fact that our calling is to the "priesthood of all believers." This teaching of the Reformation is related also to the teaching of Vatican II that lifts up the apostolate of the laity.

The lessons thus provide a wonderful occasion for celebrating the ministry of all God's people and particularly the ministry of the laity and their vocation for God's epiphany in Christ. It is a good time to acknowledge the manifold gifts of the Spirit (1 Cor. 12:4ff.), which reflect the manifold blessings of the gospel. The works of love, which John's epistle enjoins, and the works of healing, justice, and peacemaking, which mark the revelation of the Messiah we follow, find expression in the lives of God's people as they go about their work in family, community, and workplace. It is a good time to sanctify their places of service. As Jesus' identity as Son of God was manifest in his baptism, so also our identity as children of God in our baptism is the identity that frames all our other identities. Parenthood, work, community service, and citizenship become venues for the service of Christian love.

> BAPTISM INTO CHRIST BESTOWS THE SPIRIT AND ORDAINS US TO THE MINISTRY OF THE WHOLE PEOPLE OF GOD. IT IS THE START OF A LIFELONG CALLING AND ETERNAL MEMBERSHIP IN THE COMMUNION OF SAINTS.

THE GOSPEL
MARK 1:4-11 (RCL);
MARK 1:7-11 (BCP, RC)

Interpreting the Text

In Mark's account, as in all the other Gospels, we read of John the Baptist's claim that one is coming who is greater than he, one whose sandals he is not fit to stoop down and untie. The statement speaks for itself, and its ubiquitous presence in the Gospel accounts alerts us to its importance. It also sets the stage for what some have seen as a problem.

Whenever John's baptism is discussed, it is always described as "a baptism of repentance for the forgiveness of sins" (see v. 4). As John the Baptist is himself the one who prepares the way for the Messiah, so his baptism prepares the way for baptism in the name of Jesus, which, as we have just observed, is baptism with the Holy Spirit (v. 8).

The fact that Jesus submitted to John's baptism has sometimes caused consternation among the faithful. If Jesus is truly the sinless Son of God, why should he have undergone a baptism of repentance and the forgiveness of sins? Mark is silent on the matter. However, in Matthew's account (Matt. 3:13-17) the problem is recognized. John does not think it appropriate to baptize Jesus and tries to resist. However, Jesus says, "Let it be so now; for it is proper for us in this way to fulfill all righteousness" (v. 15). In Matthew, then, it is a symbol of solidarity with the people, and we might hazard the further thought that it is a foretaste of the atonement drama in which Jesus takes upon himself our sins. Perhaps this implication is completed in both Mark and Matthew, since immediately after his baptism they both have him driven into the wilderness where he is tempted by Satan and shows his power over sin, as indeed he would soon do in his atoning work.

In other ways as well the baptism of Jesus reveals his unfolding identity. The appearance of the Spirit makes a clear connection for us with Isa. 42:1. Jesus is the Servant upon whom God bestows the Spirit. The rich nuances of the Servant Songs now become a part of the color and texture of our emerging portrait of Jesus.

The descent of the Spirit not only fulfills the prophecy of Isa. 42:1 but also suggests that the connection of the Spirit with baptism on this occasion inaugurates the new era of baptism in the name of Jesus that John himself foresees (v. 8).

Finally, it is noteworthy that in Mark's telling it is Jesus alone who sees the dove and hears the voice from heaven. For the other evangelists it is an event of public disclosure. For Mark it is an intimate moment of personal epiphany for Jesus. The man Jesus is thus strengthened for his bout in the wilderness.

Responding to the Text

The theme of baptism and Christian vocation that we discussed in response to the second reading selections for this day certainly is appropriate in relation to the Gospel reading as well. Moreover, the Gospel enables us to bring even greater depth to our sense of call as Christian people. The example of John the Baptist's desire to show the way to Jesus, who is the one who really counts, is germane.

Christians are no less susceptible to the pleasures of recognition and applause than anyone else. The allure of praise and admiration is quite seductive. Frequently our occupations in life are the venue for our pursuit of success and its rewards of personal aggrandizement. However, as people of God in Christ, we are called to show the way to Jesus as John the Baptist did. We need the help of the Spirit to transform our self-serving motivation to do well in our callings into a loving, others-serving motivation so that in our conduct people may get a glimpse of Jesus. In everything from parenting to plant management, we need to ask if it is only our own interests we serve or rather, as Jesus did, the needs of others.

We do have the help of the Spirit in being faithful witnesses. It comes with baptism. Like Jesus who, strong in the Spirit, went from baptism to wilderness to conquer the devil, we too are strong in the Spirit. The same intimacy and love Jesus experienced in the Father's words and the touch of the Spirit are ours as well. We are baptized into Christ, members of his body, the church. As such we are his brothers and sisters and children of the Father. Luther said we should begin each day by making the sign of the cross and remembering our baptism. It sets the tone for the whole day. And, then, when we pray in the Lord's Prayer, "Abba, Father," we are reminded once again that we are among the beloved with whom, because of Jesus, God is well pleased.

IN EVERYTHING FROM PARENTING TO PLANT MANAGEMENT, WE NEED TO ASK IF IT IS ONLY OUR OWN INTERESTS WE SERVE OR RATHER, AS JESUS DID, THE NEEDS OF OTHERS.

SECOND SUNDAY AFTER THE EPIPHANY

SECOND SUNDAY IN ORDINARY TIME
JANUARY 19, 2003

REVISED COMMON	EPISCOPAL (BCP)	ROMAN CATHOLIC
1 Sam. 3:1-10, (11-20)	1 Sam. 3:1-10, (11-20)	1 Sam. 3:3b-10, 19
Ps. 139:1-6, 13-18	Ps. 63:1-8	Ps. 40:2, 4, 7-8, 8-9, 10
1 Cor. 6:12-20	1 Cor. 6:11b-20	1 Cor. 6:13c-15a, 17-20
John 1:43-51	John 1:43-51	John 1:35-42

FIRST READING
1 SAMUEL 3:1-10, (11-20) (RCL, BCP);
1 SAMUEL 3:3b-10, 19 (RC)

Interpreting the Text

Samuel was a prophet and the last judge of Israel before he anointed Saul as king and later David as Saul's successor. He was an extremely important religious figure in the history of Israel. Having ushered out the period of the judges, he then presided over the institution of the monarchy, a rather traumatic turn of events for a people whose only king was Yahweh.

This is one of a number of call narratives in the Bible. In Isaiah 6 the prophet's encounter with God in the temple is astounding and awesome. The prophet is filled with fear at this vision. The Lord comes to the boy Samuel in the temple also, but it is in the quiet of the night, reminding us again of the different modes of God's revelation as God enters our lives with both immense power and gentle love.

As with all calls from God, this call is accompanied by the sure promise that God will be with Samuel to empower his work and to assure him that none of the words that he speaks as God's prophet will be discredited (1 Sam. 3:19-20).

Responding to the Text

God's call comes to us in diverse ways, as the narratives of call in the Bible point out. Sometimes it is a dramatic event that shakes us up and turns our eyes toward God's beckoning, as in the case of Isaiah or of Paul on the road to Damascus. Sometimes it comes in quieter ways that, as in the case of Samuel, require repetition, perhaps over time, before it dawns on us that God is calling us in some specific way to some new expression of discipleship. That call itself is a blessing of God's grace, just as we are called in baptism and ordained to the priesthood of all believers, a theme that keeps suggesting itself in the texts for this season.

Being God's servant in the world often involves some messy and trying involvements. Look at the turmoil that punctuated so much of Samuel's prophetic career.

When you are God's person with a word to speak or a deed to do—and that includes all of us—you can't simply walk away from troubles or continually seek to avoid them. Moreover, the difficulties of life that you encounter will not only be other people's difficulties. God tapped Samuel to be his prophet but did not spare him the personal grief of corrupt sons (1 Sam. 8:1-3). Often as we reach out to serve others as Christ has taught us to do, we do so in the midst of personal pain and failure. But through it all God is there to hold us up, even as the Lord promised Samuel. When we answer the call to be disciples, saying, "Speak, Lord, your servant is listening," the answer we receive is that which was given to Paul struggling with his mysterious "thorn in the flesh": "My grace is sufficient for you" (2 Cor. 12:9).

RESPONSIVE READING
PSALM 139:1-6, 13-18 (RCL);
PSALM 63:1-8 (BCP);
PSALM 40:2, 4, 7-8, 8-9, 10 (RC)

The verses chosen from Psalm 139 are words of praise that put one in mind of the traditional divine attributes of omnipotence, omniscience, and omnipresence. The thrilling thing about this recitation of God's knowledge and power is that it is not an abstract formulation. Rather, the psalmist understands these transcendent attributes of God in terms of God's immanent presence with him.

Ps. 63:1-8 is a prayer of longing for communion with God and praise for God's steadfast mercy. The opening verse conveys a sense of deep need, the need of one who has been pushed to the edge. Yet this neediness shifts to confidence and trust in God's love and faithfulness so that praise and joy are blended in.

Psalm 40 extols the saving work of God in the life of the psalmist and inspires in him the will to be faithful and the desire to bear witness to God's faithfulness and salvation. Here, as in the other lessons for this day, it is God's prevenient grace that enables us to be God's faithful witnesses.

1 CORINTHIANS 6:12-20 (RCL);
1 CORINTHIANS 6:11b-20 (BCP);
1 CORINTHIANS 6:13c-15a, 17-20 (RC)

Interpreting the Text

Verse 11b tells us that we are washed, sanctified, and justified in the name of Jesus and the Spirit. This is a tight synopsis of the gospel and life in Christ. This is a powerful *indicative*. What follows then is the *imperative* of life in Christ.

The imperative of Christian living in this particular case deals with fornication or sexual sin. Corinth was a notorious center of debauchery in the pagan world, so it is not surprising that such issues should arise. The target of Paul's concern, however, is more specific than just the indulgent attitudes and behavior of Corinthian society. Paul's conflict is with the "libertines" within the Christian community who thought indulgence of sexual appetites was virtually on the same level as satisfying hunger by eating. They saw the freedom of Christians from dietary laws as a license for freedom from other constraints of tradition as well (vv. 12-13). He rejects their thinking.

Paul counters that their bodies (ours too!) are members of Christ. How can they be united with a prostitute? Never! Our bodies are made for the Lord, not for fornication (v. 13b). Being united with a prostitute as "one flesh" just can't happen, because we are one with Christ. So, Paul is saying in effect, "Be what you are!" The imperative and the indicative of life in Christ co-inhere.

The imperative and the indicative always exist in tandem in Paul's thought. The verses that follow develop that theme. Reminding the Corinthians that their bodies are temples of the Holy Spirit (v. 19) is an imperative to be chaste, but it is also an indicative promise that the Spirit is ours to strengthen us against temptations that threaten to lead us away from our true being.

Finally, being true to our identity in Christ by turning away from sexual license has an epiphany edge as well. Paul says we should "glorify" God in our bodies. The Greek word here is *doxasate,* "praise, honor, and magnify," from *doxa,* meaning "brightness, splendor, radiance."

Responding to the Text

Certainly this text provides a strong basis for a sermon on sexual morality. Our situation today and that of the Corinthian Christians is woefully similar in many respects. There seems to be very little that is considered out of bounds for consenting adults in our society. Sex sells everything from movies and cars to toothpaste. We are bombarded with images of sex. The entertainment industry treats sexual license as perfectly normal and gives no hint that there might be a moral issue involved. Christians are exposed to the allure of a sexually charged culture along with everyone else. Moreover, like the libertines of Corinth, Christians in today's world can be quite adroit at finding a rationale from within the faith for considerable latitude in sexual relations.

When a society places very few sanctions of disapproval or shame on sexual promiscuity, the incentives to chastity are greatly diminished. Christians, however, have other incentives than the avoidance of a fast-disappearing social censure. First of all, the indicative of God's grace has made of us a new creation in Christ. The tug of the sinful nature still exists, but the power to realize the ideal of a sexual union in the bonds of love that mimics the unity of love in the body of Christ is the birthright of our baptism. And the ministry of the Spirit continually renews that power. Second, we realize that the moral choices we make are neither to escape the consequences of moral failure nor to gain the approval of a society that doesn't really care. Rather, the witness of a sexual ethic that reflects the caring, self-giving love of God is part of our witness to that glorious divine love in Christ.

> THE TUG OF THE SINFUL NATURE STILL EXISTS, BUT THE POWER TO REALIZE THE IDEAL OF A SEXUAL UNION IN THE BONDS OF LOVE THAT MIMICS THE UNITY OF LOVE IN THE BODY OF CHRIST IS THE BIRTHRIGHT OF OUR BAPTISM.

THE GOSPEL
JOHN 1:43-51 (RCL, BCP);
JOHN 1:35-42 (RC)

Interpreting the Texts

In this pericope we have two focal points in complementary relation to each other. The one is the further revelation and dawning awareness of who Jesus is. The second primary feature of the narrative is the calling of the disciples, who, along with John the Baptist, sense the fulfillment of messianic hope in their experience of Jesus.

John leads his readers to a fuller understanding of who Jesus is through two powerful allusions to Jesus' fulfillment of the Hebrew scriptures. In v. 35 John the Baptist echoes his earlier statement (v. 29) that Jesus is "the Lamb of God who takes away the sin of the world!" The point is obvious. The lamb was the predominant sacrificial victim offered for the atonement of sin by the faithful of Israel. Jesus as the Lamb of God is the sacrifice to end all sacrifices, the final act of atonement. Philip makes this connection between Jesus and the lamb led to the slaughter in Isa. 53:7 during his encounter with the Ethiopian eunuch (Acts 8:32ff.).

The second fulfillment utterance comes from Jesus himself in v. 51. God's promise to Jacob in his dream of angels ascending and descending (Jacob's "ladder" in Gen. 28:12ff.) is about to be fulfilled in Jesus. It may also be helpful to see the connection between seeing the heavens open to reveal the Son of Man in Jesus' statement and Stephen's dying vision of that very thing recorded in Acts 7:56. The "heavens being opened" suggests that in these events earthbound humankind is afforded a vision of the transcendent God.

Meanwhile the call of the disciples couched in the unfolding revelation of messianic fulfillment shares center stage. The word *follow* occurs four times in this reading. The call to follow requires a response of obedience, but it is one prompted by the revelation of messianic promise, not by the demand itself.

Responding to the Text

We need to gather up some of the observations we have made. The call to be a follower of Jesus comes in a variety of ways. We can compare Samuel's call from the first reading with Isaiah's call in Isaiah 6 and the disciples' call in our Gospel as well as other instances in the New Testament, such as Paul's call on the road to Damascus. All have their own peculiar features. How has God called you? What were the features of those key times when your discipleship was begun or renewed?

Regardless of the different circumstances of one's calling, the various call narratives we can cite share the common feature that it is God's grace and promise that make it all possible. Samuel is assured that his word will not fail; God will sustain him. The disciples follow Jesus because he is the Lamb of God, the Messiah in whom they can hope and to whom they can entrust their lives. This is the same sort of insight we got from Paul's admonitions to the Corinthians in the second reading for the day. The imperative of a life of Christian witness flows from the grace of God's indicative, God's "yes" to us.

So we are launched by grace into a Christian calling of discipleship in which the operative word of our text is "follow." What does it mean to follow? Physically speaking, to follow is to walk behind another. It means then that the primary thing we see, if not the only thing, is the person directly in front of us who is leading the way. To follow means to look only to Jesus and the way he is leading. It is the sort of single-minded response required in the astounding statement Jesus makes in Matt. 8:22, "Follow me, and let the dead bury their own dead."

> WE ARE LAUNCHED BY GRACE INTO A CHRISTIAN CALLING OF DISCIPLESHIP IN WHICH THE OPERATIVE WORD OF OUR TEXT IS "FOLLOW."

In discipleship Jesus leads us down many paths of service in life, many activities, occupations, and roles, but the disciple is always playing a serious game of "follow the leader," for our leader provides not only direction but the power and grace to persevere.

THIRD SUNDAY
AFTER THE EPIPHANY

THIRD SUNDAY IN ORDINARY TIME
JANUARY 26, 2003

REVISED COMMON	EPISCOPAL (BCP)	ROMAN CATHOLIC
Jon. 3:1-5, 10	Jer. 3:21—4:2	Jon. 3:1-5, 10
Ps. 62:5-12	Ps. 130	Ps. 25:4-5, 6-7, 8-9
1 Cor. 7:29-31	1 Cor. 7:17-23	1 Cor. 7:29-31
Mark 1:14-20	Mark 1:14-20	Mark 1:14-20

FIRST READING
JONAH 3:1-5, 10 (RCL, RC)

Interpreting the Text

In much prophetic literature the setting and details in the history of Israel are essential to grasping the full meaning of the text. The absence of genuine clues to the historical situation of Jonah, however, leads us directly into the message of the story itself: A merciful God is ready to forgive those who turn in repentance (v. 10).

By contrast, the larger context of the book presents us with the portrait of Jonah who is bitter over God's mercy. Jonah was sent to "cry out against [Nineveh]" (1:2). After trying to escape God's commission and then being delivered from the belly of the great fish, Jonah finally goes to Nineveh to voice God's warning (3:4). Now, however, the reluctant prophet is put out that God has not destroyed Nineveh and thereby vindicated Jonah in the message of judgment he was sent to proclaim (chap. 4). God showed Jonah mercy when he cried out from within the great fish, but Jonah was not ready for God's mercy toward the Ninevites when they cried out in repentance.

Responding to the Text

Jonah's message is simple but powerful. The divine character of mercy is contrasted with the moralistic character of Jonah. One thinks immediately of Jesus' parable of the unforgiving servant. The king forgave this man a huge debt, but the ingrate turned around and threatened his fellow servant with imprisonment if he did not repay him the pittance he was owed (Matt. 18:23-30). No wonder we are taught to pray, "Forgive us our sins as we forgive those who sin against us."

Jonah may have been facing the same problem others face when they find the gospel to be a scandal, a stumbling block, because they are convinced that one must do something to gain God's favor or face judgment if they fail. As far as Jonah was concerned, the Ninevites should have been punished and Jonah's word upheld. He could not fathom that God's justice is made known in mercy. We who are in Christ know God's mercy and therefore stand ready to forgive and focus our vision of justice through the lens of compassion.

JEREMIAH 3:21—4:2 (BCP)

Interpreting the Text

The text begins with a call for repentance. Some have noted the similarity of Jeremiah's mission "to pluck up and to pull down, to destroy and to overthrow" (1:10) and Jonah's call to cry out against Nineveh (Jon. 1:2). However, the prophet Jeremiah is also "to build and to plant" (1:10). Our passage moves in that direction.

If Israel will but turn from the idolatry of their faithlessness (3:21-23) and remove the "abominations," the idols of other gods (4:1), and confess God in word and deed, they will again become what they were called to be, a blessing to the nations (4:2).

In this last verse we hear the words of God's covenant promises to Abraham and Isaac reverberating down through the centuries. Moreover, we see in the same breath as this renewal of the covenant vision the marks of true religion so common to the Hebrew scriptures: truth, justice, and uprightness, the underlying Hebrew words associated with God's steadfast love and righteousness (see Pss. 85:10; 86:15; Jer. 23:5; Amos 5:24).

Responding to the Text

The world is more often than not a place of cruelty and vengeance both in the violent expressions of our behavior and in our nonviolent but still hurtful ways. Yet we who have heard God's call to repentance and have received God's mercy in Christ know another way.

The way of the world is often marked by deceit and injustice. Individuals and governments alike lie about what is really going on in order to hide the truth of unfair dealings, exploitative relationships, and oppressive policies. As Israel sought security in false gods, so it is just as easy to seek security in falsehood itself. However, we who have known the

GOD'S EARNEST COVENANT FAITHFULNESS NEVER LETS GO OF US. THE ASSURANCE OF THIS LOVING ACCEPTANCE SETS US FREE TO BE TRUTHFUL AND SEEK JUSTICE.

mercy of God can stand the truth. We do not need to be "whitewashed tombs" (Matt. 23:27) hiding the truth of our sin behind a false face of righteousness. God's earnest covenant faithfulness never lets go of us. The assurance of this loving acceptance sets us free to be truthful and seek justice. We can own up to the truth of our flawed relationships and deal fairly with others. We can face the truth about injustice in our communities and begin to work for change. As we exercise our freedom in this way, the light of God's mercy, justice, and steadfast love is showered abroad through the witness of his people as a blessing to others.

RESPONSIVE READING

PSALM 62:5–12 (RCL); PSALM 130 (BCP); PSALM 25:4–5, 6–7, 8–9 (RC)

Psalm 62 is a psalm of trust in God's steadfast love. God is the "rock" of salvation, a rich biblical metaphor for the trustworthiness and durability of God's promises. So the psalmist urges others to trust in God as well. Human power and the evil designs of human greed are vain hopes. Power belongs to God.

Psalm 130 is what the scholars call an individual lament. It is one of the seven penitential psalms in Christian liturgical tradition. The others are Psalms 6, 32, 38, 51, 102, and 143.

Luther's hymn *"Aus tiefer Not schrei ich zu dir"* ("Out of the Depths I Cry") is a well-known rendition of this psalm. The psalmist cries out to God for forgiveness knowing that God will forgive; that is God's promise. Once again, God's steadfast love is invoked as the grounds for our assurance. In this way Israel is reminded of God's faithfulness to the covenant, God's unflagging refusal to abandon them.

> THE PSALMIST CRIES OUT TO GOD FOR FORGIVENESS KNOWING THAT GOD WILL FORGIVE; THAT IS GOD'S PROMISE.

The opening verse of Psalm 25 tells us that the psalmist is fearful of his enemies who would put him to shame. However, he also knows that to seek God's help against his foes, he must also appeal to God's mercy to blot out the memory of his sins and to lead him in God's ways. God's mercy both justifies and sanctifies the humble, those who know their need before God. Throughout the psalm we are reminded of God's covenant virtues of steadfast love and mercy or goodness.

1 CORINTHIANS 7:29-31 (RCL, RC);
1 CORINTHIANS 7:17-23 (BCP)

Interpreting the Texts

Although both readings are part of an extended discourse mainly on marriage, a larger message is involved that concerns devotion to Christ as the norm of life in all circumstances.

Verse 17 has Paul telling us that he customarily gives instructions to the churches on various matters (see also 1 Cor. 4:17; 11:34; 14:33). Such instructions may not always be a "command of the Lord," but Paul appeals to their respect as one who by grace can be considered trustworthy (v. 25). Here, then, we get a glimpse of the early church engaged in moral deliberation under the leadership of Paul, seeking God's will for the challenges of the time.

Paul's apparent sense of an imminent eschaton (vv. 29, 31; see also Rom. 13:11 and 1 John 2:15-17) prompts him to counsel that persons should stay in their present state of affairs and eschew the distractions of life (vv. 29b-31). This sense of the nearness of the end seems strange to us two thousand years later, but the core lessons of the text are not strange at all. We can serve Christ in any occupation or station in life. The Corinthian Christians were therefore not to seek to be free of their present circumstances. True freedom is ultimately in Christ (see also John 8:36), the freedom from sin that was bought with the price of his sacrifice. Christians don't allow their freedom to be defined by any other standard (v. 23). All affections and emotions and circumstances are relativized by devotion to the coming Savior (vv. 29-31).

Responding to the Texts

Occasionally there are events in our lives that make everything else seem trivial, at least for a time. They may be negative intrusions, such as the untimely death of a loved one, a huge natural disaster, or an outbreak of war. Such all-embracing events may also be positive, such as a new job or a demanding new project, getting ready for marriage, or welcoming a new baby.

If we consider how these kinds of experiences take over our minds and feelings, we begin to appreciate what Paul is saying. To be in Christ and live in anticipation of his coming is to be dominated by that faith and hope so that all our strivings and experiences are placed in the perspective of that faith and hope.

Anticipating Christ's coming does not mean that we should stay put and not seek desired changes in life or embrace life's natural emotions and relationships; rather, we should understand them in terms of our faith and its promises.

Furthermore, living within the horizon of God's future enables us to find meaning in the present. We can see meaning in our present activities of Christian calling because we have been shown our future in him. And, at the same time, because we have been shown our future, we know that present activities in life are not the last word. We work at our tasks as being important yet as though they are passing away. We plan seriously for tomorrow yet as though there is no tomorrow. In this manner we are faithful both to our callings and to our hope.

THE GOSPEL
MARK 1:14-20

Interpreting the Text

Mark has narrated the events that point the way to our understanding of Jesus' identity: the prophecy of John the Baptist, Jesus' baptism with the descent of the Spirit and theophany, and his triumph over Satan in the wilderness. Now in v. 14 Jesus proclaims and claims the significance of his person and work for which those events have prepared us. The expectations of the kingdom of God were in process of realization in the person and work of Jesus. The dozens of references to the kingdom of God in the Synoptic Gospels only serve to underscore the centrality of this proclamation to our interpretation of the Christ event.

It is interesting to compare our text with the parallel in Matt. 4:17, where the call to repent precedes the announcement of the kingdom's nearness. By starting with "The time is fulfilled, and the kingdom of God has come near . . ." (v. 15), Mark accentuates the positive, gospel character of Jesus words, as well as emphasizes their eschatological significance.

The Greek verb behind "has come near" is the perfect tense, suggesting both completion and continuance. Without hanging too much on the interpretation of a verb, the "already-not-yet" character of the divine reign hinted at by this construction connects with the fact that the Bible sees the kingdom as present and fulfilled in Jesus' victory and yet future and still coming.

Having stated what must have been a stunning and exciting, if not audacious, claim to be the agent of a long-expected hope for God's reign, Jesus calls disciples to follow after him. They are from the ranks of humble fishermen. Jesus' affinity for the humble and the lowly in society's estimate is everywhere in the Gospels. These are those who will "fish for people," those who will proclaim the good news revealed in Jesus. "And immediately they left their nets and followed him." The abrupt and unquestioning response implied by these words is almost as astounding as Jesus' claim concerning the kingdom.

In *The Cost of Discipleship,* Dietrich Bonhoeffer talks of the call of the disciples in terms of single-minded obedience. Certainly that appears to be the response of those who left their nets without hesitation. Bonhoeffer then contrasts single-minded obedience with the response of the rich young man who went away sorrowfully when told he must sell all, give the money to the poor, and follow Jesus (Matt. 19:16-22). We don't have to delve into Bonhoeffer's discussion of that story to recognize that the conditions of discipleship appear to be daunting indeed.

Only an eschatological claim of ultimacy could justify the call for such single-minded devotion, and only an ultimate promise of God's favor could equip the followers to be fishers of people. That, of course, is the point. Here, as in the other call narratives we have touched upon this season, the daunting call is couched in the grace of divine promise and the power for obedience that comes with it.

> ONLY AN ESCHATOLOGICAL CLAIM OF ULTIMACY COULD JUSTIFY THE CALL FOR SUCH SINGLE-MINDED DEVOTION, AND ONLY AN ULTIMATE PROMISE OF GOD'S FAVOR COULD EQUIP THE FOLLOWERS TO BE FISHERS OF PEOPLE.

Nonetheless, as we follow Jesus through this world, we walk by faith and hope in the in-between time, not by sight. For centuries the church has plied its "nets," but many are still outside the faith. Much of the world's population has been effectively cut off from a real hearing of the gospel. However, many of those who are surrounded by Christianity and churches seem impervious to the Good News. People hungry for some kind of spirituality gravitate toward sectarian movements or something like the theologically amorphous New Age phenomenon. Why do they turn away from faith in Christ? Such agonizing questions can undermine discipleship or send us scurrying after gimmicks in an exercise of misplaced trust. The struggle is ours. God gives the fulfillment. That is Jesus' message: "The time is fulfilled. . . ."

THE PRESENTATION
OF OUR LORD

FEBRUARY 2, 2003

REVISED COMMON	EPISCOPAL (BCP)	ROMAN CATHOLIC
Mal. 3:1-4	Mal. 3:1-4	Mal. 3:1-4
Psalm 84 or Ps. 24:7-10	Psalm 84 or 84:1-6	Ps. 24:7, 8, 9, 10
Heb. 2:14-18	Heb. 2:14-18	Heb. 2:14-18
Luke 2:22-40	Luke 2:22-40	Luke 2:22-40 or 2:22-32

FIRST READING
MALACHI 3:1-4

Interpreting the Text

It is helpful to the overall understanding of our text if we begin with 2:17 and end with 3:15. Interpreters often regard 2:17—3:15 as a unit. It frames the text, then expresses God's judgment against injustice and moral and spiritual apostasy.

Malachi, whose name means "messenger," appears to have been a prophet associated with the cultic life of Israel, judging by allusions to cult worship and the priestly caste of Levi. God has sent his messenger to announce his coming. It will be a day of judgment against injustice but also a day of purification when the sacrifices of the people will once again be acceptable to God and God will turn things around. This is, after all, the "messenger of the covenant" who is coming and who evokes immediate connotations of God's favor. To be sure, there is confirmation of Israel's unfaithfulness to the covenant, but there is also the assurance that God is changeless in faithfulness. Verses 6-7 carry forward this theme.

Responding to the Text

Malachi's association with the cultic life and priesthood of Jerusalem contributes to the priestly and ritual character of the readings chosen for this day. Epiphany is here mediated by the motifs of priestly leadership in the worship life of the people.

The eschatological message of God's coming to purify and refine injustice and profligacy into justice and righteousness is central to this reading. We are invited to connect John the Baptist with the messenger of the covenant and the coming of Jesus, the Christ, as the fulfillment of God's covenant promise and the ultimate act of purification. We can hardly help but look ahead to the book of Hebrews where Jesus is the perfect sacrifice and the priest who offers it at one and the same time.

The context of Israel's worship life in our reading is an open invitation to reflect on our own eucharistic worship. There we celebrate the once and for all pure sacrifice acceptable to God. There is no need for further sacrifices to be offered on our altars. There is, however, a sacrifice of praise and service. It is implicit in the word *liturgy* itself, which of course means service. Indeed, the Lord's Supper is the very fountainhead of Christian service for justice and the common good. In this supper we are fed, and we rise from table to feed others. Just as the one body and blood of Christ makes us one in communion with him, so our response in neighbor love creates community and solidarity.

RESPONSIVE READING
PSALM 84 OR PSALM 24:7-10 (RCL);
PSALM 84 OR 84:1-6 (BCP);
PSALM 24:7, 8, 9, 10 (RC)

Psalm 84 offers us an elegant and fervent song of praise for the joy of dwelling in God's temple. The lines are memorable. One gets the sense that in God's temple there is peace and security that even the birds who nest there can sense. The reference to the king, the anointed one, in v. 9 leads to the conclusion that this is preexilic. Perhaps with the monarchy intact, the sense of well-being the psalm conveys is further heightened. In any case, in the presence of God in the temple, one feels God's blessing. One feels in worship a foretaste of promised bliss. The psalmist cannot remain in the temple all the time. Neither can we. But when we worship in the presence of God, we receive blessings that go with us into the world.

Psalm 24:7-10 is the second half of a processional hymn sung antiphonally as worshipers move toward the temple. Some suggest that it may have been sung during processions bearing the ark. In our verses the song goes up to the gates, and the response comes back from within. The call is to offer praise at the entrance of the King of glory and the Lord of hosts who is mighty in battle. God is the mighty warrior for Israel. This image is one of many faces of God's faithfulness to the people. When we feel beleaguered in life, we take refuge in God's love, but we also long for one who will be our champion in the good fight.

SECOND READING

HEBREWS 2:14-18

Interpreting the Text

The themes of priesthood and sacrifice are dominant in the book of Hebrews. Christ is our high priest and our sacrifice alike. Only the high priest of the people could offer the sacrifice on the Day of Atonement.

In this reading we have an explanation of the atonement accomplished in Christ. This means freedom from death and from slavery to the fear of death (vv. 14-15). Atonement for the sins of the people (v. 17) means making them as though they were not. That is the sense of the Hebrew that lies behind the Greek (see John 3:16; Rom. 3:25; 2 Cor. 5:19; 1 John 4:10).

ONE IS IMMEDIATELY REMINDED OF ANSELM'S ANCIENT TREATISE *Cur Deus Homo?* (WHY DID GOD BECOME HUMAN?). THE AUTHOR OF HEBREWS ANSWERS THAT AGE-OLD QUESTION BY SIMPLY SAYING, "IT WAS FITTING."

Only by sharing in our humanity could Jesus enter death in order that he might conquer it (v. 14). One is immediately reminded of Anselm's ancient treatise *Cur Deus Homo?* (Why Did God Become Human?). The author of Hebrews answers that age-old question by simply saying, "It was fitting" (v. 10). There is more to say, however. We have the additional assurance that, because Jesus was tested in every way, as we are, being one with us in the flesh, he is able to help those who are being tested (v. 18). This point is then reiterated in 4:15, where we are reminded that we have a high priest who has shared our trials and can sympathize with us.

Responding to the Text

God in Christ has mercifully entered into our sorrow, sin, and death that we might be delivered from their power and have life. That is the message of atonement here, dressed in the cultic imagery of priesthood and sacrifice. As in the corollary texts cited above from John and Paul, the picture is one of God taking matters into God's own hands. It is the story of God with us and God for us, at once both mysterious and clear.

It follows from this note of divine grace that Jesus, as God with us in the flesh, bearing our sorrows and our sins, remains God with us in the lingering trials of our "not yet" world. Those trials are legion. So many things can drive one to despair: the loss of a loved one, perhaps even a child, disgrace, rejection, debilitating illness, reversal of fortune. Even in the absence of personal troubles, sensitivity to the brutalities and terrors of our troubled world alone can cast us deep into doubt.

Adult children often go to their parents for support in times of trial, because they know that their parents have seen much of life's suffering and temptation and will show them understanding, empathy, and love. It is much like that when we go to Jesus, who has undergone all that we have and who can be counted on for love and support. Paul adds a further assurance that is a sibling to our text when he writes to the Corinthian Christians that God is faithful and will not test them beyond their endurance (1 Cor. 10:13).

THE GOSPEL
LUKE 2:22–40 (RCL, BCP, RC);
LUKE 2:22–32 (RC, alt.)

Interpreting the Text

As Jesus was brought for circumcision and naming (2:21), so he is now brought for presentation in the temple. This was in accord with the command laid down in Exod. 13:2 and 12 that all firstborn of the people and their animals should be consecrated to the Lord in remembrance of and in response to God's deliverance of the people from slavery in Egypt.

Now, in this capstone event of Luke's infancy narratives, Jesus is consecrated and set apart, and the ultimate meaning of the theme of deliverance underlying this tradition and ceremony finds expression in Simeon's song. Once more "epiphany light" is shone upon Jesus' messianic identity (vv. 30–32; see Isa. 42:6; 49:6; 52:10), this time in particular before the eyes of Jesus' amazed parents.

Simeon's warning that people will be divided over Jesus (see also 1 Cor. 1:23; 1 Pet. 2:8) certainly proved true then and now. However, his words seem addressed especially to Mary, who must face the piercing of her own soul in the pain of her son's rejection and suffering.

Anna completes the picture. She had been keeping vigil, waiting on the Lord for the redemption of Israel in the revelation of the Messiah. Her response of praise is further affirmation of Jesus' person and work. Being of great age and a widow devoted to prayer and fasting for most of her life, Anna represents the best of a durable faith practiced in patience and grounded in profound trust.

Responding to the Text

The dedication of Jesus in the temple provides another instance of messianic revelation occurring in the context of an event in which Jesus is placed under the law. Later, at his baptism by John, a theophany confirms his sonship. Now at his presentation, we have Simeon's song and Anna's testimony.

Jesus' submission to the law in circumcision and dedication seems to do two things. First, it presages his fulfillment of the law, and second, it reinforces his solidarity with us in all things, a solidarity begun in the incarnation and completed on the cross. The connection with the reading from Hebrews provides a rich combination of meanings and images.

Simeon's promise was fulfilled and Anna's vigil rewarded. He and she were ready to "depart in peace." Yet, while their struggles were about over, as Simeon's warning now suggests, the struggles that were imminent in the conflict that would ensue over this infant Messiah only foreshadowed the hundreds of years of conflict still to come. The sword that pierced Mary's soul in the unspeakable pain of seeing her son crucified is the wicked sword that still pierces our souls in a world of enmity still living at the foot of the cross.

JESUS' SUBMISSION TO THE LAW IN CIRCUMCISION AND DEDICATION SEEMS TO DO TWO THINGS. FIRST, IT PRESAGES HIS FULFILLMENT OF THE LAW, AND SECOND, IT REINFORCES HIS SOLIDARITY WITH US IN ALL THINGS, A SOLIDARITY BEGUN IN THE INCARNATION AND COMPLETED ON THE CROSS.

So we find ourselves, like Simeon and Anna, awaiting the redemption of a world in which corrosive forms of conflict can be found at virtually every level of human interaction. It seems we are unable to receive Jesus' word and way of peace. Anna and Simeon clung to the promises until the sign finally came. So do we. This is the walk of faith on the way to sight. Yet in the child presented at the temple who would one day be the Easter Christ, our eyes too have seen God's salvation.

FOURTH SUNDAY AFTER THE EPIPHANY

FOURTH SUNDAY IN ORDINARY TIME
FEBRUARY 2, 2003

REVISED COMMON	EPISCOPAL (BCP)
Deut. 18:15-20	Deut. 18:15-20
Psalm 111	Psalm 111
1 Cor. 8:1-13	1 Cor. 8:1b-13
Mark 1:21-28	Mark 1:21-28

FIRST READING
DEUTERONOMY 18:15-20

Interpreting the Text

A helpful place to start is at vv. 13-14, which precede the assigned text. Here we see the call to be loyal to God and give no heed to the soothsayers and diviners of the pagan gods. This is the stuff of the first table of the Law, to have no other gods, framed in terms of giving heed only to the word of God spoken through the prophet God appoints. The people's faithfulness to God will then be vindicated by God's faithfulness to them.

Moreover, God will raise up for them a prophet from among the people that they might receive God's word on a human scale. The background to this promise in answer to the people's wish can be found in 5:23-31, where the people hear the word of God at Horeb out of the fire of God's presence and fear they will be consumed. Moses is the first edition of this promise; another will follow.

The command to disregard prophets of other gods or unauthorized prophets is then reiterated in v. 20, another echo of the command to have no other gods (Exod. 20:3).

Responding to the Text

People who keep their promises inspire our trust. We are willing to take their word and count on it. We entrust ourselves to them. Many of life's problems begin when our trust is betrayed. Sometimes this is malicious disregard for us and for the sanctity of a promise. Often it is simply that finite persons and institutions caught in the contingencies of life find themselves unable to keep their promises. Then we may not feel betrayed, but we are still bereft.

At still other times the problem is ours. We trust in "other gods" of success, social status, wealth, power, or romance to bring us happiness and security. But like the pagan prophets Israel was to avoid, these prophets of our culture gods are fickle, unreliable, and ultimately impotent. Nonetheless, they have a powerful allure because they are something near to our world that we can grasp, something we believe we can possess.

God, however, has come near to us, and God is faithful. God gave Moses to the people so that they might receive God's word on a human scale, and God promised a successor to Moses that they might not be abandoned. The fullness of that promise is seen in *the* Word on the truly human scale of the incarnation (see esp. Acts 3:22).

In faith and in life God's actions create our reactions: faithfulness begets faithfulness, faith, and trust.

RESPONSIVE READING
PSALM 111

Psalm 111 is quite obviously a psalm of praise, as the opening verse declares. The focus of the psalmist's praise of God is God's wonderful deeds. Those wonderful deeds include mercy and grace, care for basic needs, justice, and redemption. These qualities of divine activity are at the heart of God's awesome holiness. In sum, God is faithful to the covenant promises made with the people. We in response find God's precepts worthy of trust and obedience. Indeed, in concert with the authors of Job (28:28) and Proverbs (1:7), the fear of the Lord that such trust and obedience signals is the beginning of wisdom (v. 10). The prominent theme of God's faithfulness calling forth our faithfulness makes a fine companion to the similar theme we lifted from the first reading in Deuteronomy.

SECOND READING
1 CORINTHIANS 8:1-13 (RCL);
1 CORINTHIANS 8:1b-13 (BCP)

Interpreting the Text

The initial concern Paul is dealing with is that eating meat sold in the marketplace that had been sacrificed to an idol (v. 4) or eating it in the temple of an idol at a banquet was a problem for "weak" believers. The "strong" in faith, knowing that idols were of no account because there is only one God, our Father, and one Lord, Jesus Christ (vv. 4-6), felt free in this faith to eat without qualms.

Legitimate though this freedom may have been, it was being exercised with a certain prideful disdain and disregard for those who were struggling in conscience over this matter. Therefore, Paul issued a twofold warning. First, those who think they know it all and are enamored of their spiritual superiority only demonstrate that they don't know it all. The important thing is not the pride of knowing but to be known by God in loving God (vv. 1-3). Second, those who truly care about their sisters and brothers in Christ will take care not to cause others to stumble in the faith by the way they exercise their freedom (vv. 9-13).

The factious Corinthians could ill afford to let difference over the eating of meat sacrificed to an idol be yet another cause for division among them.

Responding to the Text

The issue in our text is one that has often been dubbed "giving offense." Christian freedom in the gospel means that many religious practices and prohibitions fostered by legalistic attitudes are not binding on Christian consciences. We do not need nor should we cultivate these practices in order to win God's approval. We are accepted by God in Christ. Spiritual disciplines like certain practices of Lenten self-denial, abstaining entirely from alcohol, or strict adherence to tithing as the only formula for giving are matters open to individual choice in Christian freedom. Similarly, forms of worship and patterns of church governance are also open to the exercise of freedom in the gospel.

However, as with some in the Corinthian congregation, there are those today who have scruples about matters that are in the realm of freedom and may be offended by those who think and act differently. When faced with this challenge in personal relationships or congregational life, we need to recognize that there is one thing we are not free to dispense with: the loving concern that maintains the unity of the faithful in the gospel of Jesus Christ. Sometimes we will have to defer our freedom so as to place no barrier of offense between ourselves and another. Sometimes congregations will need to give extra effort to consideration of making changes in certain practices so these changes do not cause division and strife unnecessarily.

> WE NEED TO RECOGNIZE THAT THERE IS ONE THING WE ARE NOT FREE TO DISPENSE WITH: THE LOVING CONCERN THAT MAINTAINS THE UNITY OF THE FAITHFUL IN THE GOSPEL OF JESUS CHRIST.

At the same time, there are occasions when the freedom of the gospel and its integrity must be maintained by deliberately asserting that freedom as Paul did in resisting the legalistic demand that Christians be circumcised (see Gal. 2:3-5; 5:1-6). Christian love will discern when that response is needed to protect the liberating message of the gospel from compromise, and love will discern when sensitivity to the conscience of another is required, but an arrogant spirit will not.

THE GOSPEL

MARK 1:21-28

Interpreting the Text

The opening verses (vv. 21-22) focus on the revelation of Jesus' teaching authority. In this respect he is obviously superior to the scribes, who were of lesser rank than the rabbis. This comparison, however, is a minor detail in the narrative. Most noteworthy is the fact that Jesus' teaching amazes the people and they are drawn to this magnetic authority. This is a recurrent theme in Mark's Gospel (6:2; 7:37; 10:26; 11:18). There are intimations here of Jesus' messianic identity, especially as his teaching authority is punctuated by his power over unclean spirits (v. 27).

Jesus' exorcism of the demonic spirits (vv. 23-28; see also Luke 4:33-37) completes the messianic picture being constructed here by showing his power over the forces of evil as his first miracle in this narrative (a companion to his defeat of Satan in the wilderness, 1:12-13). Indeed, it is the demon himself who testifies that Jesus is the "Holy One of God" (v. 24).

The Greek word behind the word "unclean" (v. 23) has both cultic and moral nuances. In its cultic association it designates the sort of ritual impurity that separates a person from the worshiping community. But the word is most prominently used in the New Testament in its moral sense reflecting the vices and wickedness of the demonic. Such manifestations of evil are also a manifestation of separation from God.

Responding to the Text

The revelation of God's grace in Jesus Christ is a revelation not only of our salvation but also of our sanctification. The teaching authority of Jesus is able not only to point the way; blended as it is with the power of his person and work, it is also able to empower us to walk the way. Christ's triumph over the evils that assail us restores us to community with God and one another. This is a restoration *to* life and *for* life.

> THE TEACHING AUTHORITY OF JESUS IS ABLE NOT ONLY TO POINT THE WAY; BLENDED AS IT IS WITH THE POWER OF HIS PERSON AND WORK, IT IS ALSO ABLE TO EMPOWER US TO WALK THE WAY.

The very real demonic forces of our world, manifest in enmity, jealousy, greed, lust, and manifold forms of cruelty and disregard for life, are divisive. The demonic is mean spirited in its drive to separate us from God and one another and to divide us within ourselves, pitting the impulses of selfishness against the desire to love. The grace of God in Jesus Christ exorcises the demonic. It reunites us with God and sets us on a path of love and reconciliation with our neighbors.

It heals our torn spirits and makes us whole again. The lingering struggle with evil, within and without, does not go away this side of God's ultimate future, but neither does the Christ.

Once again, the sacramental life of the church undergirds our proclamation. Baptism and the Lord's Supper are both means of grace by which God effects a unity of us all in the body of Christ. As we embrace the newly baptized and gather together at the Lord's Table, we exorcise the divisive impulses of the demonic as God's grace strips away every barrier.

FIFTH SUNDAY AFTER THE EPIPHANY

FIFTH SUNDAY IN ORDINARY TIME
FEBRUARY 9, 2003

REVISED COMMON	EPISCOPAL (BCP)	ROMAN CATHOLIC
Isa. 40:21-31	2 Kings 4:(8-17), 18-21, (22-31), 32-37	Job 7:1-4, 6-7
Ps. 147:1-11, 20c	Psalm 142	Ps. 147:1-2, 3-4, 5-6
1 Cor. 9:16-23	1 Cor. 9:16-23	1 Cor. 9:16-19, 22-23
Mark 1:29-39	Mark 1:29-39	Mark 1:29-39

FIRST READING
ISAIAH 40:21-31 (RCL)

Interpreting the Text

In these verses the prophet extols the majesty of the all-powerful creator God. The ruler of the universe who sits above the heavens in transcendent power is also the ruler of history and the power above all earthly powers (vv. 21-24).

The prophet voices God's challenge: "To whom then will you compare me?" It is a rhetorical question. Moreover, the all-powerful creator and ruler of history is also the all-knowing God who knows the people's struggles and cares about them, even though they may doubt this at times (vv. 25-27).

> THE ALL-POWERFUL CREATOR AND RULER OF HISTORY IS ALSO THE ALL-KNOWING GOD WHO KNOWS THE PEOPLE'S STRUGGLES AND CARES ABOUT THEM, EVEN THOUGH THEY MAY DOUBT THIS AT TIMES.

The everlasting, all-powerful, all-knowing ruler of the universe is beyond our grasp. God does not grow weary or faint, and God gives that same strength to those who *wait,* those who look to God in faith, hope, and trust (vv. 28-31). These words are comfort and encouragement to an Israel exiled in Babylon, doubtless wondering if God is really in charge.

Commentators often note that the Hebrew word for "create," *bara,* used in Genesis 1, is hardly used again in the Hebrew scriptures until Second Isaiah, who uses it sixteen times, including in v. 26 of our reading. This linguistic connection with the Genesis 1 creation narrative summons up a vision of the universal power of God over chaos and the creation from chaos of life, beauty, and order.

It is almost trite but still true that there are often times when our personal world or the world around us seems to be spinning out of orbit. We wonder if God is really in control and, if so, what is going on. What does it all mean that so many things are distressing and out of whack?

Such times are times of exile. We are weary and no longer at home in a world continually gone awry with suffering that we seem helpless to alleviate or estrangement that we cannot mitigate. On the personal level it seems as though we have lost the supports that spell security.

Isaiah gives us a call to faith, not simply that God is in charge and one day that will be clear, but also that we will be strengthened to stand up to the trials of our smaller and larger worlds—worlds that are ultimately not our true home—and even to make a contribution to the common good.

God the creator has overcome the chaos of the void and made a world of awesome beauty and astounding intricacy and order. That same God is our redeemer who has overcome in Christ the chaos of sin and death to make a new and everlasting creation.

2 KINGS 4:(8-17), 18-21, (22-31), 32-37 (BCP)

Interpreting the Text

The prophet grants this barren Shunammite woman her wish to bear a son, one would presume both to insure their family's posterity as well as for the joy of having a child (vv. 8-17). One is immediately reminded of Abraham and Sarah, Hannah (1 Samuel 1), and Elizabeth (Luke 1:5ff.). God brings new life where it seems unlikely.

God also overcomes death when it seems unlikely (vv. 18-37). Elisha's life-giving ministry to the dead son of the Shunammite woman recalls Elijah's very similar miracle in 1 Kings 17:17-24. Snatching life from death is, of course, a powerful theme in the miracles of New Testament record, not to mention Jesus' ultimate victory over death on Easter morning.

Responding to the Text

What parent has not felt the utter dread that comes with the very thought of losing a child to untimely death by disease, accident, or a senseless act of brutality? We stand in stunned silence before the horror of such an event, like Job, unable to fathom the sense of such evil.

What makes this story so poignant and so important? Perhaps the terrible sense of loss we feel or can imagine at the death of a child is a way to present with inescapable power the profound truth of death itself and all the unanswered questions it raises. In so doing, we see the profound necessity of Jesus' triumph over it.

JOB 7:1-4, 6-7 (RC)

Interpreting the Text

We are all familiar with the story of Job. It draws us into the often impenetrable and enigmatic nature of human suffering in which bad things happen to good people for no apparent reason, yielding no apparent meaning unless we are prepared to concede that life is simply absurd.

Within this larger thematic context our text presents Job's comments on the simple fact that human life in general, and Job's life in particular, is a hard journey marked by striving and struggles virtually like that of a slave laborer (vv. 1-2). We endure misery and worse, one might aver, a sense of emptiness of meaning that brings restless nights devoid of peaceful sleep (vv. 3-4). Moreover, this life is transient and ends seemingly without hope (v. 6). Finally, Job ends his soliloquy and begins to address God concerning his fleeting and abandoned state (v. 7).

Responding to the Text

Job's story is a classical locus for the age-old question of why there is evil in a world ruled by a benevolent and omnipotent God. It wouldn't be so vexing a question if we could simply say that God allows us to suffer the consequences of our misdeeds, but the book of Job seems to gainsay that by pointing out at the beginning that Job is "blameless and upright" (1:1). Thus, it is an explanation that works only some of the time.

Instead, we are forced to face the fact that the reality of human sin runs deeper than can be detected in the contrast between morality and immorality. Rather, all of us are caught in its web of brokenness and death. Even the so-called decent and the prosperous among us cannot escape that reality as Job, himself both decent and prosperous, discovered, albeit in a most dramatic way. And what of all the "innocents" of the world whose lot is misery because an accident of birth placed them in the midst of oppression, poverty, disease, and starvation?

Job nevertheless speaks to God (7:7ff.), and God also speaks to Job. The relationship is not destroyed in the mystery of Job's suffering. Therein is the signal of hope.

PSALM 147:1–11, 20c (RCL);
PSALM 142 (BCP);
PSALM 147:1–2, 3–4, 5–6 (RC)

In general, Psalm 147 is a psalm of praise that lifts up the testimony that God the creator is also God the provider and the God who cares for the down-trodden. More specifically, this divine activity is focused on God's steadfast love for Israel. Themes that recur in Second and Third Isaiah have their counterpart here. Verse 2 suggests the end of the exile. Verse 3 brings to mind Isa. 61:1, and v. 4 reminds one of Isa. 40:26. Finally, God's covenant with Israel is recalled in v. 20 (see Deut. 4:7-8).

If Israel was "imprisoned," so to speak, in its exile at the time of Psalm 147, the individual crying out in Psalm 142 is actually imprisoned by his persecutors (v. 7). As he pours out his heart to God and airs his suffering, he does so in the confidence that God will deliver him (v. 7b). God is his only hope and advocate (vv. 4-5).

SECOND READING

1 CORINTHIANS 9:16–23 (RCL, BCP);
1 CORINTHIANS 9:16–19, 22–23 (RC)

Interpreting the Text

In this reading we learn about yet another dimension of our freedom in the gospel. Paul tells us that to live in the gospel and preach the gospel is its own reward. The call to preach is both compelling and liberating (vv. 16-19). This freedom for which we have been set free is a freedom to serve.

Paul therefore puts the call to serve by sharing the grace of the gospel for the sake of others ahead of the rights the gospel itself bestows. This is the other-directedness of neighbor love, which the Lord exemplifies in his self-emptying love and calls on us to imitate.

Responding to the Text

Two focal points for our response leap into view almost automatically. The first is the connection we can make with Luther's *Treatise on Christian Liberty,* and the second is the significance of Paul's admonition for our own practice of evangelism.

Those familiar with Luther's writing on the freedom of the Christian will remember that his treatise is based on the apparent contradiction that the Christian is perfectly free and subject to none yet dutiful servant to all. The freedom that we have in Christ is freedom from the condemnation of the law through the freely given grace of forgiveness that we embrace with the arms of faith. Our freedom in Christ is the freedom to be bound—bound to the needs of our neighbor in love. We serve not to please God and gain God's favor, but out of the joy of being loved and set free from self-concern. This is the foundation of the Christian ethic as a witness to the gospel. When we preach about service to our neighbor and the witness of active Christian concern for the manifold needs of our world, we should do so not by making people feel guilty and shaming them into action. Rather, we should start with the gospel and what God has set us free to do. Loving as we have been loved is an integral part of our gospel proclamation. The history of the Christian church is filled with glowing examples of persons who have given freely in Christlike love. Some you know personally, and some are well known to all.

The counterpart to this servant-freedom in the matter of evangelism is in our readiness to give of ourselves for the sake of the neighbor and our witness to Christ. When we set out to share the gospel, we are to do so by meeting people where they are. As much as is humanly possible, we should try to put ourselves in our neighbor's place so that we can better understand how the gospel speaks to them and we can then help them to hear it. It means moving out of our comfort zone and getting involved with people. Evangelism is not a program or a technique; it is an intimate process of sharing.

Though Paul sought to be all things to all people, few of us can pull that off. Together, as a collection of Christians with many varied gifts, however, we have what we need to meet people where they are.

THE GOSPEL
MARK 1:29-39

Interpreting the Text

Jesus restores Simon's mother-in-law so completely that she is able to get up and serve them (vv. 29-31). Here and in Matthew's account (Matt. 8:14-15), the verb in the phrase "lifted her up" is the same Greek verb that is used frequently in the New Testament for Jesus' resurrection. Was this event then intended as a prefiguring of Jesus' resurrection as some have wondered? It may be a stretch to hang that conclusion on a verb, but it is consistent with Jesus' self-revelation to say that the miracles of healing and exorcism (vv. 32-34), signifying power over

evil, are among the marks of the expected Messiah and point to the ultimate healing of Jesus' resurrection and its triumph over evil.

Jesus' forbidding the demons, who recognized him, to speak further signals that
miracles are intended to point beyond themselves (v. 34). This "messianic secret"
passage is one among a number in which Jesus enjoins silence, scholars have
concluded, because he did not wish to be identified with false understandings of
the Messiah as a mere miracle worker. God's messianic agenda was far greater
than those individual acts of immediate blessing or even than the fortunes of Israel
itself. Furthermore, this view is consistent with Jesus' refusal to remain in Caper-
naum and take advantage of the popularity his works had generated. Instead,
he went on the road to preach in the neighboring towns of Galilee (vv. 37-39).
Luke 4:43 adds Jesus' statement to this account that he must fulfill his mission to
"proclaim the good news of the kingdom."

Responding to the Text

God's plans for us are greater than our own hopes. Given the choice, we
often settle for less than is possible. We want comfort, security, and peace for our
own lives and our families. In Jesus' works of healing
and in his concern for all human need, he shows that he
cares about these very real and very understandable concerns and desires. Even at that, however, he wants us to
see how the goods of life in the present point beyond themselves to a coming
reign of God in which a perfection of life beyond our best hopes awaits our
world.

GOD'S PLANS FOR US ARE GREATER THAN
OUR OWN HOPES.

In the meantime, as Peter's mother-in-law was raised up to serve, so are we,
seeking in love the healing of persons and of our world as Jesus himself did. As
Jesus also taught us by his own actions, we understand how these acts point
beyond themselves as anticipations in concrete terms of the wonderful promises
of the coming reign of God, which we preach as the good news Christ came to
reveal. Individuals engaged in service, congregational ministries of healing and
outreach, social ministries of care and advocacy, and global ministries feeding the
hungry and seeking justice are all partners in the same mission of pointing the
way to the future by healing broken lives and a broken world in the present.

SIXTH SUNDAY
AFTER THE EPIPHANY

SIXTH SUNDAY IN ORDINARY TIME
FEBRUARY 16, 2003

REVISED COMMON	EPISCOPAL (BCP)	ROMAN CATHOLIC
2 Kings 5:1-14	2 Kings 5:1-15b	Lev. 13:1-2, 44-46
Psalm 30	Psalm 42 or 42:1-7	Ps. 32:1-2, 5, 11
1 Cor. 9:24-27	1 Cor. 9:24-27	1 Cor. 10:31—11:1
Mark 1:40-45	Mark 1:40-45	Mark 1:40-45

FIRST READING

2 KINGS 5:1-14 (RCL);
2 KINGS 5:1-15b (BCP)

Interpreting the Text

Elisha's healing of the Syrian commander Naaman ("Aram" = the later Greek designation, "Syria") parallels the healing of the leper in the Gospel for this day. As we shall see, however, the Gospel account has a somewhat different emphasis.

Leprosy is an imprecise term in the Bible, covering a variety of skin diseases as well as the leprosy we know today as Hansen's disease. Naaman either had something other than Hansen's or was in the early stages of it, for he was still actively involved among his troops. Nevertheless, his concern was obviously great considering the size of the tribute brought to the king of Israel (v. 5).

Notwithstanding this detail, the focus is not on compassion for one who suffers or fears for his life, though that may be inferred. Rather, the point is that Naaman's healing at the instruction of the prophet showed that the God of Israel alone is God (v. 15). Elisha's refusal to come out to Naaman, who was determined in his pride not to go to Elisha, can be construed as faithful representation of the one God who is above all rather than a reciprocal act of pride on Elisha's part.

Responding to the Text

One might suppose there is a little Naaman in many of us at times. We want God's favor but on our own terms or in line with our own reasoning as to how things should go. We want to be numbered among the disciples but wish to choose our own path, our own idea of what discipleship involves. What receiving God's favor might involve, however, is giving up our pet notions and comfortable assumptions for the unfamiliar territory to which God calls us. Seminaries are full of people who have left successful careers behind to prepare for the ministries of the church. They have felt called to a place far from where they thought they would be. At the same time, some who come in their zeal to serve the gospel discover that this was their idea and not God's. God had other modes of service in mind for them. Even high-minded commitments can be off the mark. Not a few Christians have yet to face the tough questions of how their practices in their workplace lives may be dramatically out of sync with the values of their faith. All of us, no matter what our station in life, are likely to face garden-variety questions of stewardship and faithfulness in prayer and worship.

Just as Jesus in our reading from Mark wanted to prevent people from imposing on him their false notions and expectations about the Messiah in order that they might eventually see the truth, so Elisha had to challenge Naaman to be open to God's leading. What we find when we are open to God's bidding is that God wants to heal us of all our ills of body and spirit and make us God's own.

LEVITICUS 13:1-2, 44-46 (RC)

Interpreting the Text

These verses provide background to the Gospel reading and help to spell out the significance of Jesus' healing of the leper. As noted in the discussion of 2 Kings 5:1-15, *leprosy* is an imprecise term for a variety of skin diseases. When the disease reached a certain degree of severity, as determined by the priest, the person was rendered ceremonially unclean and excluded from the worshiping community and the community in general, being forced to warn anyone who might draw near that he or she was "unclean."

Responding to the Text

People are created for community with God and with one another. The tragic condition of lepers was not only their disease, as sad as that may have been, but also their isolation from their physical and spiritual communities. They were outcasts living with public humiliation. God's will, however, was to restore all people to community and to heal their brokenness. As the psalmist says, "God gives the desolate a home to live in" (Ps. 68:6). Or, if you prefer the King James Version, "God setteth the solitary in families."

Responsive Reading

PSALM 30 (RCL);
PSALM 42 OR 42:1-7 (BCP);
PSALM 32:1-2, 5, 11 (RC)

Psalm 30 gives thanks for healing and thus fits nicely with the other readings. In vv. 4-5 the congregation is encouraged to join in this praise and acknowledge that, while we weep in this life, God's favor endures and joy outlives sorrow. In v. 9 there is a touch of bargaining as the psalmist makes the point that it is hardly in God's interest to let him die and have his words of praise and testimony thereby silenced.

Psalm 42 expresses hope in God in the midst of illness and suffering, which have kept the psalmist from the temple worship he longs for (vv. 1-2) and brought taunts from those who cry, "Where is your God?" (vv. 3, 10). One can readily see how this might be the troubled prayer of a leper and thereby appreciate the greater depth of the pathos involved in the leprosy we meet in the other readings.

Psalm 32 deals with gratitude for healing but offers the additional observation that healing goes hand in hand with repentance and forgiveness. One thinks of Jesus connecting forgiveness and healing (Matt. 9:1-8; Mark 2:1-12; Luke 5:17-26) in a story we will read next Sunday.

SECOND READING
1 CORINTHIANS 9:24-27 (RCL, BCP)

Interpreting the Text

This metaphor for the life of discipleship would certainly communicate to a Greek audience familiar with athletic games as an integral part of the culture (see also Phil. 3:12-14 and 2 Tim. 4:7-8 for parallel ideas). Athletes in Paul's day competed for a prize that was no more than a wreath of vegetation that would soon shrivel up and disintegrate. If these athletes were willing to submit themselves to severe training for a moment of honor as transient as the perishable wreath that symbolized it, how much more should we who seek an eternal goal be willing to discipline our lives in that cause? This form of argument has a rabbinic flavor: "If for a perishable, how much more for an imperishable?" (see, e.g., Matt. 6:26, 30). Paul also admonishes his readers to be imitators of him as he is of Christ (1 Cor. 11:1).

THIS METAPHOR FOR THE LIFE OF DISCIPLESHIP WOULD CERTAINLY COMMUNICATE TO A GREEK AUDIENCE FAMILIAR WITH ATHLETIC GAMES AS AN INTEGRAL PART OF THE CULTURE.

Placed in the larger context of Paul's writings, we know that the discipline he encourages is not a condition of salvation but an imperative that arises out of the indicative of God's acceptance. It is a call to be what we are, children of God, saints, members of Christ's body, and to act in ways that serve the gospel out of the freedom we have in Christ (recall the previous week's reading from 1 Cor. 9:16-23).

We all have heard stories of athletes who made it to the top of their game then became so smug and cocky that they began to neglect the discipline required, ending their sports career tragically.

To choose another example common to human experience, we know of marriages or other precious relationships that disintegrate due to neglect. We take one another for granted and fail to pay attention to each other's needs.

Our relationship to God can suffer the same sort of neglect. We drift away from the disciplines of faith, such as hearing the Word, partaking of the means of grace, praying, and participating in the faith community. From these come the strength to run the marathon race of discipleship and the joy that comes with the presence of God along the way.

1 CORINTHIANS 10:31—11:1 (RC)

Interpreting the Text

Paul is now summarizing his discussion of freedom and offense, which we encountered in the readings of the previous two Sundays. He enjoins the Corinthians to give no offense to Jews, Greeks, or any in the church (10:32). This admonition reflects the inclusiveness of the gospel and of Paul's very mission as a Jew sent to the Gentile world and as one concerned for the "unity of the Spirit in the bond of peace" (Eph. 4:3; see also Phil. 1:27).

The context tells us that Paul's statement about trying "to please everyone" (10:33) is not an effort to curry favor for himself in some obsequious manner. Rather, he is attempting to faithfully present the faith with sensitivity to his audience and therefore in a manner that places no unnecessary barriers to its reception. Similarly, it can be easy to misconstrue Paul's encouragement to be imitators of him as an arrogant claim (11:1) unless we look carefully at the second half of the statement and recognize that it is a call to imitate Christ (see also Phil. 2:4ff.; 1 Thess. 1:6).

Responding to the Text

The call to be imitators of Christ perhaps had its popular contemporary incarnation in the recent spread of "What would Jesus do?" (WWJD) bracelets. The inventor hoped that we would wear the bracelet and be reminded of and guided by Jesus' example and teaching as we faced life's challenging decisions.

In matters of moral choice, we certainly have much to go by in the Bible, and we have the Spirit to guide us and to form us in the love exemplified by and commanded by Christ. Still there remain many questions as we try to cope with the dilemmas of a very different world. For this we need the help of the community of believers engaged in moral deliberation and discernment of what it means to be imitators of Christ.

In our text Paul is quite clear about what the imitation of Christ entails. We need to put the gospel first. However, here too we need one another to discern as a Christian community what putting the gospel first requires in our increasingly multicultural world. We need to nurture an understanding of others and sensitivity to their ways rather than insisting on our own modes of thought. In what ways, then, can our faith community become a more welcoming community?

THE GOSPEL
MARK 1:40-45

Interpreting the Text

The first readings of the day have already given us the occasion to note that *leprosy* is a term that can stand for a number of different diseases and that severe forms—whatever the actual disease of the skin—could by priestly decision render a person unclean and isolate him or her from the worshiping community and from society in general (Leviticus 13; see esp. vv. 44-46). This is important background for understanding the significance of the healing of this leper in our Gospel.

"Moved with pity" (v. 41) is a translation of a strong Greek verb of compassion in which one's inward parts are figuratively poured out in intense response to the plight of others. We might say, "My heart goes out to you," although that would be a weak contemporary variation made even less vivid by overuse.

Matthew and Luke also have this story but not with this description of Jesus' compassionate response. In other contexts in both those Gospels, however, this verb used of Jesus' pity occurs in association with a variety of human needs (Matt. 15:32; 20:34; Luke 7:13; 10:33; 15:20).

Again, as before, Jesus wants to keep the focus on his true mission to which his miracles point rather than on the miracles themselves. So he enjoins silence, but he cannot keep this joyous former leper quiet (vv. 43-45).

Responding to the Text

There are two related points to consider in our response to the Gospel story. First, it is helpful to reiterate comments made in connection with the Leviticus 13 reading that Jesus' healing restores persons to community just as Jesus' saving work of reconciliation restores us to community with God and one another. Anyone who has been estranged from spouse and family knows the terrible loneliness and loss of identity that come with it. We have a need to belong, even in our rather mobile and individualistic society. So it is that we are not saved simply as individuals but brought into the body of Christ, the communion of saints. This is a good connection with our discussion of baptism earlier in Epiphany. The worshiping community of the baptized is an anticipation of the heavenly community despite its evident warts.

Second, the community of Christ's people is a compassionate one, following in the steps of its Savior, imitating him as Paul calls us to do in the epistle reading. That compassion takes shape in our caring outreach to all people, especially those who are without a caring community, lonely, and on the margins of life, perhaps because they are disdained as unfit like the leper Jesus healed. In any case, whether it is concern for ordinary lonely people, homeless people, orphans, prisoners, the mentally ill, the senile, or the dying, that Christlike caring punctuates the gospel message we are called to proclaim. As that powerful combination of word and deed brings others into God's family, we realize our epiphany mission.

AS THAT POWERFUL COMBINATION OF WORD AND DEED BRINGS OTHERS INTO GOD'S FAMILY, WE REALIZE OUR EPIPHANY MISSION.

SEVENTH SUNDAY AFTER THE EPIPHANY

SEVENTH SUNDAY IN ORDINARY TIME
FEBRUARY 23, 2003

REVISED COMMON	EPISCOPAL (BCP)	ROMAN CATHOLIC
Isa. 43:18-25	Isa. 43:18-25	Isa. 43:18-19, 21-22, 24b-25
Psalm 41	Psalm 32 or 32:1-8	Ps. 41:2-3, 4-5, 13-14
2 Cor. 1:18-22	2 Cor. 1:18-22	2 Cor. 1:18-22
Mark 2:1-12	Mark 2:1-12	Mark 2:1-12

FIRST READING

ISAIAH 43:18-25 (RCL, BCP);
ISAIAH 43:18-19, 21-22, 24b-25 (RC)

Interpreting the Text

God is going to do a new thing (v. 19). A new act of deliverance will overshadow the memory of even the exodus (v. 18) as well as other past acts of divine largesse. Israel is in exile in Babylon as it once was enslaved in Egypt. As God made a path through the sea for their deliverance from Pharaoh, so God will now make a way in the wilderness, a way that promises new life even as "rivers in the desert" bring life to an arid landscape (v. 20).

GOD IS GOING TO DO A NEW THING.

God is doing this new thing despite Israel's faithlessness (vv. 22-25) and the way they have wearied God with their sins. Moreover, that "new thing" also involves the forgiveness of their sin in its promise of a new beginning (v. 25).

Responding to the Text

God does a new thing. That is the key thought. In creation God brings a new universe of beauty and order out of the nothingness of the chaos (recall our discussion of Genesis 1 on Epiphany 1). In the deliverance of Israel from Egypt, God makes a new people out of a slave people. God makes out of "no people" a "royal priesthood" and a "holy nation," "God's people" (1 Pet. 2:9-10). Anyone who is in Christ is a "new creation" (2 Cor. 5:17).

So it is that God makes rivers of new life arise from the barren desert. This is a metaphor for the life-giving power of God's forgiving mercy. Through forgiveness of sin in Christ, God brings life to the arid soil of our sinful humanity, a life that prevails even in the face of death.

Living in the light of that solid promise, we should not be surprised that God does new things in our lives at times when we feel burdened by sin, exiled from our spiritual home, or dried up in spirit and body like the desert itself. Perhaps it is hearing the word of God's forgiveness and love speak to us with new and unexpected clarity and power. Perhaps it is the presence of support from those around us that we never realized was there for us. Perhaps it is a brand new opportunity or a new lease on life in the midst of vexing illness. The manifestations of God's new things are more than we can name.

The idea of the "new" is a great Epiphany idea. It connotes something revelatory, unexpected, and wonderful.

RESPONSIVE READING
PSALM 41 (RCL);
PSALM 32 OR 32:1-8 (BCP);
PSALM 41:2-3, 4-5, 13-14 (RC)

The psalmist of Psalm 41 is very sick, and his enemies relish his pain and misfortune (vv. 5-8). Even his good friend has turned against him (v. 9). Despite it all, however, the psalmist has faith in God (vv. 1-3, 11-12), so he prays for healing, deliverance from his enemies, and forgiveness of sins (v. 4), a complex of concerns we have seen addressed in the Isaiah 43 reading as well.

The combination of healing, forgiveness, and deliverance is pronounced in Psalm 32 as well (vv. 1-7). This time the interconnected character of these aspects of God's mercy is expounded in the context of a song of praise and thanksgiving for these blessings from God. Once again, as in so many texts with this sort of theme, the recognition of God's peculiar covenant love, God's promising love, that is, God's "steadfast love," is lifted up as the abiding hope of the faithful (v. 10).

SECOND READING
2 CORINTHIANS 1:18-22

Interpreting the Text

The immediate background provided by vv. 15-17 tells us that Paul was being criticized for being fickle, because he had apparently changed his plans to visit Corinth both before and after his trip to Macedonia.

Our reading then begins with Paul's emphatic denial that he is fickle. You can count on Paul no less than you can count on God (v. 18). Paul and his colleagues have faithfully proclaimed the reliable promise of God in Christ. Mention of the reliability of God's promise, then, prompts a shift of ground. Paul now lifts up God's unambiguous "yes" in Christ, who is the fulfillment of all promises and hopes and the ground of our certainty (vv. 19-20).

The gift of the Holy Spirit through the gospel in baptism is further basis for trust (see also Rom. 8:16, 23; Eph. 1:13; 1 John 2:27). The Spirit secures the truth of Christ and is also a sign, a first installment (also can be translated "pledge" of "earnest money" or "down payment") of the dawn of God's eschatological rule, a point that further underscores the theme of promises kept.

Responding to the Text

An unqualified "yes"? Where do you get something like that? People and organizations in whom we put our trust certainly make a lot of promises and guarantees. Often they can be relied upon; but often, due to fickleness or the contingencies of finitude, we find ourselves disappointed or even disenchanted. This is why we frequently require some pledge in advance to ensure the sincerity of the promise. When we purchase a house, we are required to put down some "earnest money" at the time we sign an agreement to purchase. When we make other major purchases, we provide a down payment. When we take marriage vows, we commit ourselves legally through the instrument of a license and ceremony recognized by the state as the first installment of a lifelong promise. All these devices are a hedge against the frailty of human arrangements.

God's "yes" to us is unconditional, and God's love for us is unqualified: God is unaffected by the contingencies of finitude, and God does not waver from steadfast love. Yet God still gives us "earnest money" or a "first installment" by which to secure our faith in the divine promises. In the Christ event, whose truth is sealed in our hearts by the Spirit, we have a definitive experience in the present of the future of life, peace, and harmony that awaits us in the culmination of God's promised future. By the Spirit we also, then, join Paul, Silas, and Timothy in the confident proclamation of this unconditional "yes!"

THE GOSPEL
MARK 2:1-12

Interpreting the Text

Scholars wonder about the unity of this passage, suggesting that perhaps the healing miracle account (vv. 1-4, 11-12) has been spliced together with an account of a controversy over forgiveness (vv. 5-10). This seems especially probable to some since the section on forgiveness includes both a divine claim (v. 7) and a messianic claim (v. 10; the "one like a son of man" in Dan. 7:13-14 [NIV] was often thought to be the Messiah) at a place in Mark's narrative where Jesus has been deliberately secretive concerning his person and work.

Although we need to note this commonplace observation about the text, the fact is that it is a perfect unity from a theological perspective; it is consistent with the strong biblical theme of linking healing and forgiveness that is also present in the Isaiah 43 reading and the two psalm selections for the day. Added to that linkage is the aspect of faith. Jesus saw how much faith they had before he proceeded (v. 5). Faith and healing also have strong connections in Jesus' ministry (Luke 7:9; 8:48; 17:19) and faith, healing, and forgiveness come together in the prayer of Psalm 41.

THE NARRATIVE ENABLES US TO SEE JESUS' HEALING MIRACLES IN THE LARGER CONTEXT OF TRUST IN THE PROMISES OF GOD'S SAVING WORK NOW REVEALED MOST FULLY IN THE CHRIST.

Once again the narrative enables us to see Jesus' healing miracles in the larger context of trust in the promises of God's saving work now revealed most fully in the Christ. Because Jesus' works of healing are portrayed in this larger context, we hardly have here a proof text for sensationalist faith healers.

Responding to the Text

One might readily imagine the paralytic thinking to himself, "Thanks for the word of forgiveness, but that's not exactly what I had in mind." He was soon to find out, however, that God had a larger plan for him than he had imagined and that he was about to play a part in a drama of revelatory significance. Several thoughts seem to follow.

Could we not consider the possibility that God's plans for us are often larger than our immediate concerns, even concerns as monumental as those of the paralytic? Given the limits of our finite vision, it is sometimes hard for us to see beyond the need to solve the present problem or to satisfy the present desire. The solution of immediate problems or the satisfaction of present desires leave unanswered the question of the overall meaning of life and the outlook with which we face a parade of ever new problems and desires that march along through our lives. That outlook is the outlook of faith, and God's larger plan for us is to live out that faith in the promise of God's forgiveness and the ultimate healing of Jesus' victory.

Living out that faith as members of Christ's body, the church, means that we, like the paralytic and those who were there with him, are witnesses to the revelation of God in Christ with a call to carry forward that witness. It is a witness in word and deed after the manner of the Christ who showed forth his divinity and his messianic identity in both healing and forgiving. Our proclamation of God's forgiveness in Christ is punctuated by acts of mercy and advocacy for those conditions in our world that make for peace and enable all life to flourish. The healing of the paralytic paired with the word of forgiveness reminds us of the unity of our Creator and Redeemer in the unity of the Trinity and the unity of the work of creation and redemption that is ultimately manifest in the resurrection of the whole person.

THE TRANSFIGURATION OF OUR LORD / LAST SUNDAY AFTER THE EPIPHANY

EIGHTH SUNDAY IN ORDINARY TIME
MARCH 2, 2003

REVISED COMMON	EPISCOPAL (BCP)	ROMAN CATHOLIC
2 Kings 2:1–12	1 Kings 19:9–18	Hos. 2:16b, 17b, 21–22
Ps. 50:1–6	Psalm 27 or 27:5–11	Ps. 103:1–2, 3–4, 8, 10, 12–13
2 Cor. 4:3–6	2 Pet. 1:16–19, (20–21)	2 Cor. 3:1b–6
Mark 9:2–9	Mark 9:2–9	Mark 2:18–22

FIRST READING
2 KINGS 2:1–12 (RCL)

Interpreting the Text

Elijah's greatness as the prophet among all prophets is underscored by his being taken into heaven directly without passing through death. On his way to that moment of his assumption, he replicated the exodus miracle of parting the sea by the analogous miracle of parting the waters of the Jordan with his mantle (v. 8). Elijah stands in the train of Moses.

Elijah was a man strong in the Spirit. He was a truly inspired prophet whose spirit was known and revered by the community of prophets. This reverence for Elijah is evident in the reaction of these prophets when they perceived that Elisha now possessed the spirit of Elijah (v. 15). Elisha asked his master for a double portion of his strong spirit. Elijah promised it if Elisha was permitted to witness his departure to heaven, and he was. This transfer of spiritual authority was confirmed when Elisha picked up Elijah's mantle and parted the waters of the Jordan as his master had done.

Responding to the Text

God's Spirit is faithful in raising up new voices in each generation that will proclaim the Word of God. The mantle is passed from generation to generation as leaders fit for the particular demands of their time and place arise by God's prompting from among the people.

The vision of Elijah's assumption, which confirms Elisha's succession; the passing of the mantle of authority from Elijah to Elisha; and the recognition of Elisha's preeminence by the company of prophets all remind us that our leaders in the community of faith are not self-appointed. Rather, they are sealed by God's Spirit, and there are outward signs of succession and attestation by the community.

This pattern of confirmation is a great gift to be cherished by the people of God as signs that reassure us of the faithful proclamation of God's Word. This same message of conferred authority is implicit in the apostles' presence with Jesus at his transfiguration. Like Elisha, they too shall be heirs of the spirit of their Master; only he is a Master who is more than a prophet. This implicit promise is, of course, made explicit with great power at Pentecost, and it is carried forward in the life of the church in a variety of ways. We are ordained to the priesthood of all believers in our baptism, as we observed earlier. We lay on hands in ordination to the ministry of Word and Sacrament. We commission people for various ministries and pray for them to receive the gift of the Spirit.

1 KINGS 19:9-18 (BCP)

Interpreting the Text

Even prophets can get discouraged and start feeling sorry for themselves (vv. 10, 14). Look at Jeremiah and his personal laments (six of them can be found in Jer. 11:18—12:6) as another prominent example.

We know from a variety of biblical accounts that powerful natural phenomena usually accompany the presence of God and some form of theophany. Here these signs usher in the voice of God out of the "sheer silence," a sudden, contrasting, penetrating quiet (not the "still small voice" that has launched so many sermons, I'm sorry to say) that followed (vv. 11-13).

"Get up and go about the business I've assigned you." That is basically the message Elijah received. And with the call to get back into action and overcome the fears for his life that accompanied his discouragement (v. 10, repeated in v. 14) is a promise from God: There are those who are not apostate and they will be spared (v. 18).

Perhaps the seven thousand to be spared are somehow related to the notion of the "righteous remnant" in Isa. 10:20 and 11:11, an assurance that God's Word will not be denied. Perhaps, then, the promise of the seven thousand could be likened to Jesus' purpose in telling the parable of the sower to his disciples. One can well imagine that some of them may have been discouraged at the progress or lack of progress in their mission in those heady early days. The parable certainly describes the various reasons why faith fails to take root or to flourish. The real point of the parable, however, is reassurance that fertile soil exists and that God's Word will take root and grow (Matt. 13:8).

Responding to the Text

Pastors, like prophets, can get discouraged at times. They work hard to spread the gospel in their community and long to see an increase in the number of the faithful, but often they find that people seem impervious to the invitation. There are so many competing agendas in a culture that no longer even regards Sunday morning as sacred time to be reserved for worship. Perhaps the mission never gets off the ground because the congregation is torn by conflict. Caught in the middle of this conflict, a pastor may feel almost like Elijah did, alone and threatened.

Others trying to do God's will in their lives can have the same sorts of feelings. Caregivers for the elderly, the infirm, and the disabled may feel as though they have given their all and are unappreciated, wondering at times whether they were simply fools to sacrifice their own ambitions. Persons engaged in advocacy can certainly be tempted to think that true justice is always elusive, and every partial gain seems overmatched by setbacks. Indeed, Christians in all walks of life may for any number of reasons be filled with terrible questions about the meaning of being a faithful Christian.

Yet, despite it all, God is at work and things are happening, sometimes without our realizing them or appreciating their significance. I still remember a pastoral visit to a young woman in the hospital who was in deep distress. I fumbled trying to find something meaningful to say and left her bedside totally discouraged; I was sure I hadn't helped her in any way. Months later, after church, she came to me in tears thanking me profusely for all that I had done for her. I had done nothing at all effective, but I had brought the Word of God's grace to her, and God had given her healing and hope.

> GOD IS AT WORK AND THINGS ARE HAPPENING, SOMETIMES WITHOUT OUR REALIZING THEM OR APPRECIATING THEIR SIGNIFICANCE.

HOSEA 2:16b, 17b, 21-22 (RC)

It will be helpful as we discuss this reading to see it as a unit of vv. 16-23. Set in the eighth century after the Assyrian conquest, the book of Hosea in general brings a message of redemption to God's beleaguered people. This text is no exception.

As in Israel's honeymoon period with God after her deliverance from Egypt (v. 15), she will again call God her "husband," and the name of "Baal," the Canaanite deity, will vanish and no longer be voiced.

The context of this promise is God's renewal of a universal covenant of peace and harmony among all people and among all creatures (v. 18; see also Lev. 26:6; Job 5:23; Isa. 11:6-9; Ezek. 34:25-31). Israel will be God's bride forever. The earth shall flourish as well, along with justice and righteousness (v. 19) under the steadfast love and mercy of God presented tenderly in the persistent imagery of marriage.

Responding to the Text

The recurrent themes of God's love and redemption are here once more couched in the intimate metaphor of marriage to describe the loving relationship God has with the people. To be sure, this imagery has a patriarchal cast, as does the analogy of Christ's relation to the church in Eph. 5:23ff. Still, the message in those historical contexts is clearly one of tender loving care and faithfulness on God's part. This same orientation is also implied in those places where the Gospels describe Jesus as the "bridegroom." An example of this is in the Gospel reading from Mark 2:18-22, which is paired with this lesson from Hosea. A few points of significance follow from these observations.

First, as in the preeminent event of the incarnation so in the metaphor of marriage, God chooses visceral modes of communication that are anchored in the core of human experience. Second, there is an eschatological dimension to God's promise, which Jesus, the bridegroom and the greater fulfillment of Hosea's prophecy, picks up in the Gospel reading from Mark 2. Finally, included in this eschatological vision is a harmonious, peaceful, and abundant creation in the grand tradition of Isa. 11:6-9. Again and again in the texts we have reviewed we are invited to see how God's creating work and saving work coalesce. Again and again, then, we are invited to consider how our work for peace and harmony in *this* world is a part of our testimony to the hope that is within us.

AGAIN AND AGAIN IN THE TEXTS WE HAVE REVIEWED WE ARE INVITED TO SEE HOW GOD'S CREATING WORK AND SAVING WORK COALESCE.

RESPONSIVE READING

PSALM 50:1-6 (RCL)

God is coming to judge God's people. The whole of creation is called as witness (cf. Isa. 1:2). The powerful signs in nature of God's coming are typical of signs that accompany theophany (see the notes above on 1 Kings 19:9-18). We anticipate again the definitive theophany in our Gospel for Transfiguration Sunday.

Covenant is a key term (v. 5), and for the covenant people the proper sacrifice is not one of animals but of righteous behavior and thanksgiving, as the psalm goes on to spell out (vv. 7-23), even as God is a righteous judge (v. 6).

PSALM 27 OR 27:5-11 (BCP)

This is an individual prayer for deliverance and a lament over the oppression the psalmist is suffering from his enemies. It is mingled with expressions of trust in God's deliverance even as he pleads with God not to forsake him (vv. 9-10). So it is with us in prayer as well. We plead for God's intervention in our struggles or in the troubled lives of others, but the very act of offering that prayer is itself an expression of trust based on the manifestations of God's mercy as we have come to know them. We embody this outlook in the collects of the church. These brief prayers normally begin with a recitation of God's action on our behalf that forms the basis of the petition to follow and the trust that drives it.

PSALM 103:1-2, 3-4, 8, 10, 12-13 (RC)

The psalmist's joy and gratitude and the portrait of a merciful God in these verses almost overwhelm us with their beauty. The psalmist has been healed and saved from death (vv. 3-4), but he has also been forgiven and praises God's steadfast love and compassion in removing our transgressions (vv. 10, 12). God is like loving parents who have compassion for their children. One is immediately reminded of how Jesus connected healing and forgiveness (see notes on Mark 2:1-12 under the Seventh Sunday above) and how he taught us to pray to "Abba" as to a loving parent.

SECOND READING
2 CORINTHIANS 4:3-6 (RCL)

Interpreting the Text

In this section of the epistle, Paul is defending his apostolate and the authority of his proclamation by asserting that in his kerygma God is revealed through the preaching of Christ who is the very image of God (v. 4). "Image of God" here is a designation of divine revelation. Christ is the image of God in the unique sense that in him God is most fully revealed; God's presence, God's "glory," is made known through God's gracious action toward us. We, in turn, are transformed through the Christ into the divine image (2 Cor. 3:18) for which we are created (Gen. 1:26).

Here once more we have a blending of creation motifs and salvation or Christological motifs punctuated by the epiphany motifs of "light" and "glory."

Paul's argument in the larger context of 3:18—4:6 is that he does not preach his own message but the revelation of God in Christ. Paul's message in that regard is analogous to the revelation of God in Christ, the divine image.

Responding to the Text

In a time when marketing virtually dominates the culture, techniques and programs for "marketing" the church are inevitable. As in the marketing of commercial products, one begins to see the same techniques repeat themselves from market to market. Thus, across denominational lines and geographic boundaries, features that seem to work in attracting people begin to proliferate, such as multimedia worship services, a variety of social outlets for different age groups, attention to demographic affinity, and a singular focus on mission as congregational expansion.

Characterizing these approaches as marketing rather than mission is perhaps unfair. It biases our outlook on such strategies and tends to disparage their successes as counterfeit expressions of church. That judgment would be altogether too simplistic, because the church has always carried forward its mission existing in and using the forms of specific cultures. The church has, at its best, always tried to contextualize its message. In some sense this is akin to what marketing attempts to do. The problem arises when the marketing becomes the message.

We need a discerning evaluation of contemporary trends in church outreach that goes beyond what is possible in these brief remarks. Paul provides a benchmark. The critical test by which to evaluate all forms of mission and ministry is whether or not Christ is faithfully preached and, through him, God is truly revealed. This means no less than a full vision of God, for Christ is the very image of God. Does God's unconditional grace predominate? Does God's desire to include all people find embodiment in mission? Are the values of God's reign, such as peace-making, justice-making, and the care of all creation, a prominent theme in proclaiming the good news? As with Paul, our only authority as the church is in the call to faithfully preach Christ.

> THE CRITICAL TEST BY WHICH TO EVALUATE ALL FORMS OF MISSION AND MINISTRY IS WHETHER OR NOT CHRIST IS FAITHFULLY PREACHED AND, THROUGH HIM, GOD IS TRULY REVEALED.

2 PETER 1:16-19, (20-21) (BCP)

Interpreting the Text

Whether the author is actually Simon Peter is doubted by some scholars. The intended message of this particular text within the larger letter is plain

and transcends the issues of authorship. That message is that the gospel proclamation of Christ is based on historical occurrences witnessed by the apostles. This
claim of historicity, of course, does not prove the Christian kerygma; it does,
however, state clearly that the kerygma is not a collection of spiritual stories, but
an account of God's self-revelation in human history. The reference to the experience of the transfiguration obviously points the way to the Gospel lesson and
serves to underscore the revelatory importance of this event in the mind of the
early church (vv. 16–18).

The message of the Christ is a lamp shining in a dark place and a morning star.
The author employs these now familiar epiphany metaphors of light and star to
convey revelatory power (v. 19) and returns our minds to the prophecy of the
light to the Gentiles, to those in darkness, now confirmed in Christ.

Finally, the Spirit confirms the truth of all prophecy (v. 21). This verse and 2
Tim. 3:16 have been favorite proof texts for the inspiration of scripture, but it is
hazardous to draw from these texts some of the specific conclusions for that doctrine that have been posited. The assurance of the Spirit's inspiration and the truth
of God's revelation are clear messages of this reading and important ones.

Responding to the Text

The incarnation as the definitive event of the one God's self-revelation
is unique to Christianity among the monotheistic religions. It takes the experiences of God's mighty acts for Israel to a new and unprecedented level of divine
presence among human beings.

Christianity is not an otherworldly faith in a god who lives outside the world
and cares little for it. Christianity is not faith in some impersonal cosmic force.
Christianity does not believe that "god" is reducible to some undifferentiated spiritual reality as seems to be the case in various forms of popular religiosity. Instead,
God is with us and for us. God enters our lives in the unprecedented and seismic
event of Christ's birth. God leaves witnesses to this event, and God gives us the
Holy Spirit to continue to be here for us. In common parlance we say of those
who are true friends, "You've always been there for me." These are the persons
we truly trust. One message we can cull from this reading from 2 Peter is that
God has always been there for us and continues to be with us.

2 CORINTHIANS 3:1b-6 (RC)

Interpreting the Text

Apparently Paul was under fire for supposedly recommending himself
or perhaps seeking the recommendations of others (v. 1). Were that the case, Paul
would be no more than any other teacher coming with references and pitching

his own worth. That would mean that the measure of his stature would be judged according to the same performance criteria as anyone else.

The point is that there is more to Paul's ministry than that; its results are its own testimonial, and they don't actually point to Paul. The vital faith and life of the Corinthians forged by the Spirit through Paul's ministry are a living letter (v. 3). These are the fruits of a new covenant in the life-giving Spirit (v. 6) that supersedes the old covenant of Sinai; the Corinthians are living letters not written on tablets of stone.

The idea of the Corinthians as living letters of recommendation seems in line with Jesus' words in John 5:36 that his works testify that the Father has sent him. The Word of God is self-authenticating in its power to reveal God and change lives.

Finally, the theme of a "new covenant" is a strong one in the Bible, stretching from the memorable promise of Jer. 31:31-34 to the introduction of that new covenant in the institution of the Lord's Supper by Jesus (Luke 22:20; 1 Cor. 11:25). It is a covenant of life in the Spirit as opposed to an oppressive legalism (v. 6).

Responding to the Text

Proclaiming the gospel of Jesus Christ is not a matter of argument, proof, or persuasion; it is, quite simply, a matter of proclamation. As the notes above point out, the Word of God has the power to establish its own authority by the way in which it brings people to faith and shapes their lives in the service of the gospel and in the hope of the gospel. Nevertheless, there have always been some in the Christian church who, for their own reassurance, have felt that they must somehow validate the truth of God's revelation in Christ by some additional means.

THE WORD OF GOD HAS THE POWER TO ESTABLISH ITS OWN AUTHORITY BY THE WAY IN WHICH IT BRINGS PEOPLE TO FAITH AND SHAPES THEIR LIVES IN THE SERVICE OF THE GOSPEL AND IN THE HOPE OF THE GOSPEL.

Sometimes people insist that Christians must display a certain kind of morality, usually focused on specific behaviors. If there is evidence in their lives of this moral obedience, they reassure themselves that they are truly Christians and by inference that the Gospel is also true. Similarly, others have sometimes believed that specific spiritual experiences are the signs one can rely on to confirm the truth of God's Word and the authenticity of one's faith. Still others have sought to protect the truth of God's Word in Christ and to buttress their own faith by insisting on a rigid doctrine of the verbal inspiration of scripture.

All these efforts and others we could name seek the sort of "recommendations" Paul disdained. There is no need to add anything to God's Word in Christ. Morality, spirituality, and concern for biblical inspiration have their place, but the assurance of the gospel, which gives birth to these dimensions of Christian life, is in its proclamation of God's promise. Realizing this, we can approach morality, spirituality, and doctrine in the new covenant of life in the Spirit, not in legalism.

THE GOSPEL
MARK 9:2-9 (RCL, BCP)

Interpreting the Text

In the biblical world we are well aware that mountains are places of divine revelation. Their very height suggests transcendence and rarefied air. So it is fitting that the pinnacle of the Epiphany season should be on a mountaintop. Furthermore, Jesus' dazzling bright appearance at the moment of his transfiguration caps off a season of readings in which brightness and light illuminate for us what God is revealing to the world. And there is more.

The presence of Moses and Elijah, representing the Law and the Prophets, focuses our attention on the fact that Jesus is the summation of all that has gone before. The precepts and the promises reach their definitive expression in him. So we are invited to gather up the various instances of "fulfillment" we have noted throughout the Epiphany cycle under the heading of this appearance. There is no doubt that Jesus is the Messiah, for along with all the other signs packed into this episode, the presence of Elijah makes that statement. The return of Elijah was expected as a herald of the Messiah (see Mal. 4:5-6).

Finally, there is the theophany that provides the climax. It repeats the words of the theophany at Jesus' baptism, but here it is heard not only by Jesus but also by those with him, and the words "Listen to him!" (v. 7) are added. These words tell us that we are being addressed now, and along with his disciples on the mount, we are being called to follow him. Beyond that, these additional words of command draw us back to the Fourth Sunday after the Epiphany. There we had a reading from Deuteronomy 18 in which the people of Israel received the promise that God would raise up for them a prophet like Moses from among the people. The text then goes on, "You shall heed such a prophet" (18: 15), which is to say, "Listen to him!" This is a connection a number of interpreters have made and, if valid, provides yet another detail in this picture of fulfillment, which is already rich in texture.

What about the disciples in this piece? We know they were astounded and terrified (v. 6). We can't be sure of the extent to which they were able to comprehend the meaning of the event. Peter proposed making three booths, one each for Moses, Elijah, and Jesus. He had put them together in his mind. Does he see them then at this point as coequals—each having their own booth—in the line of God's signature prophets? (He had earlier confessed his belief that Jesus was the Messiah.) We can't know with certainty. We only know that Peter thought it was good to be there (v. 5). Despite the terror the disciples felt, Peter at least thought this was a very special time, a moment to be preserved. But it was not meant to be preserved, and the trip down the mountain simply provided another message to puzzle over when Jesus commanded their silence until after his resurrection (v. 9). What was this rising from the dead to be about (v. 10)? In the end, for the immediate and long-term future, the key to reality for them is found in v. 8, "They saw no one with them any more, but only Jesus."

Responding to the Text

The readings for the Epiphany season have given us a veritable feast of revelations. Transfiguration Sunday pulls them together in a marvelous way. This gives us an opportunity to pause on our way to the Lenten season and appreciate the incredible profundity of the passion that is stretched out ahead of us; it is not just the terrible suffering of a good man, but the suffering of the very Son of God. Without the revelations of Epiphany and the connections made with centuries of hope for God's Messiah, the events that would follow in the life of Jesus would make little sense. His death and resurrection would be hard to decipher were they not set against this backdrop.

> THE READINGS FOR THE EPIPHANY SEASON HAVE GIVEN US A VERITABLE FEAST OF REVELATIONS. TRANSFIGURATION SUNDAY PULLS THEM TOGETHER IN A MARVELOUS WAY.

The moments on the mountain must have been very important for Jesus and his followers alike. Trials lay ahead that Jesus understood all too well and that the disciples would discover as they moved ahead. To hear again the Father's confirmation must have been strength for the journey from the mountaintop to the ugly little hilltop of Golgatha. To see their Lord transfigured, to be let in on such a moment of revelatory glory, however frightening and confusing, must have given Peter, James, and John resources of strength for the faith that would be required as they left the rarefied air of the mountain for the plain and the hill.

So it is with us as well. We need moments of divine confirmation for a life on the plain, which is often devoid of spiritual mountaintop moments. As the joy of hope and life born of the Nativity and revealed in the Epiphany gives way to the passion of Lent, so our lives move from moments of joy to stretches of sorrow, from triumphs to trials, from gain to loss, perhaps simply to drudgery and the challenge to endure.

For the three disciples and ultimately for us, what was even more important, however, was that Jesus went with them down the mountain. The transfiguration would live in their memory and excite their spirits, but the Lord would always be with them (Matt. 28:20). That seems to be the importance of the detail that, after the voice from heaven, "they saw no one with them, only Jesus." Their Lord and their friend, their companion and their Savior, is now their sole support and the hope on which they will bet their lives.

Jesus, only Jesus, has walked and continues to walk our way with us. The mountaintop moments of Christmas and Easter worship, for example, live in our memories and excite our spirits; we need them as Jesus and his followers did on that far-off day. But what about the world of Mondays that stretches out for a lifetime? The days of gladness when God's blessings overwhelm us are true gifts to the spirit, but what about the long dry spells when, blessed though we may be, the big thing is simply to get through the day, minimize the conflicts, and solve whatever problems seem possible? The final stanza of that familiar transfiguration hymn is the perfect prayer to go with these thoughts.

How good, Lord, to be here!
Yet we may not remain;
But since you bid us leave the mount,
Come with us to the plain.

MARK 2:18-22 (RC)

Interpreting the Text

The reading from Hos. 2:16bff. that is paired with this Gospel reading has already alerted us to the imagery of marriage to portray God's covenant relationship with people. Two other examples that illustrate this use of metaphor can be found in Isa. 54:6 and Jer. 2:2. The reference to Jesus as the bridegroom appears to stand in that tradition. (See also the remarks above in response to the Hosea passage regarding Eph. 5:23ff.) Casting himself as the bridegroom is, then, a bold messianic/divine claim.

The foil for this disclosure is the fasting being undertaken by the Pharisees and the disciples of John the Baptist. The fact that Jesus' disciples are not fasting stands out and raises questions (v. 18). Jesus' response that one does not fast when the bridegroom is present—weddings are feasting occasions—has a narrower and broader significance.

The narrower and immediate point is that at some point later on the disciples will be on their own and there will be occasions for spiritual discipline as they undertake their mission. Now, however, while Jesus is with them, fasting is inappropriate (vv. 19-20), because this bridegroom is *the* bridegroom. That brings us to the broader point. As the bridegroom, Jesus brings to fulfillment God's covenant marriage with the people. The eschatological character of this revelation is clear; the bridegroom, the Messiah, the fulfillment of all God's covenant promises, is with them. John the Baptist and his followers were anticipatory, called to pave the way. They and the Pharisees represent what is now the old order; the new has come. Therefore, a new vision and a new piety are in order; you can't sew a new patch on an old garment or put new wine in old wineskins (vv. 21-22).

Responding to the Text

The bridegroom has come and solidified God's covenant of grace and love. All things are new. As Paul says it, "So if anyone is in Christ, there is a new creation: everything old has passed away; see, everything has become new!" (2 Cor. 5:17). In Christ our future with God is revealed. It is present to us, and still it is "not yet." We await the return of the bridegroom even though we know he has come and is with us in the Spirit. In other words, as theologians are fond of saying, we live in an already-not-yet situation. As noted earlier, ours are the in-between times.

The seasons of the church year reflect our circumstances. We rejoice with high delight at Christmas and Easter, for example, but we recognize the abiding significance of the cross in our broken and sinful world as we move through Lent. The event of Pentecost is an exciting and powerful follow-up to the Easter victory, but it leads us into a long string of Sundays in the Pentecost season devoted to the daily tasks of discipleship, with all the questions and ambiguities involved in that winding journey.

In the already-not-yet time, it is important to stay close to one another in the body of Christ and to gather around the meal of his presence among us. In this way, Christ our future is reasserted in our present. We are thus renewed for our Epiphany mission to make that future present for others.

THE SEASON OF LENT

PHILIP H. PFATTEICHER

Introduction

A principal organizing image for Lent is the evocative picture of a pilgrimage. It is, of course, an important image for the Bible. Abraham is the archetypal pilgrim, directed by God to leave his homeland and relatives and go on an epic journey in search of spiritual truth. Without hesitation he set out, not yet knowing the destination and not yet understanding the purpose of the long and difficult journey. His condition became the condition of all his descendants, who are described by the writer to the Hebrews as "strangers and pilgrims" (Heb. 11:13 KJV) on earth. This world is not our home; the promised land of heaven is "our true native land" (as the eucharistic hymn "O Saving Victim" calls it). Our life here is a journey through this passing world to our heavenly home. The Prayer of the Day for the First Sunday in Lent in the Lutheran Book of Worship derives from this image. "O Lord God, you led your ancient people through the wilderness and brought them to the promised land. Guide now the people of your Church, that, following our Savior, we may walk through the wilderness of this world toward the glory of the world to come." (We might wish that the prayer would ask not simply that we walk "toward the glory of the world to come" but that we might at last arrive safely there.)

A pilgrimage is a journey to a holy place made with a devotional intention. The journey begins, as it did for Abraham and his family, with turning in a new direction, with what the New Testament calls *metanoia*, conversion. It requires a separation from one place and set of conditions and instead of them a concentration on the goal of the journey. It requires not just looking around but looking ahead with focus and determination. The Lenten pilgrimage is a journey to a specific holy place, Jesus' cross and tomb. Most of us, however, make the journey without

> A PRINCIPAL ORGANIZING IMAGE FOR
> LENT IS THE EVOCATIVE PICTURE OF
> A PILGRIMAGE.

leaving our city or town and accomplish the journey as a spiritual pilgrimage made in heart and mind. We are called to leave those places in our lives where we are not living our Christian identity, where we are not truly at home or at peace. One of the great purposes of Lent is to bring us to ourselves, so that, like the prodigal son, we may realize that the condition in which we find ourselves is not our true home and that as comfortable as we usually feel, we are aliens in a foreign land and need to come home. So the Lenten pilgrimage is made with a clear purpose in mind. It is a journey home, although, as it was for Abraham, the home to which we go is a place we have never yet been.

This Lenten pilgrimage is accomplished not merely within our mind without leaving our present location. It requires a physical journey (if we are able to make it, of course). We must decide to leave home and walk, or more often drive, to a specific holy place, our church. There ritually we are in Jerusalem, and there we are at the cross and the tomb of Jesus. The journey is repeated week after week, year after year, but, one hopes, it is an ever new experience with still more discoveries to be made, still more insights to be gained, still greater depths to be explored each time we make the journey.

The pilgrimage, we learn as we walk, becomes an all-embracing, all-consuming activity. When we are on a pilgrimage, everything can be understood to be part of the way. Every step is as important as the last. Everyone and everything we encounter along the way is part of the pilgrim experience. A good bit of the route may seem ordinary and prosaic, but that does not mean that it is insignificant.

When God renewed the covenant with Abraham, changing his name from Abram to Abraham (Genesis 17, the RCL first reading for the Second Sunday in Lent), God said to Abraham, "Walk before me, and be blameless" (Gen. 17:1). The verb "to walk" is used in this way throughout the Bible, in both Testaments, and it is often translated or interpreted as "to live." Walking is a more active and suggestive verb, however. It implies movement: living is not a static activity. Walking also implies having a clear direction. Walking is not a casual stroll or an aimless meandering; it is going to a specific place with a specific intention. Walking before God (Ps. 116:9) is walking in God's law, going in the way of God's commandments, walking carefully along a prescribed path. "And when you turn to the right or when you turn to the left, your ears shall hear a word behind you, saying, 'This is the way; walk in it' " (Isa. 30:21). It is walking with God as with a friend (Mic. 6:8). Nearly always, it should be noted, such walking is a community activity. "It is you, . . . my companion, my familiar friend, with whom I kept pleasant company; we walked in the house of God with the throng" (Ps. 55:13-14). Such companionship on the journey affects our behavior. "Whoever walks with the wise becomes wise, but the companion of fools suffers harm" (Prov. 13:20).

In the New Testament, the female counterpart to Abraham is the Virgin Mary. She was, like Abraham, summoned by God to be the progenitor not just of a new family but of a new race, those who became part of her Son, the new Adam. Abraham was called to leave home and to travel to a distant and as yet unrevealed place. Mary too received a transforming visit from God, but it was not necessary for her to travel far geographically. Her vocation was to be carried out where she was. There was a visit to her cousin Elizabeth in the hill country and the flight into Egypt to escape Herod's murderous orders, but mostly she stayed home. Her spiritual journey, however, was no less revolutionary than that of her distant ancestor Abraham. The pilgrimage of Lent, therefore, need not be geographical, but that does not lessen its call to a radical redirection and transformation of our lives.

In a sense, Lent does not bring anything new, only an intensification of what are already the constant themes and elements of the Christian life. The solemn season begins with a call to conversion, a summons to travel a different road, the way that leads to God. It is a road that leads out of the confinement of our mundane existence and into the uplands to open wide vistas for those who travel this way. The difficult path expands the horizon that has been confined by sin, which curves sinners into themselves. Lent opens our eyes to see others who travel with us, to see larger possibilities for our lives, to feel the exhilaration of walking to our true home.

ASH WEDNESDAY

MARCH 5, 2003

REVISED COMMON	EPISCOPAL (BCP)	ROMAN CATHOLIC
Joel 2:1-2, 12-17	Joel 2:1-2, 12-17	Joel 2:12-18
or Isa. 58:1-12	or Isa. 58:1-12	
Ps. 51:1-17	Psalm 103 or 103:8-14	Ps. 51:3-4, 5-6,
		12-13, 14, 17
2 Cor. 5:20b—6:10	2 Cor. 5:20b—6:10	2 Cor. 5:20—6:2
Matt. 6:1-6, 16-21	Matt. 6:1-6, 16-21	Matt. 6:1-6, 16-18

Abraham's pilgrimage began with the sudden and unexpected call by God to leave home and to set out for an undetermined place. Into the comfort and security of familiar surroundings and people and a settled life came the disruptive word "Leave." And he did.

Lent for Christians begins with another disruptive and deeply disturbing message. Ash Wednesday always comes as an interruption. Into the richness of the pleasure of living comes the grim reminder, "You are dust, and to dust you shall return" (Gen. 3:19). It was God's word to Adam and Eve after their disobedience, and it is God's word to us all. Cutting into life abruptly when we are enjoying it the most comes the warning, "You too must die." It is a fact of life that we would rather not face, so we turn aside and raise our voices and laugh a little louder and quicken the pace of our pleasure; but still the hollow voice insists, "You too shall die." The certainty that no life lasts forever is always there, jumping out from behind an automobile in a near-accident, waiting in the corner of a hospital room. There is an inevitability about this unwelcome fact that makes it upsetting, sometimes frightening. The truth that Ash Wednesday will not let us forget is that life—our life—will someday end.

> THE TRUTH THAT ASH WEDNESDAY WILL NOT LET US FORGET IS THAT LIFE—OUR LIFE—WILL SOMEDAY END.

Ash Wednesday with its disruptive intrusion into our pleasure may well be considered the real beginning of the liturgical year. It marks the one abrupt change in the yearly cycle. Advent follows without a break from the final weeks after Pentecost and takes up the proclamation of the Sunday of Christ the King on the Sunday following, which is the First Sunday in Advent, "Behold, your king comes to you." The secular New Year's Day does not mark a new beginning in the church's calendar; for the church, January 1 is the eighth of the twelve days of Christmas. But Ash Wednesday is not a continuation or extension of the themes of the time after the Epiphany nor even a bridge between Epiphany and Easter. It is not related to the recalling of the stages in the life of Christ. It comes as an unexpected interruption, almost without warning. It always catches us up short with its unwelcome reminder. But it is with the message of this day, "Remember that you are dust, and to dust you shall return," that Lent begins, and with it in a sense, the new church year begins. The Jews conclude the high holy days marking the beginning of their new year with the most solemn day of the year, Yom Kippur, the Day of Atonement. For Christians, the year may be understood to begin with the Christian version of the Day of Atonement, which we call Ash Wednesday.

FIRST READING
JOEL 2:1-2, 12-17 (RCL, BCP);
JOEL 2:12-18 (RC)

Interpreting the Text

Joel, unlike earlier prophets who stood outside the cultic life of Israel, carried out his ministry within the liturgical life of the temple. He is therefore an appropriate prophet to hear at the beginning of the church's time of fasting and prayer. He is interested in the worship of the temple, its priesthood, and its services.

A plague of locusts had ravaged the country, probably in the late fourth century B.C.E., and Joel understands this to be God's work to call the people to repentance. The land did not even yield enough produce to supply the daily offerings in the temple. Joel therefore calls for a fast, lamentation, and mourning on the part of the priests and the elders, and all the inhabitants of the land—not only Hebrews but everyone who happened to be living in the land and sharing in its condition.

In ancient Israel the trumpet was used to warn of imminent danger, the punishment of Israel, the coming of the day of wrath. The trumpet also summons Israel to religious gatherings and hence will be the signal for the gathering of the elect on the last day. Verses 12-17 issue the call to repentance. The people are to assemble as an expression of their corporate penitence, and the priests are to intercede with God on their behalf so that the other nations will not be able to charge that the people have been abandoned by God.

The "day of the Lord" was coming. This day was popularly thought to be a glorious time of restoration of power and prominence among the nations of the earth, a time of unprecedented luxury. But it was in fact not something to be eagerly anticipated. It would be a day of terrifying devastation, foreshadowed by the present plague and famine. Because the plague announces the impending day of the Lord, the chilling sound of the trumpet is to announce the beginning of a fast. Everyday life, even extraordinary life such as a marriage celebration, is to be interrupted for a time of prayer and fasting. The priests take their place outdoors where they can be seen, between the porch of the temple and the outdoor altar where sacrifices were offered. There they do their priestly duty and intercede for the people, pleading with God for mercy. In the face of impending disaster, the people are commanded to match their fasting with an interior change of heart, so that the exterior fasting becomes a sign of an interior conversion.

The RCL and BCP reading ends with the priests' prayer, "Spare your people." No response by God is heard. That will be delayed in the liturgy for six weeks, until Easter. Allowing the desperate cry to hang there, echoing through the temple courts and through the minds and souls of those who listen to the reading, gives powerful effect to the cry and requires the hearers to ponder it in their own lives. The RC reading, however, does not leave the cry of repentance unanswered, as if such a cry of desperation without a reply is intolerable. The reading therefore includes the comforting words of v. 18, and we are not required to wait for God's reply and consoling promise.

ISAIAH 58:1–12 (RCL, BCP, alt.)

Isaiah here speaks the traditional prophetic condemnation of empty exterior rituals. "To obey is better than sacrifice" (1 Sam. 15:22) has been a consistent insight since the earliest days of prophecy under Samuel. It is too easy to pay for a sacrifice and then keep on living an unchanged life; it is too easy even to make the personal sacrifice of fasting and not reflect in one's conduct what fasting implies. The selfish lives and display of false humility on the part of those who claim to be seeking God contrast with God's requirement to perform acts of mercy.

The first portion of the reading condemns the self-centered attitude of the people in their fasting (vv. 1–5). In the second portion of the reading (vv. 6–7), Isaiah is quite specific in telling the people exactly what God expects them to do and describing what a godly fast looks like. Then, in the grand final portion of the reading, Isaiah tells how God will again bless the people who obey and practice what God commands and expects. It is noteworthy that this section of hopeful promises is the longest section of the reading and its principal emphasis.

The reading from Joel opens with a terrifying alarm announced by the atonal voice of the *shofar,* an other-worldly sound that disturbs our security and contentment. It warns of imminent danger: The day of the Lord is coming with terror; it will be a time of punishment and retribution. Yet the prophet is insistent that we hear the other side of the message as well, the call to repentance, for God never wants simply to threaten and terrify. Total calamity may yet be avoided. Notice that the prophet does not make God's response to the fast automatic. Joel as a faithful prophet is careful not to claim or promise too much. He does not say, "Repent, and everything will be all right." Repentance is never to be undertaken in order to get unpleasantness behind us and get back to normal again. It is because we have done wrong that we must repent, and we must do so without an eye on the outcome. We repent out of shame for what we have done, and what will be done with us because of our sin is God's business.

The ancient practice of fasting is not to be deprecated, and we must be careful not to cheapen it by implying that we in the modern church do not need to fast but need simply to live a good life. (As if that were easy to do.) Fasting, abstaining from certain foods and drink, and limiting our consumption of other food are difficult and unpleasant and are worth doing for a number of reasons as a part of the Lenten discipline. Then, when we have learned to discipline ourselves in that way, we are ready to move on to the more demanding change in the pattern of our life and works.

RESPONSIVE READING
PSALM 51:1-17 (RCL);
PSALM 51:3-4, 5-6, 12-13, 14, 17 (RC)

The great and profound psalm of repentance is a natural choice for Ash Wednesday. The lament is said to have been composed by David as his response to the prophet Nathan's condemnation of his affair with Bathsheba. Whether or not that is true, this powerful appeal for cleansing by God has close affinity with the preaching of the prophets, and each one of us can take the psalm into our own mouths and sing or speak it from the heart. It gives us words with which to express the intolerable burden of our sin, which has been ours from our conception in our mother's womb, and to ask for cleansing and renewal. This requires nothing less than a new creation, a clean heart and a right spirit. Then, restored to God, we will teach transgressors God's ways, not necessarily by our words but by the quality of our renewed life. The psalm teaches us that a deep sense of sin is a step toward our Creator and opens the door for God's abundant and eager mercy. The prayer offered by this psalm is similar to the appeal made in Eph. 4:23-24, "Be renewed in the spirit of your minds, and . . . clothe yourselves with the new self, created according to the likeness of God in true righteousness and holiness."

PSALM 103 OR 103:8-14 (BCP)

As Isaiah 58 is a more optimistic alternative to the traditional reading from Joel, so Psalm 103 is a more comforting alternative to the profundity of Psalm 51. The attributes of God invoked here are those revealed to Moses (Exod. 34:6ff) and here stress mercy and kindness. The Ash Wednesday connection is made in v. 14, "He remembers how we were made; he remembers that we are dust." Throughout the psalm, but especially in the shorter version (vv. 8-14), God's being, justice, and eternity are contrasted with our transient, sinful, and frail nature. The praise of God's compassion expressed in this psalm anticipates the song of Zechariah, "By the tender mercy of our God, the dawn from on high will break upon us" (Luke 1:78).

SECOND READING
2 CORINTHIANS 5:20b—6:10 (RCL, BCP);
2 CORINTHIANS 5:20—6:2 (RC)

Interpreting the Text

Paul's relations with the church in Corinth had been strained. God's goodness is available to us as "ambassadors for Christ," and the reading begins with the urgent appeal Paul makes on behalf of Christ, "Be reconciled to God," that is, accept the forgiveness that is being offered. "Now is the day of salvation," he announces (6:2), echoing Isa. 49:8, but it is a warning too, for we dare not presume that the "acceptable time" and "day of salvation" will always be there for us. Time passes and days come to an end. For Paul, this implied that we must accept the offer before the day of the Lord arrives and Christ returns. We are to seize the opportunity for conversion while we can. We notice Paul's careful language. God did not make Christ "a sinner" for us, because the sinless one could never be a sinner. Rather, God made Christ "be sin" for us and suffer death, the punishment for sin. He did so in order not that we might become "righteous" before God, for we remain sinners, but that we might become "the righteousness of God." Christ took on our condition so that we might receive his character. Thus the work of God and our unworthiness are emphasized. Paul then describes his triumphant sufferings on behalf of Christ and his church, but in so doing he is describing the life of all who seek to follow the crucified Savior.

Responding to the Text

The word at the beginning of Lent is "now." The urgency of the appeal is emphasized, and the opportunity may not always be available. We must not put off the summons to receive what is being offered, to take the way that is opened and become a pilgrim, to leave the comfort of our usual life and change our pattern and purpose of living. Lent

CHRIST TOOK ON OUR CONDITION SO THAT WE MIGHT RECEIVE HIS CHARACTER.

lies ahead of us as an invitation and an appeal to make the journey and to walk in the steps of Christ our Lord and Master. As Paul describes his life, it is in stark contrast to what the world seeks and honors, and yet it is the only way to purpose and peace.

Examining the organization of this passage may be helpful. William Barclay has noted that the passage consists of a pair of three groups of three. The first category describes the trouble and trials that are to be overcome through the grace of endurance, bearing up under impossible weight in such a way that these adversities are transformed into strength and glory. There are first of all the internal conflicts of the Christian life: "afflictions," severe, distressing trials that weigh upon us and press us down; "hardships," the unavoidable sufferings of life; and "calamities," the straits or narrow places that shut us in and from which no escape seems possible. Second, there are the external sufferings of the Christian life that characterized Paul's life but that we may not be required to endure: "beatings" with rods or whips; "imprisonments"; and "riots," the hostile violence of a mob. Third, there is the effort of the Christian life: "labors," for Paul his preaching as well as his employment at tent-making, work that drains us of all energy to the point of exhaustion; "sleepless nights," repeated vigils because of night work or prayer and concern for the churches; and "hunger," going hungry for the sake of the work, forced upon him by travel or poverty. Balancing these is the equipment that God supplies for victorious living. In the first category of this equipment are qualities of mind: "purity," the complete integrity of a thoroughly cleansed life; "knowledge" of what must be done, of the gospel; and "patience," enduring illtreatment without retaliation. The second category includes qualities of the heart: "kindness" to all, friendly or hostile; "holiness of spirit," the spirit directed entirely to God; and "genuine love" that seeks nothing else than the other's highest good. The third category includes equipment for the preaching of the gospel: "truthful speech," which is nothing less than the gospel that cannot lie or deceive;

"the power of God" by which Paul is able to endure all that would otherwise overwhelm him, and "weapons" for right and left hands for both defense and attack. The passage concludes with lyrical contrasts of seven conditions as Paul moves through honor and dishonor, ill repute and good repute: His outward reputation to the world (impostor, unknown, dying, punished, sorrowful, poor, impoverished) is more than matched by his situation before God (true, well known, alive, not yet killed, rejoicing, making many rich, possessing everything). Such a life was Paul's own imitation of Christ. Ours may not be so dramatic or violent, but our call as Christians is to share in the suffering of Christ so that we may share his glory.

THE GOSPEL
MATTHEW 6:1-6, 16-21 (RCL, BCP); MATTHEW 6:1-6, 16-18 (RC)

Interpreting the Text

The reading is, of course, from the Sermon on the Mount and treats the three "evangelical counsels" (that is, counsels drawn from the Gospels) of almsgiving, prayer, and fasting, which are the principal work of Lent. By these three activities we make use of our baptismal incorporation into Christ and his life. The first verse introduces and summarizes what is to follow. "Beware of practicing your piety before others in order to be seen by them; for then you have no reward from your Father in heaven." "Piety" (NRSV) or "righteous deeds" (NAB) or "acts of righteousness" (NIV) includes and implies the activities of almsgiving, prayer, and fasting.

> THE READING TREATS THE THREE "EVANGELICAL COUNSELS" OF ALMSGIVING, PRAYER, AND FASTING, WHICH ARE THE PRINCIPAL WORK OF LENT.

Almsgiving is mentioned first probably because Jews of Jesus' time considered it to be the foremost act of piety. Giving alms involves giving away something that is undeniably ours, for which we have worked. Prayer is opening ourselves to receive what is first of all God's. Fasting puts worldly and bodily needs in perspective. Together, the three evangelical counsels teach the wisdom of a treasure that cannot be touched by earthly decay or loss.

We may consider each of the three evangelical counsels separately, but in the Christian tradition, as in the Hebrew tradition, all three are parts of a whole way of life. In ancient times the catechumens who were preparing for baptism at Easter were expected to demonstrate proficiency in these disciplines during the forty days of Lent as a condition for their admission to the company of the baptized. Those who had fallen away from the church were expected to fast, to pray, and to serve during Lent as evidence that they had once again shouldered the cross and were walking with Christ in the company of God's family along the pilgrim's way. In the present church we all practice the evangelical counsels together. (It is easier to be humble about such service and discipline if they are something we are all doing together.)

The monk and bishop Caesarius of Arles (470–542), reflecting a profound understanding of the discipline of the church, speaks of two forms of almsgiving: giving bread to the hungry and also promptly forgiving those who injure us. "We learn from our Lord's teaching in the gospel how we should impart the remedies of true charity to our enemies, even though they do not ask for it." Those who injure us inflict a grave wound not only on us but more importantly on themselves, and it is our duty to help heal that wound. They, by their wound, are perishing, and we by keeping silent are doing worse than their reviling us. "When you correct and reconcile others, you make them free on earth; free on earth, they will also be free in heaven. You give much to them, not to yourself; because they who sinned against you harmed themselves greatly, not you" *(Sermon 28)*. Almsgiving is thus to be understood as a participation in the generosity of God.

Fasting is not unique to Christians and Jews. All religions practice it. Just as almsgiving expands to include reconciliation, fasting has to do with more than just the way our bodies work. Jews under the original covenant did without food on Monday and Thursday in order to better watch and pray for the coming of the Messiah. The early Christians fasted on Wednesday and Friday, the day on which Jesus was betrayed and the day on which he was crucified, as a way of helping them pray and remember the cost of their redemption.

In the Bible fasting was part of the rhythm of life for the people of God. It was woven into their life like day and night, summer and winter, waking and sleeping. Everyone did it: Moses the lawgiver and David the king, Elijah the prophet, Esther the queen, Daniel the seer, Anna the prophet, John the baptizer, Paul the apostle, Jesus the Son of God. From Judaism fasting passed into Christian life and practice. Jesus assumed that it would be so. He said to his disciples and to his followers of all the ages, "When you fast . . ." not "Should you choose to fast . . ." or "If you fast. . . ." After the Reformation fasting eventually declined in the Protestant churches, but the practice persisted in remarkable places. It was never completely forgotten in Lutheran practice. More remarkably, John Wesley refused to ordain anyone who did not fast twice a week.

Fasting humbles us by showing us our limits and our frailty. It reminds us of our dependence on God and on one another—farmers and millers and truckers and bakers and storekeepers. It brings us down to reality by showing us that we are not self-sufficient. Fasting helps us get control over our body and its desires and cravings. It breaks our self-indulgence, our self-centeredness, our selfish wills. By fasting we submit ourselves to God and allow his work in us to grow. Paradoxically, fasting strengthens us and so helps us to pray, and prayer is the principal activity of Lent—prayer for ourselves, for the church, and for the whole world.

Responding to the Text

Both Old Testament readings and this Gospel examine the proper motivation for devotional actions. Jesus' sermon exaggerates to make his point, and it is amusing to picture what he describes: a trumpet blast to announce that someone is about to give alms (compare the trumpet in Joel), praying loudly and conspicuously on street corners (we've seen people do that, and we usually think they're crazy), making up one's face to look unattractive so that people will believe that fasting is the cause.

By itself an act of almsgiving, praying, or fasting may have some value. (Luther said that even a prayer said by rote makes the devil tremble.) But, as Isaiah and this Gospel teach, even worthy acts can be misused by calling attention to themselves and to those who do them or by being thought themselves to be sufficient to discharge one's religious obligations. All of us are tempted to make a show of our good works. Also, we must beware of pointing to others and saying, "That's what Jesus is condemning." The Bible is always to be heard speaking first of all to us. The danger of hypocrisy or misuse, however, is not a reason to avoid any of the three activities or to replace them with something else. Wearing an ashen cross this day may be a way of calling attention to one's piety, or in our time it may be a confession and proclamation of the lordship of Christ. So Jesus' counsel to "wash your face" does not condemn the imposition of ashes any more than his counsel to pray behind the closed door of your room prevents you from coming to church for prayer. The real question is who is being served by such actions, God or oneself? Thus Jesus continues and deepens the teaching of Isaiah 58.

> AS ISAIAH AND THIS GOSPEL TEACH, EVEN WORTHY ACTS CAN BE MISUSED BY CALLING ATTENTION TO THEMSELVES AND TO THOSE WHO DO THEM OR BY BEING THOUGHT THEMSELVES TO BE SUFFICIENT TO DISCHARGE ONE'S RELIGIOUS OBLIGATIONS.

When we have progressed to a level where we are no longer conscious of the good we do, we are content to know that the standards of judgment of good belong to God, not to us, and that we are simply doing what is expected of God's servants. We must hide our goodness even from ourselves, and our acts of devotion should be spontaneous and not self-conscious.

Although we may intercede for others and offer thanks on their behalf, the focus of prayer is God. When we pray, as Pastor Martin Hauser frequently reminds his congregation in New York, what God sees is not a pious and devout human being but the face of Jesus Christ, and God's final comment on all of us is, "You are my child, the one whom I love; with you I am well pleased." God loves all our prayers—the little prayers we offer at odd moments, our secret thoughts while driving or riding the bus, the prayers we offer the last thing at night but never quite finish before we fall asleep. God loves all our prayers, because all God hears when we pray is the voice of the Holy Spirit praying within us.

FIRST SUNDAY IN LENT

REVISED COMMON	EPISCOPAL (BCP)	ROMAN CATHOLIC
Gen. 9:8-17	Gen. 9:8-17	Gen. 9:8-15
Ps. 25:1-10	Psalm 25 or 25:3-9	Ps. 25:4-5, 6-7, 8-9
1 Pet. 3:18-22	1 Pet. 3:18-22	1 Pet. 3:18-22
Mark 1:9-15	Mark 1:9-13	Mark 1:12-15

Anciently, before the additional four days beginning with Ash Wednesday were included to make the season exactly forty days long (excluding Sundays, which are always feast days), this day marked the beginning of Lent. It still retains this character. The constant theme of the First Sunday in Lent in all of the three years of the lectionary cycle is the temptation of Jesus. Thus the first station of the Lenten pilgrimage is in the desert with our Lord, and it continues the themes of fasting and prayer, which are so prominent in the traditional discipline of Lent. The time in the desert recapitulates the testing of Israel. As it was for the Israelites a time of purification and preparation before their entrance into the promised land, so for us it is a time of testing and purification before our celebration of the opening of the gates of eternal life at Easter.

THE FIRST STATION OF THE LENTEN PILGRIMAGE IS IN THE DESERT WITH OUR LORD, AND IT CONTINUES THE THEMES OF FASTING AND PRAYER, WHICH ARE SO PROMINENT IN THE TRADITIONAL DISCIPLINE OF LENT.

FIRST READING

GENESIS 9:8-17 (RCL, BCP); GENESIS 9:8-15 (RC)

Interpreting the Text

The reading is an extract from the conversation that God had with Noah after the flood. It marked a new beginning. Just as Adam was the father of humanity, so too Noah is the progenitor of the race that descends from him. God made a covenant with Adam, and here God makes a covenant with Noah. Echoes of creation are heard in this narrative of new beginnings. God said to the man and the woman, "Be fruitful and multiply" (Gen. 1:28). He says the same to Noah and his sons (Gen. 9:1). But notable too are the subtle differences between the first creation and this new beginning. The world that emerges from the flood is a step removed from the perfection of the original creation. The original command was, "Be fruitful and multiply, and fill the earth and subdue it." The renewed charge is "Be fruitful and multiply, and fill the earth." The first charge said simply "have dominion," but with the new charge a more sinister note enters: "The fear and dread of you shall rest on every animal of the earth. . . ." Human rule over the rest of creation is affirmed, but it will no longer be tranquil. In the unfolding age humanity will be at war with animals and with one another, and the peace of paradise will not return until the last days (Isa. 11:6ff.). The first people and animals were to be vegetarian (Gen. 1:29-30); after the flood, meat eating was permitted (Gen. 9:3) but with a warning to respect life symbolized by blood and a proscription of murder. We may slay animals, but we must not kill other human beings. So precious is humanity that even animals are not permitted to take human life. The new covenant after the flood includes not only all human beings but "every living creature." It is a covenant with the whole creation. All living things are under God's promise and God's law.

Moreover, preservation of the entire natural order is guaranteed by the universal covenant that God makes with all humanity (Noah's sons are regarded as the ancestors of the diversity of humankind) and with every living creature and even with the earth itself (Gen. 9:13).

The sign of the covenant is the rainbow. Ancient people imagined that the bow was the weapon with which a divinity shot lightning (Ps. 7:12-13; Hab. 3:9-11). Here it is hung up in the clouds as an indication that God will not use it. God alone can promise that "the waters shall never again become a flood to destroy all flesh" (Gen. 9:15), because God alone is the Creator who controls creation. The regularity and dependability of the world of nature, on which all life is utterly dependent, will be preserved by God and is evidence of God's faithfulness and fidelity.

Responding to the Text

Genesis 1 is notable for its grand view of the place of human beings within creation, for the text emphasizes our lordship, mastery, and control over the rest of what God has made. The second and third chapters show humanity from a quite different perspective: We who have been made from the earth (as we were forcefully reminded on Ash Wednesday) are lowly, weak, and easily led astray, and therefore we deserve God's punishment. Yet even there, what God punishes with one hand (the left hand, Luther would say), God

GOD'S GOODNESS REVEALED IN THE WATER OF THE FLOOD INESCAPABLY POINTS TO BAPTISM.

blesses with the other (the right hand). God drives the sinful couple from Paradise but gives them clothing to wear for protection in a hostile world. Here in the renovated creation after the flood, the focus is on God's goodness and desire to bless humanity and to preserve the fruitfulness of the earth on which we live.

Especially in the context of Lent, with one of its original purposes to prepare candidates for baptism at Easter, God's goodness revealed in the water of the flood inescapably points to baptism. The account of the flood since ancient times has been seen as prefiguring baptism. The second reading explicates the connection.

RESPONSIVE READING

PSALM 25:1-10 (RCL);
PSALM 25 OR 25:3-9 (BCP);
PSALM 25:4-5, 6-7, 8-9 (RC)

This psalm of lament is an acrostic, each verse beginning with a successive letter of the Hebrew alphabet, and this pattern accounts for the lack of a clear and logical structure to the psalm. The psalm is a prayer for guidance and protection, and the central expression of trust (vv. 3-9) may be heard as the voice of Christ in the wilderness and the voice of the church under attack by the world. The repeated references to God's "ways" and "paths" remind us of the road that is Lent. It is an invitation to leave contentment and security and to travel the pilgrim's way, led by God deeper into the mystery of the divine life. The brief and fleeting life of human beings is set against the ancient and abiding mercy and steadfast love of God. In this psalm God is the teacher, the loving guide, who goes in front of us and who, we may imagine, turns around from time to time to see whether we are following.

SECOND READING

1 PETER 3:18-22

Interpreting the Text

This reading suggests how the first lesson is to be understood in the context of the church's keeping of Lent. The flood is an image of baptism. The ark that saved Noah and his wife, their three sons and their wives, eight people in all, is a prefiguring of baptism by which salvation is offered to all people. Then water drowned nearly all living creatures; now water drowns all that is unworthy in us. Then eight people were preserved through the flood; now the water of destruction is transformed into a saving and life-giving water. As Noah and his family, together with the animals, were led out of the ark to populate the new world, so now new Christians arise from the waters of baptism to a life of promise and possibility that opens before them. (Many regard 1 Peter as a baptismal catechesis.)

The text sets forth a threefold activity of Christ: He redeems humanity by his death (v. 18), he preaches to the spirits in prison (v. 19), and he receives the submission of angels in heaven (v. 22). This threefold activity reminds us that no one act of Christ's life can be isolated from the rest. All are part of one whole. Most of all, his passion, death, resurrection, ascension, and glorification are one great action. The events are each usefully the focus of examination and devotional meditation, but it must always be kept in mind that the great events are one act of redemption.

Christ's atoning death for the unjust, to restore the broken relationship between God and humanity, took place once and is unrepeatable. His single sacrifice was sufficient, unlike the repeated deaths of the victims in the Levitical system. The rotund redundancies of the eucharistic prayer in the *Book of Common Prayer* declare that Christ on the cross "made there, by his one oblation of himself once offered, a full, perfect, and sufficient sacrifice . . . for the sins of the whole world." He died "for all" to bring us to God. If this access is indeed open to "all," then those who lived before his death and resurrection must somehow also have this access. The text therefore speaks of Christ going and preaching to "the spirits in prison."

The reference to Christ's "proclamation to the spirits in prison, who in former times did not obey" (vv. 19-20) is a difficult passage. The church's traditional interpretation of the activity may be helpful here. After the crucifixion and before the resurrection, Jesus descended into hell, the place of the dead (the Apostles' Creed in the International Consultation on English Texts [ICET] translation declares that he "descended to the dead"). He went there not as punishment, for hell was not understood to be reserved for the wicked but was the place where all the dead were gathered, and Jesus went to the dead as the first act of his victory over death. There he preached to the spirits in this prison "who in former times did not obey," apparently those in Noah's time who were drowned, to announce his victory. But later in this letter the passage was opened to include all who lived before his coming into the world. Christ preached "even to the dead" (4:6). In Acts 2:25-27 Peter applies to Jesus the words of Ps. 16:10: "David says concerning him . . . , 'For you will not abandon my soul to Hades, or let your Holy One experience corruption.'" In Luke 4:17-18 Jesus had applied to his own work Isa. 61:1, where the servant of the Lord is "to proclaim liberty to the captives." Thus in 1 Peter Jesus is pictured as going down "in the spirit" into Hades between his death and resurrection to offer salvation to those who had died without hearing the gospel and having the opportunity to repent. He went to the dead to set free those who had lived and died without benefit of the good news. It was his first act of triumph. Eph. 4:8 quotes Ps. 68:18, "Therefore it is said, 'When he ascended on high he made captivity itself a captive; he gave gifts to his people.'" The passage then explains, "When it says, 'He ascended,' what does it mean but that he had also descended into the lower parts of the earth?" (4:9). So, as this passage in 1 Peter implies, the descent to the dead is the opening of the Easter events and a prelude to his rising on the third day.

Responding to the Text

Christ's descent to the dead, wherever precisely they are (the ICET deliberately resisted the translation "to the place of the dead" as being more localized than is warranted), is first of all a declaration that he really died and that his death was complete. This was no "near death" experience. He was as dead as one can be. Vital signs stopped, and he went where the dead go. He has undergone the full limits of human life, from birth to death, plumbing the depths of the entire human experience. The descent to the dead is first of all a proclamation of the fullness and the completeness of the incarnation. Christ's descent to the dead is at the same time a proclamation of his lordship over all of creation. No place is without his victory. The three areas of the old picture of the universe—heaven, earth, and hell—are all subject to the reign of Christ, and all three domains are incorporated into his empire. The old Easter hymns understood this. John Ellerton's translation of Venantius Fortunatus's hymn "Welcome, Happy Morning," for example, has the last stanza begin, "Loose the souls long prisoned, bound with Satan's chain; All that now is fallen raise to life again." Christ's destruction of hell is not just rising from the dead but breaking down the doors of that gloomy castle. Opening the way to paradise would be incomplete without a corresponding opening of the prison of Hades and leading those set free to the light of heaven.

> OPENING THE WAY TO PARADISE WOULD BE INCOMPLETE WITHOUT A CORRESPONDING OPENING OF THE PRISON OF HADES AND LEADING THOSE SET FREE TO THE LIGHT OF HEAVEN.

Christ's time in hell is not a sleep but an active time that is part of his victory on behalf of the spirits who are there and his victory over those who hold them in that prison. He announces the decisive defeat of the rulers of hell, and he sets free those who are their captives. The descent to the dead is thus a proclamation of God's all-inclusive concern. Even the ancients who died before the coming of Christ are included in his victory. In Noah's time, eight people were saved. Now Christ descends to the dead to liberate others, sinners though they were, and baptism is shown to have the capability of rescuing the whole world through its universal saving power. The dereliction that "hell" suggested before the victory of Christ by that victory has been transformed into a condition of intimacy with

God. He has made every corner of creation his own. Now, as Paul declares in his ringing affirmation (next week's RC and BCP second lesson), nothing "will be able to separate us from the love of God in Christ Jesus our Lord" (Rom. 8:39).

If it is true that Jesus is the way to God and eternal life, we sometimes wonder, what about those holy men and women who lived before Christ? It was not their fault that they did not know him. Can they be confined to the realm of the dead, excluded from heaven, just because of when they were born? What about Abraham and Sarah, Moses and Elijah, Isaiah and the prophets, Deborah the judge, and Huldah the prophet (2 Kings 22:14)? Heaven would not be quite satisfying if they and the other great people of the Old Testament were not there. Jesus' work of redemption would not be complete if it included only those who were living at the time of the crucifixion or even those, like us, who would live in future centuries and would learn the story. Those who had lived before Christ must hear the Good News too. They must have an opportunity to make belief their own. So, while Jesus' body rested in the tomb, his living spirit went and preached to the spirits in the prison of Hades. For they too must know that Jesus has offered a way out of the prison of death, a deliverance from the confinement of ruined and sinful lives, an exit from hopelessness. Even those who with prophetic vision and confidence knew that one day the promised one would come had to know that the day had at last arrived and that his name was Jesus. So this passage in 1 Peter gives a satisfying understanding of the completeness of the saving work of Christ. Such is God's all-embracing compassion and care.

THE GOSPEL
MARK 1:9–15 (RCL);
MARK 1:9–13 (BCP);
MARK 1:12–15 (RC)

Interpreting the Text

The heart of this reading is Mark's account of the temptation (vv. 12-13). In typical Markan style, it is the briefest of the three synoptic accounts and yet, as is often true with Mark, it has significant details the other reports lack. The RCL and the BCP readings include the context: the baptism by John in the Jordan with the Spirit descending and the voice from heaven. The very next event in each of the synoptic accounts is that Jesus, coming up out of the Jordan, goes into the wilderness to be tempted by Satan, the adversary (1 Chron. 21:1) and the accuser of God's people (Zech. 3:1). Moreover, it is the Spirit who descended upon him at his baptism who brings Jesus into the wilderness. Luke has the simplest statement: Jesus was "led by the Spirit" (4:1); Matthew has "led up by the

Spirit" (4:1). But Mark with his typical haste has this happen "immediately" after the baptism and with his typical vigor and energy has the Spirit not just leading but driving Jesus "out into the wilderness" (v. 12). It is not to be understood as driving an unwilling prophet to where God wants him to go nor forcing a reluctant prophet to confront the old enemy. Jesus, after all, has just received the commendation of the Father, "with you I am well pleased" (v. 11). Therefore, being driven by the Spirit is to be understood as we use the phrase "a driven man." Jesus is under the compulsion of the Spirit's irresistible energy and in that sense is driven "out" into the wilderness, beyond the limits of civilization, to the very edge of human experience. The time in the wilderness recalls the experiences of Moses (Exod. 24:18) and Elijah (1 Kings 19:8) as well as the wilderness testing of Israel after their deliverance through the Red Sea (a type of baptism). Jesus was, as Mark alone notes, "with the wild beasts" (v. 13). The beasts emphasize the loneliness and the desolation of the place where no human being is at home. The beasts are also traditionally associated with evil powers (Ps. 22:11-21; Ezek. 34:5, 8, 25) and also with the triumph of righteousness (Job 5:22-23; Isa. 11:6-9; 65:25; Hos. 2:18). Whereas Matthew says angels "came and waited on him" after the devil had left (there are no angels in Luke's account), Mark has Jesus waited on by angels apparently throughout his time in the wilderness. Mark may have known the *Testament of Naphtali* 8:4, "And the devil will flee away from you [plural] and the wild beasts will fear you and the angels will come to you." That verse may perhaps have suggested Mark's brief but powerful account of the temptation.

The RCL and RC lectionaries include vv. 14-15, the beginning of Jesus' ministry for which the ordeal of the temptation was preparation. The essence of his preaching, "Repent, and believe the gospel," is in the Roman rite an alternative formula for the imposition of ashes on Ash Wednesday.

Responding to the Text

We do well not to try to fill in Mark's account of the temptation with details from Matthew and Luke, as if Mark has given us only an abbreviated version of the "real story." Mark's brief but powerful account should be taken as it stands, and it is sufficient in itself. While Jesus was in the wilderness enduring temptation, his cousin and forerunner John was arrested. When Jesus returned to society, he surely recognized that what had been done to John would probably happen to him as well. The *agon* of the temptation prefigures the great ordeal of the passion. Indeed, as the story unfolds, John was the forerunner of Jesus in birth and life and was the forerunner also in death. But this adumbration did not make Jesus retreat from what had been begun in him. It impelled him to begin his own work of announcing the gospel in words

IN ALL OF IT—BAPTISM, TEMPTATION, AND PREACHING—GOD WAS AT WORK REMAKING THE WORLD.

and in deeds of power. The Spirit drove him into the wilderness, and John's imprisonment forced him to take up where John had left off. In all of it—baptism, temptation, and preaching—God was at work remaking the world. At the beginning of his ministry, the temptation, and at the end, the passion, Jesus faced his enemy alone, and by the strength of his purity, in both situations he was victorious. But he does not remain alone for long. He comes from the exalted experience of his baptism with the voice of the Father and the descent of the Spirit to the loneliness of the wilderness, but he must soon return to the world in a yet more public way to begin his ministry of teaching, preaching, and healing.

We not only watch what is happening. We are part of it. Our baptism sets us against the prevailing culture of the world and makes us walk a different path. Our life after baptism is a continual struggle against the wiles of our old enemy. But in these struggles we are not left alone. As Jesus in the wilderness was ministered to by angels, so the unseen but powerful armies of God surround God's people still, and we rejoice in the strength of the bread of angels given to us in the Holy Supper as our nourishment for the journey through the wilderness. Thus we fast and struggle along our pilgrim's way through the wilderness of this world not alone, not just as a community, but with Christ and in Christ. In Mark's sparse account, the presence of the angels implies fasting and hunger, but it is also a significant aspect in the Gospels. Jesus' victory over Satan is marked by the ministrations of angels (cf. Luke 22:43). So here the angels are an assurance of heavenly support and a promise of ultimate victory. The angels also encourage us in our spiritual warfare against the old enemy and all his attractive but ultimately empty promises. Powerful forces, the whole army of God, surround us to strengthen our resolve and clarify our vision.

The odd detail of Jesus being "with the wild beasts" may be there to emphasize the desolate and threatening scene. In the context of this Sunday, however, with the first reading still sounding in our ears, the wild beasts serve another function. The covenant that God made with Noah after the flood allowed the eating of meat, and by a relaxing of the strictures of the original intention of the Creator expressed in the covenant made with Adam, humans were permitted to kill animals for food. Indeed, since the fall, all relationships have been distorted by human sin: God and humanity, man and woman, humans and animals, humans and the earth and the processes of nature. What was originally a harmony of equals was turned into a hierarchy of dominance. Sin, like a disease, infected not just our first parents and their descendants down to us but everything around us. Therefore, when Jesus is in the wilderness "with the wild beasts," we see the beginning of the restoration of paradise, the fulfillment of Isaiah's vision of the peaceable kingdom, when "the wolf shall live with the lamb, the leopard shall lie down with the kid, the calf and the lion and the fatling together, and a little child shall lead them" (Isa. 11:6). It is a scene made familiar to many by the paintings by Edward Hicks of *The Peaceable Kingdom*. The peace and harmony of paradise are exemplified in the hunter and the prey living side by side in safety. "The wolf and the lamb shall feed together, the lion shall eat straw like the ox; but the serpent—its food shall be dust! They shall not hurt or destroy on all my holy mountain, says the LORD" (Isa. 65:25). Animals will no longer live by the death of other animals, and fear will be taken away. In the wilderness there is a sign of hope, even as John's voice in the desert proclaimed the coming of the Lord. No place on earth is devoid of promise and the presence of God, and the restoration will embrace all creation, not just human beings everywhere but animals and the whole natural world as well.

AS HUMAN SIN INFECTED ALL CREATION, SO THE CRUCIFIXION WILL PURIFY IT ALL.

As human sin infected all creation, so the crucifixion will purify it all. Venantius Fortunatus, in a splendid Passiontide hymn, *"Pange, Lingua, Gloriosi"* ("Sing, My Tongue, the Glorious Battle"), has given the church a magnificent conception of the far-reaching effects of the work of Christ.

> He endures the nails, the spitting, vinegar and spear and reed;
> From that holy body broken. Blood and water forth proceed:
> Earth, and stars, and skies, and ocean by that flood from stain are freed.
> (trans. John Mason Neale, *Hymnal 1982,* 165)

Here in the wilderness with the wild beasts Jesus has already begun the work of reconciliation and restoration that will be accomplished by his passion and will be brought to completion at the last day.

SECOND SUNDAY IN LENT

MARCH 16, 2003

REVISED COMMON	EPISCOPAL (BCP)	ROMAN CATHOLIC
Gen. 17:1-7, 15-16	Gen. 22:1-14	Gen. 22:1-2, 9a, 10-13, 15-18
Ps. 22:23-31	Psalm 16 or 16:5-11	Ps. 116:10, 15, 16-17, 18-19
Rom. 4:13-25	Rom. 8:31-39	Rom. 8:31b-34
Mark 8:31-38	Mark 8:31-38	Mark 9:2-10

This Sunday there is a divergence in the appointed readings. The Roman Catholic lectionary, preserving an ancient tradition, focuses on the transfiguration, which the RCL and BCP lectionaries, following a Lutheran innovation just after the Reformation, have already observed on the Last Sunday after the Epiphany. (All three traditions also observe the transfiguration on August 6. It is on the RC and BCP calendars and is an optional observance on that date in the LBW).

FIRST READING

GENESIS 17:1-7, 15-16 (RCL);
GENESIS 22:1-14 (BCP);
GENESIS 22:1-2, 9a, 10-13, 15-18 (RC)

Interpreting the Texts

Last Sunday the first reading reported God's covenant with Noah. The first reading appointed in the Revised Common Lectionary is the later priestly account of the covenant God made with Abraham and Sarah. (The earlier version was given in Gen. 15:7-21, which is the RCL first reading for the Second Sunday in Lent in Year C.) God, who is called in Hebrew *El Shaddai,* a divine name from the time before Moses meaning "God, the One of the Mountains," preserved mostly in the Priestly tradition and rarely used outside the Pentateuch (except in Job), appears to aged Abram, calls him to a holy life, and establishes a covenant with him. The initiative, as always the case with covenants that God makes, is entirely God's and establishes a relationship between a superior and an inferior party. The covenant that God promises is that Abram, through his descendants, will be "exceedingly numerous" (17:2). As Abram falls down in adoration, hiding his face from God, the promise is clarified (suggesting the skillful blending of several strands of the story into one by the Priestly editor): "You shall be the ancestor of a multitude of nations." He is to be the ancestor not merely of Israel but of a multitude of nations so that the benefits of the covenant reach out to all peoples. The covenant is permanent because it is made by God, the Everlasting. As a lasting sign of the covenant, Abram is given a new name. (A change of name marks a change of destiny.) He is no longer Abram, "exalted ancestor," but Abraham, a dialectical variant, here understood to mean "ancestor of a multitude." He will be the ancestor not only of nations but also of kings. God's personal choice of Abraham is emphasized by the words "to be God to you and to your offspring."

> THE INITIATIVE, AS ALWAYS THE CASE WITH COVENANTS THAT GOD MAKES, IS ENTIRELY GOD'S AND ESTABLISHES A RELATIONSHIP BETWEEN A SUPERIOR AND AN INFERIOR PARTY.

The lection concludes with the change of the name of Abraham's wife from Sarai to Sarah. God does not speak to her directly but tells Abraham how he is to give her a new name. It should be noted, however, that she is to be involved in the creation of the future in an even more intimate way than is her husband. Abraham will be "the ancestor of a multitude of nations" (17:4), but in her childbearing Sarah "shall give rise to nations; kings of peoples shall come from her" (17:16).

The Roman Catholic and Episcopal reading, Genesis 22, is one of the great stories of world literature. (The reading had been the Old Testament lesson in the 1958 *Lutheran Service Book and Hymnal* and the first lesson for Lent Year B in the lectionary in the *Lutheran Book of Worship.*) Kierkegaard was fascinated with the story and explored it in *Fear and Trembling.* Erich Auerbach, in the opening chapter of *Mimesis* (1946; English translation, 1953) describes the difference between this story and the method of Homer. Homer and classic epics generally are characterized by frequent digressions, designed not to keep the reader in suspense since the plot is well known, but to relax the tension. The biblical style in contrast, exemplified in the story of Abraham and Isaac, admits almost no modifiers, no digression, no distraction from the terrifying events that unfold without relaxation before our eyes. The account of God's testing of Abraham's faith in the ultimate divine purpose is the most dramatic of the stories of God's dealing with Abraham and is remarkably well told, largely in dialogue. Irrelevant details are omitted, and those few that remain are notably and movingly effective.

The introductory phrase "After these things" occurs only twice in the Abraham stories (the other appearance is at 15:1), and each time suggests a crisis toward which previous events have been leading. The powerful story in Genesis 22 is God's test of Abraham in order to know what was in his heart. The location of Moriah is not known, but later tradition identified it with Jerusalem (2 Chron. 3:1) and more specifically with the temple mount (shown perhaps by Gen. 22:14, "On the mount of the LORD it shall be provided"), and this further supports the inevitable Christian reading of the story as prefiguring the Passion of Jesus, the only Son. Behind God's incomprehensible command to sacrifice Isaac may lie a condemnation of child sacrifice (Lev. 18:21), a practice often denounced by the prophets (2 Kings 3:27; Jer. 19:4ff.; Ezek. 16:20-21). The practice may have persisted long in Israel as 2 Kings 17:31 and Mic. 6:7 show. In the background of the story may lie the more developed understanding that, like all firstfruits, the first-born belong to God; they are not to be sacrificed but rather bought back, redeemed. Since Abraham passes the harrowing test, God renews the promise to him and his descendants (Gen. 12:1-3). Abraham's response of complete surrender makes it possible for God to reaffirm his promise in a most absolute way, swearing by himself.

Responding to the Texts

The reading in the RCL opens with the call to pilgrimage renewed and transformed. It is God's command, "Walk before me," and it is a summons and command to live and move openly before God in a manner pleasing to him, unashamed, with nothing to hide.

The covenant God made with Abraham is essential to Judaism. The Jews are his direct descendants spread throughout the ages and throughout the world. The covenant is important to Christians insofar as Christians are grafted onto the ancient stem and made "honorary Jews." So the promise "to be God to you and to your offspring after you" (17:7) is heard by Christians to be spoken to them. Notable in this description is its view to the future. We are responsible to be faithful not just for our own good but also for the sake of the generations that will follow us. The related promise of the land is heard by Christians not literally but figuratively. The true homeland of Christians is not to be found on this earth but rather in the heavenly country. Also noteworthy in this reading is the inclusion of Sarah. The name of Noah's wife is not recorded in the Noah stories, and the covenant is made with him and his sons, whose wives' names are also unrecorded. The covenant with Abraham reported in Genesis 15 is made with Abraham. But now Sarah is included by name in the story as the agent through whom the promise of descendants will be fulfilled. While her change of name from Sarai to Sarah makes no essential difference in meaning (both mean "princess"), the change

> THE PROMISE "TO BE GOD TO YOU AND TO YOUR OFFSPRING AFTER YOU" IS HEARD BY CHRISTIANS TO BE SPOKEN TO THEM.

implies a change in status and is parallel to the change of her husband's name from Abram to Abraham.

The harrowing story of Abraham and Isaac is a masterpiece of the storyteller's art. God's command to Abraham builds its power by adding another element with each phrase: "Take your son," "your only son Isaac" (the name reminds us of his individuality) "whom you love" (Gen. 22:2). Without a murmur of complaint (was Abraham, who was quite willing to bargain with God in Gen. 18:23-32, too stunned to reply?), with not a word of explanation to anyone, not even his wife, the mother of the child, Abraham cut the wood for the pyre (a chilling detail) himself (he didn't have a servant do this work), and set out early in the morning (so no one would try to stop him?). When he saw the place (how, we are not told, and it does not matter), he left his two servants behind (so they would not witness what is to take place? so they would not interfere?), saying, "The boy [not using his name, not calling him my child, already trying to distance himself from his son] and I will go . . . worship [true in its way], and then we will come back to you" (a deliberate lie to put the servants at ease and also to deceive himself as to what is to take place; yet in the end it is a truthful statement). Abraham then "took the wood of the burnt offering [we are not allowed to forget its intended purpose] and laid it on his son Isaac" (we are not allowed to forget the relationship between the two even though the father, to put further distance between them, treated his son as if he were a pack animal). Abraham "himself carried the fire and the knife."

The final word acts like a knife blade on us, and we realize what is implied in making the sacrifice. The separation between the two cannot be maintained: "The two of them walked on together," side by side, still, for all the father's efforts, father and son. Names return and we are reminded of the relationship between the two; "Isaac said to his father Abraham, 'Father!' " Abraham replied almost by reflex to the boy's inquiry, "Here I am, my son." The child asked the obvious question that must have struck directly at the father's heart: "Where is the lamb for a burnt offering?" (Did he ask in complete innocence or was he somehow becoming apprehensive?) Abraham's reply is remarkably clever: "God himself will provide the lamb for a burnt offering, my son." He could not forget their relationship, even though he surely dreaded what he was about to do, but here he could not lie. The boy was to believe that God would provide a sacrificial animal; the father meant that God had indeed provided the sacrifice, the miraculously born innocent lamb who had just asked the question.

They continued to walk on together. When they arrived at the place, their words ceased. In silence Abraham built the altar and slowly laid the wood in order. Without a word of explanation or apology (what words could he say?) he bound his son (who in his confusion and horror could not speak) and laid him on the wood. "Abraham reached out his hand and took the knife [the knife that he himself had carried to the mountain] to kill [or 'slaughter' as if he were sacrificing an animal] his son." The relationship even now was not to be put out of mind. Then, at the very last minute, as countless paintings have imagined, with Abraham's hand clutching the knife raised high to plunge into his son and make the death swift and as painless as possible, an angel called Abraham's name not once but twice, so urgent was the message. God commended Abraham by saying, "You have not withheld your son, your only son, from me." Abraham had passed the test. A stray ram substituted for the no longer innocent lamb. The sacrifice was offered, and Abraham and Isaac returned home. What their relationship was after this experience is almost too horrid to contemplate.

A useful Lenten devotion for the preacher is a careful reading and meditation of Kierkegaard's extraordinary text *Fear and Trembling.*

Responsive Reading

PSALM 22:23-31 (RCL);
PSALM 16 or 16:5-11 (BCP);
PSALM 116:10, 15, 16-17, 18-19 (RC)

The RCL uses a section of the great Psalm of the Passion that offers praise for the help God has provided the psalmist in his misery. Although the psalm begins as a personal lament of an innocent person, it concludes with a view to all nations and even to those who have died. "All the families of the nations shall worship before him" indicates the response of the multitude of nations that descend from the covenant with Abraham.

The BCP uses Psalm 16, a statement of faith in God's power to deliver and an expression of gratitude for God's care, the concluding verses of which, we may imagine, express Isaac's relief and perhaps also that of his father. "You do not give me up to Sheol, or let your faithful one see the Pit." As the reading from Genesis 22 has shown, God will not permit anyone who is faithful to perish. The psalm expresses the quiet faith of one who has lived long in communion with God and, living in the presence of God, has hope in this life and in the life to come. The prayer to escape death that would break the union with God hints at the developing belief in resurrection. Because of such confidence in God's care, the psalmist can sing that, even in the grave, "My body shall rest in hope."

The RC psalm provides words that, we imagine, might have been said by Abraham and Isaac after their ordeal. "I kept my faith," says Abraham; "You have loosed my bonds," says Isaac. Together they offer a sacrifice of thanksgiving on Mount Moriah and promise to do so again in the presence of all God's people in the Jerusalem temple. The psalmist resolves to pay vows of thank offerings in the temple. The vows are continuing signs of gratitude through sacrifices and obedience. In the psalm we may also hear the voice of the risen Christ (and therefore our own voice as well), "O Lord, I am your servant. . . . You have loosed my bonds. I will offer to you a thanksgiving sacrifice and call on the name of the Lord" (116:16-17).

Second Reading

ROMANS 4:13-25 (RCL);
ROMANS 8:31-39 (BCP);
ROMANS 8:31b-34 (RC)

Interpreting the Texts

The RCL second reading is to be paired with the RCL first reading, God's covenant with Abraham and Sarah. The passage in Romans extends the covenant to include all who have faith in Christ, Gentiles as well as Jews, as true descendants of Abraham. "Those who share the faith of Abraham," as well as those who adhere to the law, are counted as his descendants. Indeed, it is because God intended his promises for all people that he made the fulfillment conditional on faith rather than on circumcision. God's creation of the world out of nothing is applied to Abraham's faith and the infertility of the aged couple: God "calls into existence things that do not exist." Isaac was born of one "as good as dead," as Heb. 11:12 bluntly puts it. God's giving life to the dead and calling into existence things that do not exist, in the context of Lent as a time of preparation for or renewal of baptism, also looks ahead to the resurrection and to the wonder of new life found within the Christian community.

Romans 8:31-39 (BCP; RC concludes at v. 34) is that most stirring affirmation of Christian hope and triumphant assertion of God's love. The death of Christ is understood from the perspective of the resurrection and thus seen as the crowning evidence of God's love.

The power of that love will preserve us in the face of any experience that may threaten us now or in the future. The love of God was poured out in and through the life, death, and resurrection of Christ, and it abides as the Spirit in the new community, which was given birth by those formative events and in which they are continued until the end of time. The order of things and beings that could be expected to interfere with God's love for us seems somewhat jumbled (angels, principalities, and powers ought logically to go together). The disorder suggests Paul's spontaneous inspiration in which his thoughts outrun logical thought and leap ahead of speech. It is noteworthy that time ("things present . . . things to come," v. 38) is understood to be part of God's creation, along with angels and the geography of the physical world, and therefore has a beginning and presumably also has an end. Also to be noted, especially in a time in which many are fascinated by angels, is the implication that not all angels are on our side.

Responding to the Texts

The passage from Romans 4 that is the RCL second lesson can easily be related to the first lesson. In Genesis 17 God makes his covenant with Abraham and Sarah; St. Paul in Romans 4 emphasizes the faith Abraham had that God could do even what seemed impossible. Abraham and Sarah, aged and infertile, nonetheless were promised not just a child but a vast number of descendants. Against all appearance and all logic, Abraham believed that what God said God would do. It was the patriarch's towering confidence in the divine promise that Paul finds so instructive. We who come long after him know that the promise to Abraham was fulfilled, and

> AGAINST ALL APPEARANCE AND ALL LOGIC, ABRAHAM BELIEVED THAT WHAT GOD SAID GOD WOULD DO.

that his descendants are spread throughout the earth. What is required of us is a similar faith in God's power to do what has been promised, even though it goes against all that is rational and sensible. We believe that God raised Jesus from the dead. God's promises are kept, and faith is the confidence that they are kept. It is not our effort—no matter how strenuous—that matters but God's grace and power. So having set aside our own desires and goals, we rest in the assurance that what God wants to be done, God will do.

The RC and BCP second reading should be connected with the RC and BCP first reading. God said to Abraham, "You have not withheld your son, your only son" (Gen. 22:16). Paul, echoing that commendation of the patriarch, says that God "did not withhold his own Son, but gave him up for all of us." God's offering exceeds even the sacrifice that Abraham was willing to make. Abraham was willing to sacrifice his beloved only son because God told him to do it, but on Mount Moriah at the last second God declared that the sacrifice was not required. On Golgotha God did not intervene in the sacrifice of his only Son. The verse that links the two passages is Abraham's attempt to allay the fear of Isaac, "God himself will provide the lamb for a burnt offering" (Gen. 22:8). The sacrifice of the Son of God had to be carried to its completion in order to make us the children of God, made in the image of Christ. The Word took our human form so that we might be reborn as children of God.

Therefore nothing in death or life, no supernatural powers or superhuman beings, nothing now or to come, no height or depth of human experience will be able to remove us from the love of God, who has in Christ gone through it all and who has shown himself to be Lord of every terror and Master of every world. A prayer at the Burial of the Dead in the Lutheran rite, borrowed from the Church of Scotland, turns the conclusion to this grand passage into magnificent and powerful comfort. "God of all grace, you sent your Son, our Savior Jesus Christ, to bring life and immortality to light. We give you thanks because by his death Jesus destroyed the power of death and by his resurrection has opened the kingdom of heaven to all believers. Make us certain that because he lives we shall live also, and that neither death nor life, nor things present nor things to come shall be able to separate us from your love which is in Christ Jesus our Lord" (*Lutheran Book of Worship*, p. 210).

THE GOSPEL
MARK 8:31-38 (RCL, BCP);
MARK 9:2-10 (RC)

Interpreting the Texts

The RCL and BCP Gospel is the first prediction of the Passion according to Mark's account. The idea that the Messiah was to suffer was in sharp contrast to Jewish expectations. "Son of Man," a favorite description that Jesus used of himself, had two meanings for the people of his time. It could emphasize his identification with humanity; he is the son of a mortal (the title used in Ezekiel 2:1ff.; "mortal" means "son of [a] man"). Or "Son of Man" could be a reference to the figure in Dan. 7:13-14, who was traditionally identified with the Messiah. While both surely appealed to Jesus, his characteristic approach is to involve the readers in deciding their own response to what is being said. Jesus rejects Peter's response to his open and clear prediction of his suffering and death as a continuation of Satan's temptation to think only in human terms. The second half of the reading invites hearers to share in Jesus' sacrificial way of life.

The RC Gospel continues the ancient Roman tradition of reading an account of the transfiguration on this Sunday. The early church gathered the catechumens preparing for baptism and on the First Sunday in Lent showed them the temptation of Christ and introduced them to an austere life like that of Moses and Elijah, who spent time in the wilderness fasting and praying. Now the catechumens are invited to climb the Mount of Transfiguration and, like the three apostles, are there given a glimpse and promise of Jesus in transfigured glory with Moses and Elijah.

In Mark's Gospel the transfiguration is more closely linked to Jesus' predictions of his passion than it is in the other Synoptics. Jesus took the inner circle of the Twelve, the elite among the apostles, and revealed to them the wholeness of the paschal mystery. In Mark's account Elijah is given priority over Moses, because Elijah was identified with John the Baptist, who by his own suffering prepared the way for the suffering of the Messiah. Moses was identified as the lawgiver. The voice from the cloud said to the three apostles, and especially to Peter, "Listen to him!" (9:7). Jesus said nothing in this episode, so the command to pay attention seems to relate to Jesus' words about the impending Passion: Confess him as the true Messiah and understand that his work leads through suffering and death to new life.

Responding to the Texts

The RCL Gospel seems to state what to us is well known: Jesus had to suffer and die and then rise. That is not news; we know the story. The prediction helps to remind us of the journey of Lent to the cross and beyond, but it does not seem to do more than focus our thoughts. The second half of the reading, however, reaches out to those who would follow this suffering Messiah and involves them in his life and death. We cannot short-circuit the process. We cannot simply assume that because Jesus is alive we have eternal life, and that's that. There is a price to be paid for that life: Jesus first had to suffer and die, and if we are to follow him into life, we must walk the path he took and have our share in his sacrificial suffering and death before life is ours. We are to renounce our self-centeredness and selfish concerns and desires and put our focus on the life of service of others rather than on what we will get out of discipleship. Life is God's gift. Our life now came from God and our new life in Christ is also God's gift to us. Our life is to be the life of Christ, a life lived not for ourselves but for others. The life lived for our own good leads to death; the life lived for others leads to the life of the world.

> JESUS FIRST HAD TO SUFFER AND DIE, AND IF WE ARE TO FOLLOW HIM INTO LIFE, WE MUST WALK THE PATH HE TOOK AND HAVE OUR SHARE IN HIS SACRIFICIAL SUFFERING AND DEATH BEFORE LIFE IS OURS.

In the RC lectionary, "This is my Son, the Beloved" (Mark 9:7), the Father's voice says at the transfiguration. We may imagine such words going through Abraham's mind as he was about to sacrifice his beloved son at God's command. He did not want to do it. Jesus, on the other hand, came willingly to offer himself in sacrifice in obedience to the Father's will. This willingness gives full meaning to the heavenly commendation, "This is my Son, the Beloved."

The perplexing command by Jesus that the three apostles "tell no one about what they had seen, until after the Son of Man had risen from the dead" (9:9) suggests that the truth about the work of the Messiah had to wait until the full revelation in the resurrection. Until then the truth is revealed in a progressive way to the inner circle of the three, in a somewhat less full way to a larger group of followers, and in yet another way when speaking to the crowds. As by the observance of the church year we are drawn progressively into the heart of God, we are able to hear more and more of the fullness of the mystery of God's being and truth. Within the community of the church, each of us is at a different stage in our Christian life, and the revelation of God and God's way is appropriate to each at each stage of our journey.

THIRD SUNDAY IN LENT

MARCH 23, 2003

REVISED COMMON	EPISCOPAL (BCP)	ROMAN CATHOLIC
Exod. 20:1-17	Exod. 20:1-17	Exod. 20:1-17
		or 20:1-3, 7-8, 12-17
Psalm 19	Ps. 19:7-14	Ps. 19:8, 9, 10, 11
1 Cor. 1:18-25	Rom. 7:13-25	1 Cor. 1:22-25
John 2:13-22	John 2:13-22	John 2:13-25

FIRST READING
EXODUS 20:1-17 (RCL, BCP, RC);
EXODUS 20:1-3, 7-8, 12-17 (RC, alt.)

Interpreting the Text

The first reading in all three lectionary cycles is the Decalogue in the version that goes back to primitive Yahwist and Priestly sources, Exodus 20. The "Ten Words," as the Greek *decalogue* translates the Hebrew (Exod. 34:28; Deut. 4:13; 10:4), epitomize the duty toward God and neighbor of those who have been liberated from slavery in Egypt. The Decalogue belongs to a distinct literary genre, the apodictic, in which precepts in the second person (You shall/shall not . . .) are grouped in tens or twelves with an established rhythm of phrase. It is sometimes supposed that in their original form the Ten Commandments were all brief commands like the present fifth, sixth, seventh, and eighth without the explanatory material later added to the others. The apodictic precept is proclaimed absolutely, setting out a decision of one with authority that cannot be debated or questioned. It is in fact so absolute that there is no mention of sanctions, as in other forms of law (if someone does A, then that person must suffer B). In the Bible the commandments are not numbered individually.

Two systems of numbering the commandments have been followed. One system is (1) vv. 2-3 (no other gods before me), (2) vv. 4-6 (no idols), (3) v. 7 (no wrongful use of the name of God), (4) vv. 8-11 (remember the Sabbath), (5) v. 12 (honor father and mother), (6) v. 13 (no murder), (7) v. 14 (no adultery), (8) v. 15 (no stealing), (9) v. 16 (no false witness), (10) v. 17 (no coveting). The other system is (1) vv. 3-6 (no other gods including idols), (2) v. 7 (no wrongful use of the name of God), (3) vv. 8-11 (remember the Sabbath), (4) v. 12 (honor father and mother), (5) v. 13 (no murder), (6) v. 14 (no adultery), (7) v. 15 (no stealing), (8) v. 16 (no false witness), (9) v. 17a (no coveting of neighbor's house), (10) v. 17b (no coveting of neighbor's wife, servants, cattle). The second of these systems, drawn up by Augustine following Deut. 5:6-21, is the one accepted by the Roman Catholic Church and the Lutheran Church. The first of these systems is followed by Anglicans and Protestants.

The law is divided into two tablets or tables based on the description of Moses descending from Sinai with two tablets or tables on which the Ten Words were inscribed by the finger of God (Exod. 32:15-16). The first table describes duty to God (commandments 1–3 or 1–4, depending on the numbering system used), and the second table describes duty toward others (commandments 4–10 or 5–10).

Responding to the Text

Mount Sinai, the mountain of God, was the place where during their time in the wilderness Israel was bound to God in solemn covenant. It was the place where God spoke directly to their representative, Moses, who delivered the law to his people. It was on this sacred mountain that God revealed himself to his people and communicated with them. While Moses spoke to God face to face, the people saw God hidden in the cloud that descended on the mountain and heard the voice of God in the thunder and felt the presence of God in the earthquake. The revelation of God was an awesome experience. It is no wonder that Christians appropriated that terrifying experience as a foreshadowing of another revelation of God in Jesus Christ. Congregations may know the Advent antiphon that addresses Christ by a title for God and prays, "O Adonai and ruler of the house of Israel, who appeared to Moses in the burning bush and gave him the law on Sinai: Come with an outstretched arm and redeem us." Many are familiar with John Mason Neale's hymn based on these "O antiphons," which renders this antiphon in verse,

> O come, O come, thou Lord of might,
> Who to thy tribes on Sinai's height
> In ancient times didst give the Law
> In cloud and majesty and awe.
> Rejoice! Rejoice! Emmanuel
> Shall come to thee, O Israel.
> (*Hymnal 1982*, 56)

Such appropriation of the giving of the law as a work of Christ is a Christian way of doing what the preface to the Ten Commandments does with its reminder of God's liberation of Israel from slavery. The commandments are set within the context of God's redemptive purpose. They present the core and sum of the Mosaic law to serve as instruction and deterrent. The commandments show us the life that God expects of his people, and in the deepened understanding that Jesus gave, searching the thoughts of the secret heart, the commandments expect and demand nothing less than perfection. The primary purpose of the Decalogue for Christians, therefore, is to show us our sin. Luther's explanation of the commandments given in his *Small Catechism* is insightful. The first commandment, "You shall have no other gods" is really the only commandment. All the rest are illustrations of what it means to "fear, love, and trust in God above all things." If God is our God, then we naturally will obey all the other commandments and revere God's name, gladly hear and learn the Word of God, honor our parents and superiors, avoid harming our neighbor, love and honor our spouse, help our neighbors improve their income and property, interpret charitably all that our neighbors do, and help our neighbors keep what is theirs. In his explanations of each commandment, Luther does what Jesus does in the Gospel and shows that it is not enough simply to avoid doing what the commandment forbids. We are to take positive action to revere God and to assist our neighbors in the conduct of their lives.

> "YOU SHALL HAVE NO OTHER GODS" IS REALLY THE ONLY COMMANDMENT. ALL THE REST ARE ILLUSTRATIONS OF WHAT IT MEANS TO "FEAR, LOVE, AND TRUST IN GOD ABOVE ALL THINGS."

PSALM 19 (RCL);
PSALM 19:7-14 (BCP);
PSALM 19:8, 9, 10, 11 (RC)

As the change in form and rhythm beginning with v. 7 shows, two older, unrelated psalms have been ingeniously combined into one, forming a united meditation on the law of God. (The BCP appoints only the second part of the psalm, vv. 7-14.) Day and night the heavens praise God without words, yet their praise is understood throughout the world. The stars, in a lovely conception from ancient Mesopotamia, are the silent "writing of the heavens." In the ancient Near East the sun, by its clear light from which nothing can hide, symbolized justice; the idea is reflected in Mal. 4:2 [3:20], "The sun of righteousness [justice] shall rise, with healing in its wings." Nature and the law both manifest the perfection of God. The order of creation is obeyed by the sun, moon, and stars; human beings are expected also to obey the law given to them. The psalm prayer for this psalm appointed in the *Lutheran Book of Worship,* a prayer borrowed from the BCP, points to a proper understanding of our obedience. "Heavenly Father, you have filled the world with beauty. Open our eyes to see your gracious hand in all your works, that rejoicing in your whole creation, we may learn to serve you with gladness, for the sake of him through whom all things are made, your Son, Jesus Christ our Lord." Our obedience to God's law is not to be a sullen or resentful doing of what we are told, but is to be our willing service of God done gladly out of gratitude for what has been done for us by Jesus Christ.

SECOND READING

1 CORINTHIANS 1:18-25 (RCL);
1 CORINTHIANS 1:22-25 (RC);
ROMANS 7:13-25 (BCP)

Interpreting the Texts

The church in Corinth was divided by factionalism (not an uncommon experience in many congregations). Paul was convinced that the factions stemmed from a reliance on systems of human thought that reduced the gospel to a philosophy. Some at Corinth took pride in their ability to talk in sophisticated philosophical ways. But human wisdom cannot comprehend the mystery of God and is inadequate to understand the way of faith. To those who follow such earth-bound systems and who therefore "are perishing" (v. 18), as all intellectual fads are transitory, the central Christian proclamation about the cross is foolishness. The apparent folly of the cross, that God should love the world to such an extent that he would send his own Son to die, is a stumbling block that trips up those who cannot approach the mystery except on an intellectual plane.

HUMAN WISDOM CANNOT COMPREHEND THE MYSTERY OF GOD AND IS INADEQUATE TO UNDERSTAND THE WAY OF FAITH.

Paul supports his claim with a free quotation from Isaiah (29:14) declaring that God saved Jerusalem by his own power without consideration of any national or personal abilities or attainments. The world, for all its knowledge and learning, has never found God and in its search is still groping after him. That very quest was God's doing to show the world its own helplessness in such a quest and its dependence on God and God's revelation. The membership of the church in Corinth included few who were wise, clever talkers, powerful, or of noble birth (v. 26). Their wisdom and cleverness and lineage did not square with the way of God. Human wisdom cannot lead us to God, and therefore God decided to reach humanity not through wisdom but through faith. And faith is available to all, no matter what one's intellectual abilities may be. Paul's approach does not denigrate human knowledge or learning in itself. God's way surpasses human power, and

"God's foolishness is wiser than human wisdom" just as "God's weakness is stronger than human strength" (v. 25).

The BCP second reading, Rom. 7:13-25, is one of the most important passages in the letter. Paul emits a cry from his heart and in so doing gives voice to a continuing human conflict that is nothing short of a war. The law is spiritual in origin, given by God, but Paul is "of the flesh" (v. 14), not just in the sense of being human but being under the power of sin, the almost personified lord who captures, imprisons, and takes up residence in human nature. It is as if Paul has been sold into slavery. It is not that the flesh is essentially or inherently sinful but, because sin has invaded and so corrupted it that we are characterized by a proclivity to sin, the flesh is inevitably sinful. Paul is thus perplexed to find himself doing what he does not want to do and is helpless to avoid what he knows is wrong. The law, which is holy, being given by God, is not itself responsible for the evil state of humanity. But under the corrupting influence of sin, the law looks like an enemy. Sin produces a counterfeit law that makes war on the true law and takes us captive and so works its will with us. Deliverance from this desperate plight is never complete in this life. The process of destruction of sin that was begun in baptism is not yet complete and will not be completed until the last day. Thus Luther could speak of human beings as being at once both justified and sinful (*simul justus et peccator*) and of death as the fulfillment of baptism.

Responding to the Texts

The gospel was a stumbling block to the Jews who remembered, "Anyone hung on a tree is under God's curse" (Deut. 21:23), and who therefore found it impossible to believe that the one who was crucified could be the Messiah. Moreover, many Jews expected the Messiah, when he came, to prove himself by confounding signs and demonstrations of his enormous power. The Christian gospel was foolishness to the Greeks who believed that a god was incapable of feeling and could be moved by no human emotion or plight. A God who suffered was therefore a contradiction in terms. Moreover, the Greeks had come to understand wisdom as little more than sophistry, the ability by mental gymnastics and a facile tongue to charm and entertain an audience. The Christian

> FOR THE WORLD, THE IDEA OF A CRUCIFIED GOD IS INCOMPREHENSIBLE, AND THE WAY OF THE CROSS AS THE ONLY WAY TO LIFE AND PEACE SEEMS LIKE MASOCHISTIC NONSENSE.

preachers with their blunt and simple message seemed crude and uncultivated and therefore not worth the time of those who loved a sparkling display of cleverness and cunning. This historical background is not so foreign from the present situation of the church. For the world, the idea of a crucified God is incomprehensible, and the way of the cross as the only way to life and peace seems like masochistic nonsense.

God does not ask people to embrace senselessness. Stupidity is not a virtue and is not to be cultivated; Christians are not know-nothings. The real point at issue is that on our own, with our own mental ability or intellectual cleverness, we cannot approach God. God must make the first move. God must first come to us. Luther in the *Small Catechism* reflected Paul and traditional Christian teaching when he explained the Third Article of the Apostles' Creed, "I cannot by my own reason or strength believe in Jesus Christ my Lord, or come to him. But the Holy Spirit has called me through the Gospel, enlightened me with his gifts, and sanctified and preserved me in true faith, just as he calls, gathers, enlightens, and sanctifies the whole Christian Church on earth and preserves it in union with Jesus Christ in the one true faith." We must be called to faith.

"We preach Christ crucified" (see 1 Cor. 1:23). That is the heart and center of the gospel, the treasure of the church. The crucifixion shows the extent of God's love, the depth of human sin, and the infinite value of each individual human life. Those who have not heard the call to faith in what God has done cannot understand or accept this preaching. In that sense the stumbling blocks of Paul's day continue to trip people up in the twenty-first century. A God involved in human affairs, both in the outcast and in the corridors of prestige and power, depending on where one is (God may be found on the opposite side), remains an uncomfortable figure. The way of suffering is still unwelcome.

The Decalogue has played an important part in the worship of the Anglican Church, perhaps more than in any other denomination. In eighteenth-century Anglican churches a prominent adornment was a large panel above the altar giving the Ten Commandments, together with a second panel giving the Lord's Prayer and sometimes the Apostles' Creed. The congregation could not escape such a confrontation with the law of God. Moreover, the Decalogue was part of the penitential rite of Holy Communion, said immediately before the confession, and it continues, as an optional element, in the present Prayer Book. In such a way worshipers can see and hear and learn that a primary purpose of the law is to show us our sin.

The law can show us our sin, but because of our slavery to sin, this nearly personified lord, which constantly overpowers our spirit, which ought to be in control, the law cannot deliver us no matter how good our intentions. Christ alone can set us free from that frustrating predicament, and he has in fact freed us from that slavery. But that saving work of Christ on the cross does not end the matter so that we may rest secure in its knowledge. Christians by baptism have put on Christ, but the process of incorporation is not immediately complete. It continues, for even as they are already part of the new creation, experienced in faith and in the sacraments, Christians must continually be encouraged to put the new creation into practice. As they do that, their bewildered helplessness turns into astonished gratitude, and their defeat is transformed into victory.

JOHN 2:13-22 (RCL, BCP);
JOHN 2:13-25 (RC)

Interpreting the Text

The RCL and RC Gospel, the cleansing of the temple, occurs at the first of three Passovers mentioned in John during Jesus' ministry (the Synoptics imply a one-year ministry). In the Fourth Gospel the dramatic cleansing takes place at the outset of Jesus' ministry and soon after the testimony of John the Baptist (John 1:19-42), the cleansing thus being understood as a fulfillment of Mal. 3:1-4. In the synoptic accounts, Jesus cites two biblical texts, Isa. 56:7 and Jer. 7:11, as justification for what he does. In John, however, he acts on his own authority, and the act therefore is a demonstration of his messianic claim. His reference to the temple as "my Father's house" (v. 16) is a further testimony to his lordship. The text seems to make clear that in his righteous anger Jesus used the whip of cords on the animals not on the people and that "he poured out the coins of the money changers and overturned their tables." The animals were sold for sacrifice, and Roman money received in the transaction was changed into Jewish money to pay the temple tax.

The second half of the reading does not have a parallel in the synoptic accounts. The disciples, seeing the cleansing action, remember Ps. 69:9, which in the context has a clear messianic meaning (Matt. 27:48; John 15:25; 19:28; Acts 1:20; Rom. 15:3). The psalmist may have been a zealot for the rebuilding of the temple after the exile who, because of his zeal, encountered opposition. Jeremiah is Jesus' favorite prophet (he quoted Jeremiah more than any other prophet), and the motif of destroying and rebuilding appears often in Jeremiah (1:10; 18:7-10; 24:6; 42:10; 45:4). On the literal level, Jesus claims that he, whose power is not of this world, has the power not only to destroy the temple but to rebuild it, even in three days' time.

A further interpretation of the incident is given in the next verses. In the light of the passion and resurrection of Jesus, the episode takes on further meaning, and it becomes clear why this reading was selected for use in Lent. The destroying and rebuilding will be not of an earthly structure but of his body, dying and resurrected. Unlike Mark, who uses the Greek verb *oikodomeo* ("to build"), John uses the verb *egeirein,* with the double sense of "raising up" and "awakening." Thus Jesus' words can refer to the reconstruction of the demolished temple and also, as John explains (2:21), to the raising of his own body from death. In this context, the "three days" take on a clear paschal meaning, already alluded to in the opening reference to the Passover (2:13). The new temple and dwelling place of the Father is Jesus' humanity, the place of perfect sacrifice (Hebrews 9–10) and the source of all blessing (John 7:37ff.). He is thus the fulfillment of the prophets' insistence that what pleases God is not external sacrifice and properly performed ritual but obedience, the sacrifice of one's will to the will and intention of God.

The final section in the RC reading (2:23-25) is a further affirmation of Jesus' divinity. On his own, he knew the heart of everyone. The verses also warn against believing because of the signs alone and not believing in the one to whom they point.

Responding to the Text

This reading is appointed in all the lectionaries for this Third Sunday in Lent because of the emphasis on the resurrection. Jesus' claim that he will raise up or awaken the temple of his body three days after it has been destroyed surely made little sense to those who heard it originally, but after the resurrection the disciples remembered and understood what it meant. Irenaeus rightly said that prophecy is not fully understood until it has been fulfilled. The original hearers, perhaps even the apostles, thought that Jesus was talking about the physical temple in Jerusalem, begun by Herod forty-six years before, in 19 B.C.E. It would not be finished for another thirty-seven years. But the new temple of which Jesus spoke was to be his risen body, the spiritual temple where disciples will worship in spirit and in truth (John 4:23). Christianity was not to be tied to a particular place, as Judaism had long had its focus in the temple in Jerusalem. The body of Christians, the church, was to be the temple of the living God. This liveliness was to be more apparent in the lives of disciples than in the stones and rare wood and precious metals of an earthly temple. The connection of this idea with Lent is not to take our eyes off the present time and to look ahead to the joy of Easter. This time of Lent is our opportunity to prepare ourselves to receive the new life, to pray for the cleansing of ourselves to make us worthy temples of the Holy Spirit. As the BCP collect for the Fourth Sunday in Advent prays, "Purify our conscience, Almighty God, by your daily visitation, that your Son Jesus Christ, at his coming, may find in us a mansion prepared for himself." The purification encouraged by Advent, once called "winter Lent," should be even more intense and thorough during the Forty Days of Quadragesima, so that when Easter comes we may be able to receive the new life and the fire of the Holy Spirit. The reticence of the final verses of the RC reading (2:23-25) reminds us that such preparation is not to be undertaken lightly nor thought to be an easy thing. Jesus wanted only followers who knew and accepted that which was involved in following him. They had to know what accepting him meant and what it cost—what it cost Jesus and what it would cost each follower.

> JESUS WANTED ONLY FOLLOWERS WHO KNEW AND ACCEPTED THAT WHICH WAS INVOLVED IN FOLLOWING HIM.

FOURTH SUNDAY IN LENT

MARCH 30, 2003

REVISED COMMON	EPISCOPAL (BCP)	ROMAN CATHOLIC
Num. 21:4-9	2 Chron. 36:14-23	2 Chron. 36:14-16, 19-23
Ps. 107:1-3, 17-22	Psalm 122	Ps. 137:1-2, 3, 4-5, 6
Eph. 2:1-10	Eph. 2:4-10	Eph. 2:4-10
John 3:14-21	John 6:4-15	John 3:14-21

This Sunday used to be known as mid-Lent in the calendar in use before 1969, and traces of the old order remain in several places. The Sunday, sometimes called "refreshment Sunday," marked a lessening of the severity of Lenten discipline. Flowers, which were not permitted to adorn the altar during the rest of Lent, were permitted on this Sunday. In some places, rose vestments were used instead of the more somber violet. The Gospel was John 6:1-15, Jesus as the living bread of heaven and nourishment for the Lenten journey. The point was to offer encouragement to renew one's strength and commitment and to continue the discipline of the journey.

FIRST READING
NUMBERS 21:4-9 (RCL);
2 CHRONICLES 36:14-23 (BCP);
2 CHRONICLES 36:14-16, 19-23 (RC)

Interpreting the Texts

The RCL (and *LBW*) reading from Numbers 21 had been the Old Testament Lesson for the Fifth Sunday in Lent (then called Passion Sunday) in the *Lutheran Service Book and Hymnal* (1958), where it began a concentrated focus on the Passion, which characterized the last two weeks of Lent called Passiontide. In the present lectionary the lesson has been included here to explain the reference in the Gospel to the event.

The Edomites had refused to grant the Israelites passage through their land, and so the wanderers had to retrace their steps from Mount Hor southward to the Red Sea in order to detour around Edom. As the Israelites moved back into the desert, understandably they grew unhappy and began to complain about Moses and about God, who had led them out of the security of Egypt (they conveniently chose not to remember that it was the security of slavery) and into the perils of the wilderness. God's response to this ungrateful challenge to his sovereignty was to send fiery serpents whose bite proved fatal to many of the Israelites. More than merely poisonous snakes, these serpents are called "seraphim," fiery, like the rank of angels called by that name (Isa. 6:2, 6), one of whom is the agent of cleansing Isaiah from his sin. The discontented and now mourning Israelites recognize their sin and appeal to Moses to intercede for them. Instead of driving the snakes off, God commands Moses to set up a miraculous sign, a bronze snake on a pole, the sight of which would cure anyone bitten by the fiery snakes. The cycle is clear—rejection of God's goodness, punishment, repentance, healing.

The BCP and RC reading is the conclusion of 2 Chronicles. Whereas in 2 Kings the blame for the destruction of Jerusalem is laid chiefly on the wickedness of the king, the blame here is spread more widely on "the leading priests and people" (v. 14). The Levites and the musicians are noticeably excluded from blame. The description of the fall of Jerusalem is very close to the description in 2 Kings 25:1-21; 2 Chron. 36:21 is drawn from Jeremiah (25:11; 29:10; see Lev. 26:34) and is designed to demonstrate that the fall was due to the neglect of the sabbath, an important topic for the chronicler, and that the warning of the prophet was not heeded, another favorite theme. Because 2 Chronicles is the last book in the Hebrew Bible, the final two verses (22-23) are almost identical to the beginning of Ezra (which follows directly) and were added to the account of the destruction of the temple to introduce a note of hope so that the conclusion of the book would not seem too discouraging. The suffering will not have been in vain but will be a harbinger of the Lord's presence among his people once more. The threatened institutions will not be completely obliterated.

Responding to the Texts

The purpose of mid-Lent in the medieval church was to encourage the faithful to persist in their Lenten discipline. Such encouragement is helpful to pilgrims still. The people of Israel were nearly in the promised land. They did not know it yet, but their wandering was almost over. On the very verge of the promised land, they began to lose heart and to lose faith. They began to grumble against God and against Moses, even daring to declare, "We detest this miserable food" (Num. 21:5). The "miserable food" they loathed was the miraculous manna, the bread from heaven, the food of angels, yet they detested it. They wanted something more, something better than bread from heaven. Familiarity and their own selfish and blind sin made them want something else, which had to be less than what God had provided for them, bread for which they did not need to work. Punishment came swiftly and in an unpleasant way. Death-dealing snakes moved among the rebellious people, as if the Garden of Eden was being experienced again. Many people died. But there was a way out. God commanded Moses to make a bronze image of the instrument of death and lift it up above the people so that the people had to look through it toward God. The punishment was transformed into a means of life. The people looked through the image of death and beyond it found forgiveness and health.

God does not abolish pain and suffering. Both Old Testament readings make this clear. God does not send all the snakes away when the people repent and cry out for help. Rather, God provides a remedy for those who are bitten by the serpents. We would of course prefer that evil, pain, and suffering just be abolished; God could surely do that with a wave of the hand. But that is not God's way. The way that God chooses is to be involved in the life of the people, using events of ordinary secular life to work the larger plan and pattern that is being woven. Thus our life and experiences are not just being made safe and pleasant but are being transformed into something we cannot yet imagine.

> THE WAY THAT GOD CHOOSES IS TO BE INVOLVED IN THE LIFE OF THE PEOPLE, USING EVENTS OF ORDINARY SECULAR LIFE TO WORK THE LARGER PLAN AND PATTERN THAT IS BEING WOVEN.

The central institutions of ancient Israel—the city of Jerusalem, the temple, and the Davidic dynasty—seemed secure, assured of God's support. But in the traumatic events of the sixth century B.C.E., every one of these was taken away. The city fell to its captors, the temple was demolished, and the dynasty was obliterated. Even these terrifying events did not interrupt salvation history; indeed, each became part of the plan that was being worked out. God's power and will are such that even those things that seem to contradict them are in fact used to carry out what God intends. There may be detours on the way (at least from our human perspective), but the road continues and the destination is assured. No longer will God rule through chosen and anointed kings; God's rule of Israel will now be direct without earthly intermediary. A foreign king will be used to further the work of God. The new temple will not be an expression of the piety of the Davidic dynasty and an extension of royal power; it will be the product of God's own will, expressed though the decree of a Gentile king and independent of dynastic structures. Paradoxically perhaps, God works through earthly events and structures, but God also asserts independence from them and sometimes judgment upon them.

Also clear in both these readings are God's anger and mercy. This is a familiar theme throughout the Bible, but it is something we never completely comprehend. There is punishment, well deserved (and the deserving is always far easier to see in others than in ourselves), and there is blessing greater than that which was previously experienced. Luther spoke of the two hands of God: the left that administers punishment and the right that bestows blessings. The meting out of punishment is God's "alien" work; it is not what God likes to do. Giving blessing is God's "proper" work; it is what his nature impels him to do. And the alien work of punishment is not done out of a sadistic sense of enjoyment giving pain but is itself an expression of loving correction to bring erring children back into the right way and give them something even greater than they had before.

RESPONSIVE READING

PSALM 107:1-3, 17-22 (RCL);
PSALM 122 (BCP);
PSALM 137:1-2, 3, 4-5, 6 (RC)

The RCL psalm (107) is a thanksgiving for pilgrims. The opening three verses invite all whom the Lord redeemed and gathered from the ends of the earth to give thanks. The second section (vv. 17-22) can clearly be related to the first reading from Numbers 21. It is the thanksgiving of those who in their sickness had cried out to the Lord and had been healed and delivered from destruction. The song is appropriate for all people who are on pilgrimage through this world toward the heavenly Jerusalem.

The BCP psalm (122) is a pilgrim's song praising Jerusalem as the goal of the journey. Jerusalem here is not just the earthly city, although Christians are bound to pray for the peace of that Jerusalem. In the context of the liturgy and Lent, it is a vision of the goal of the journey, given to encourage faltering pilgrims and to help them persist on their way. The psalm is sung by pilgrims who have arrived in the holy city and are admiring its beauty and its unity. We are permitted to overhear their wondering praise, and we are thus shown that if they have made it safely there, so can we.

The RC psalm (137) gives memorable expression to the feeling of the Israelites in exile, "How could we sing the LORD's song in a foreign land?" (v. 4). Behind the verse is the ancient question, "If God is the God of the land of Israel, how can we sing praise languishing in exile in the territory of some other divinity, beyond the care and concern of God?" In a larger view of the unlimited extent of God's power and concern and presence, the question remains. If we are not in the place God has promised to us, how can we sing praise? It is not only the lament of the ancient Hebrews but also the lament of all exiles, indeed of all of us who are in exile in this world, longing for our arrival at our true home.

EPHESIANS 2:1-10 (RCL);
EPHESIANS 2:4-10 (BCP, RC)

Interpreting the Text

The chapter begins (vv. 1-3) with a grim picture of the human condition. It is not only sinful and in rebellion against God; it is under the control of Satan, "the ruler of the power of the air, the spirit that is now at work among those who are disobedient" (v. 2). Paul acknowledges that he and his hearers once lived among those under demonic power and were therefore "children of wrath," under condemnation by God's implacable hatred of sin. That is the common human condition, the situation in which "everyone" lived. Jew or Greek—it makes no difference, for "all have sinned and fall short of the glory of God" (Rom. 3:23). The Jews have no claim to moral superiority, and we are no better than they. The RC and BCP (and *LBW*) lectionaries omit these verses and focus on the more hopeful and encouraging section, beginning with v. 4.

Out of this weakness, subservience, and death, God in mercy and love brought a resurrection and even an ascension to "the heavenly places" (v. 6). The first demonstration of the power of God is the raising of Christ from the dead and elevating him to his throne of lordship. But intimately involved with this raising and glorification of Christ is the resurrection and glorification of those who belong to him and who have a share

> INTIMATELY INVOLVED WITH THIS RAISING AND GLORIFICATION OF CHRIST IS THE RESURRECTION AND GLORIFICATION OF THOSE WHO BELONG TO HIM AND WHO HAVE A SHARE IN HIS TRIUMPH.

in his triumph. It is not just a future hope. Already we have been raised, and already we have received a share in the divine glory. It is as though we have already been exalted into heaven. The full revelation of this glory will not be until the end of the age "in the ages to come," but the divine power is at work in us already through the grace that eradicates the effect of our sin. The opening description has prepared us for the contrasting conclusion. Our salvation is in no way our own doing. "By grace you have been saved through faith" (v. 8). It is a gift for which we have done nothing. No one, therefore, can boast that salvation has been deserved or earned. Just as everyone was on the same level when under demonic control, so when we are set free we are all on the same level, all debtors to God, none of us worthy.

Responding to the Text

The story begins in death. Ash Wednesday has reminded us that, as the introduction to this reading puts it, we had been dead "through trespasses and sins." The "trespasses" are literally slips or falls. They lead to straying from the right road and losing the way, an ever-present danger for pilgrims on their way to the holy place. The "sins" are literally missing the mark, the failure to be what we ought to be, the failure to live up to what we have been made in Holy Baptism. The result of this failure is death.

In Christianity, there is no such thing as a "self-made man." In the world, some may boast of what they have achieved; they may do so with absolute accuracy and honesty. But in the radically egalitarian religious life, we are all on the same level. Each one of us must say, "What I am, God has made me. I have done nothing." The relationship between faith and works has caused enormous trouble in the history of Christianity, but here the author of Ephesians makes it clear. God's grace comes first; we receive it in faith; and then we must live the life of good deeds. Good works are not the cause but the result of our salvation. Paul presents an interesting description of the situation. God has "prepared beforehand" what is to be our way of life, and in Christ God has created us for good works. God has laid out what he wants us to do and then has recreated us to accomplish it. So a prayer from the Gregorian sacramentary asks, "O Lord, mercifully receive the prayers of your people who call upon you, and grant that they may know and understand what things they ought to do, and also may have grace and power faithfully to accomplish them" (BCP, Proper 10).

THE GOSPEL
JOHN 3:14-21 (RCL, RC);
JOHN 6:4-15 (BCP)

Interpreting the Texts

This Gospel reading is either the conclusion of Jesus' conversation with Nicodemus (NRSV punctuation) or, as some interpreters suggest (see the punctuation in NAB), is largely commentary by the evangelist on the conversation that ended at v. 15. During Lent, baptismal candidates hear this conversation with Jesus as part of their progressive initiation into Christian faith and life. The emphasis is on the saving purpose of God, who does not want people to perish but to have life. The will of God is not to save just a few or some but the whole world. The offer of salvation is made by the coming of Christ into the world. It will become explicit on the cross where Jesus will, like Moses' bronze serpent on the pole, be the means of healing and

THE WILL OF GOD IS NOT TO SAVE JUST A FEW OR SOME BUT THE WHOLE WORLD. THE OFFER OF SALVATION IS MADE BY THE COMING OF CHRIST INTO THE WORLD.

restoration of life. The text is realistic in that it recognizes that not all want or are interested in what God offers. Those who are condemned are condemned by their own preference for hiding in darkness and their refusal to come to the light.

The reading emphasizes the priority and indeed the necessity of God's love before human love can respond. "God sent his only Son into the world so that we might live through him. In this is love, not that we loved God but that he loved us and sent his Son to be the atoning sacrifice for our sins" (1 John 4:9-10). Christians are in constant danger of forgetting the basic truth that God first loved us.

The distinctive Johannine insight regarding truth is evident here also. Truth is not something to know intellectually, something to comprehend, or even something to believe. Truth for the Johannine literature is something to do. "Those who do what is true [or who do the truth] come to the light" (John 3:21). Truth is an active way of life, the impulse to live as God intends. The image of the pilgrimage is once again helpful in emphasizing the activity that the truth (who is Christ) requires.

The BCP, by choosing John 6:4-15 as the Gospel for this Sunday, preserves a connection with the old mid-Lent "refreshment Sunday" for which the Gospel was John 6:1-15. The miracle of the feeding of the five thousand takes place near Passover, even as this Sunday reminds us that the Christian Passover, Pascha, is not far away. This is the only miracle recorded in all four Gospels. Jesus, as always, especially in the Fourth Gospel, is clearly in charge and knows what he is going to do. His question to Philip is humorous; he is putting the serious disciple on. "Where are we to buy bread?" he asks, and the practical disciple thinks of the huge cost—more than six months' wages. Andrew points out what will be the solution to the crisis, although he does not yet understand it so. There is a lad with a poor boy's lunch, five barley loaves and two fish, but Andrew in his realism acknowledges that the boy's lunch is meaningless in the present situation. The detail of the grass on which the crowd sat echoes Psalm 23, "The LORD . . . makes me lie down in green pastures." The gestures with the bread recall the celebration of the Lord's Supper: taking the bread, giving thanks, distributing the loaves. The fish in ancient Christian iconography are often connected with the bread as a symbol of the Eucharist. In many cultures, fish have been a symbol of life. The people in the crowd received "as much as they wanted" (6:11); the generosity of God's provision was overflowing. The gathering up of all that was left over is an act of reverent care and economy toward the gift of God. There are twelve baskets of leftovers, for the twelve apostles and the twelve tribes, further suggesting fullness.

The people in their excitement still do not understand. They think this is "the prophet" who is to come into the world, the prophet like Moses (Deut. 18:15). It is a bold claim, but it is not grand enough. They therefore want to seize him and make him a king, not realizing that only God can make a king and that the one before them is already a king of royal lineage from none other than David himself.

Responding to the Texts

The RCL and RC Gospel is a portion of Jesus' conversation with Nicodemus, the Pharisee who, symbolically, "came to Jesus by night" (John 3:2), moving out of darkness to Jesus who will later call himself "the light of the world" (8:12). The Lenten use of this Gospel reading suggests its connection with the progressive enlightenment of candidates for baptism. The symbol of light was more powerful in a time before electricity made artificial light so abundant that we seldom experience the deep darkness of night. Nonetheless, when the power is interrupted, we are plunged into unaccustomed darkness, and the experience can be terrifying. The energy of the ancient symbols is still there, lurking just below the surface. Despite an abundance of nocturnal life, in the natural world light suggests activity and life, and darkness suggests sleep and death. The fear of the encroachment of darkness is deeply embedded in the human psyche. In ancient Israel, sin would be likened to darkness and life lived according to the Law likened to light (Pss. 18:28; 107:10-16; Prov. 4:18-19; Isa. 59:9-10). In Christianity, light is focused in Christ, the light of the world, and who the Nicene Creed declares is "God from God, light from light, true God from true God." This light of Christ passes judgment on the darkness and ends its reign (John 3:17-21; Rom. 13:12-14; 1 Pet. 2:8-10). Being in the light therefore means being in communion with Christ risen from the dead, and those who are baptized in his name become bearers of his light and in the sacrament are commissioned to carry it to the world. An early name for the baptized is "the enlightened." They have come to know truth of Christ and have been filled with his light. The image is continued in the practice of giving the newly baptized a candle. In the present Lutheran rite the accompanying words are, "Let your light so shine before others that they may see your good works and glorify your Father in heaven" (Matt. 5:16). Luther's baptismal rite and the present Roman rite use a medieval text: "Receive this candle and preserve your baptism blameless, so that when the Lord comes to the wedding you may go to meet him to enter with the saints into the heavenly mansion and receive eternal life." The eschatological promise is the final victory of life in the kingdom of unending light.

The struggle between light and darkness is carried out in the life of every Christian. Ancient baptismal rites have an even more powerful and dramatic action than giving a candle to portray this warfare. The candidates faced the west, the place of the setting sun, and renounced Satan and all his works and all his empty promises. They would then spit in his direction. Then they would turn around to face the east, the place of the rising sun, and profess their faith by confessing the Apostles' Creed. The sacrament of Holy Baptism for which the candidates were completing their preparation was not a magic ritual but a rite that required the recipient's faith and response.

God's love for the world is the essence of Christian preaching, but this salvation must be accepted. Those who do not receive what is being offered do so because they love the darkness of ignorance and error rather than the light in which truth flourishes. It seems inexplicable that people should prefer darkness, but it probably involves the love of the familiar and the comfort of what is known as well as the refusal to come to the light so that they may continue in their evil ways. Living in the light carries with it great responsibility.

The condemnation of those who prefer the darkness cannot ultimately be blamed on God. It is the result of refusing to hear and act upon what God has done, and the refusal can transform a good thing into a curse, even as St. Paul warned the Corinthians who, in the celebration of the Eucharist, did not "discern the body" that they ate and thus ate and drank judgment against themselves (1 Cor. 11:29).

For John, truth is something that is done because it is related to the person of Jesus, who can change our behavior. When we come to know Jesus, we have encountered that which has been hidden through the centuries and now is revealed. And we find that truth within us.

The BCP Gospel invites a consideration of the Holy Communion as refreshment for our journey through the world, a source of strength and hope. The meagerness of the eucharistic meal, a small piece of bread and a sip of wine, is hardly enough to satisfy physical hunger, but as in the miracle on the mountainside, the slim rations in the hands of Jesus are more than enough to satisfy the deepest needs of humanity. The note in the Gospel that the Passover was near (John 6:4) is of more than historical interest. It speaks to hearers today and is a reminder that our Passover, Pascha, Easter, is not far off. Thus the notation is to be heard as encouragement to persist faithfully in the Lenten journey and discipline, for the goal of the pilgrimage is almost in sight. If we are growing weary, if we are losing interest, if we doubt our own ability and resources to continue the rest of the journey, we have company. We are like Andrew with his eyes only on the limited resources available. We who lose heart need with Andrew to place what we have, which seems so little and so useless, into the hands of Jesus, who can still do miraculous things and give "more than we either desire or deserve" (BCP, Proper 22, p. 234), "better things than we can desire or pray for" (BCP, p. 831).

The people in the crowd received "as much as they wanted" (6:11). A Lutheran postcommunion hymn by Johann Rist (1607–1667) that derives its thought and imagery in large measure from John 6 says to Christ, the "living bread from heaven":

My Lord, you here have led me
Within your holiest place
And there yourself have fed me
With treasures of your grace;
And you have freely given
What earth could never buy,
The bread of life from heaven,
That now I shall not die.

You gave me all I wanted, [Thou givest all I wanted]
This food can death destroy [i.e., this food can destroy death]
And you have freely granted
The cup of endless joy.
My Lord, I do not merit
The favor you have shown,
And all my soul and spirit
Bow down before your throne.
    (Catherine Winkworth's translation
    with verb forms modernized; *LBW,* 197)

At the beginning of the Gospel, John notes of Jesus that "a large crowd kept following him, because they saw the signs that he was doing for the sick" (6:2). The reading concludes with the people believing him to be a prophet and "were about to come and take him by force to make him king" (6:15). We often do not know what we need, only what we want. So the Gospel ought to teach us to pray: "Almighty God, to whom our needs are known before we ask, help us to ask only what accords with your will; and those good things which we dare not, or in our blindness cannot ask, grant us for the sake of your Son Jesus Christ our Lord" (BCP, pp. 394–95).

Those who receive the sacrament must be willing to allow themselves to be drawn into the mystery of Christ and not to make of him what we might like to have.

FIFTH SUNDAY IN LENT

APRIL 6, 2003

REVISED COMMON	EPISCOPAL (BCP)	ROMAN CATHOLIC
Jer. 31:31-34	Jer. 31:31-34	Jer. 31:31-34
Ps. 51:1-12	Psalm 51 or 51:11-16	Ps. 51:3-4, 12-13, 14-15
or Ps. 119:9-16		
Heb. 5:5-10	Heb. 5:(1-4), 5-10	Heb. 5:7-9
John 12:20-33	John 12:20-33	John 12:20-33

In the calendar in use before 1969 this was Passion Sunday, the beginning of the two-week Passiontide. The Sunday marked a turn from the disciplines and lessons of Lent toward a contemplation of the passion and death of Jesus. With the reform of the calendar in all the churches beginning in 1969, Passiontide was reduced to one week, Holy Week, but, as with the Fourth Sunday in Lent, traces of the old arrangement remain, and this Sunday has its eyes turned toward the cross and passion of Christ.

FIRST READING
JEREMIAH 31:31-34

Interpreting the Text

Jeremiah's prophecy of the new covenant is the first reading in all three lectionaries. The prophet speaks against an increasing tendency to limit and confine the understanding of the original covenant delivered on Sinai. The Law was considered, naturally, to be external, outside the individual, a standard to which one was to conform individual conduct by exercising one's own effort and will. Through the prophet, God promises a new and interior covenant, inscribed on the hearts of the people. "The days are coming" is a typical prophetic indication of an indeterminate time, often an eschatological future. Jeremiah's vision expands the understanding of the covenant. It is no longer the possession of an elite group, no longer the possession of the prophets or the scholars, because the new covenant will be inscribed on the heart. It will be accessible to everyone regardless of education or social status.

This new covenant, like the old one, is God's gift. It is not by our efforts that the new covenant is made, but by God's own doing. "Says the LORD" is repeated in every verse of the reading, indicating that the message is not the prophet's opinion but the very words of God.

There is no suggestion that the old covenant was wrong. The new covenant differs only in that it is written on the heart (cf. Ash Wednesday first reading). Moreover, the new covenant, because it is inscribed in the heart, will not have to be taught, nor will any need to urge others to obey it. The new covenant will so change the will of the Israelites that they will know God without instruction, without urging or punishment. It is a small step to say that God will live in them.

> THERE IS NO SUGGESTION THAT THE OLD COVENANT WAS WRONG. THE NEW COVENANT DIFFERS ONLY IN THAT IT IS WRITTEN ON THE HEART.

Responding to the Text

The Decalogue was recounted in the first reading on the Third Sunday in Lent. The old covenant, by codifying God's high expectation and demand, shows us our sin. It reveals our inevitable failure to live up to God's standard of perfection. The new covenant promised through Jeremiah, however, will bring with it forgiveness of sin. God says, "I will forgive their iniquity, and remember their sin no more" (31:34). We must constantly emphasize to correct erroneous popular ideas that God does not desire death for his creation but life and health. His constant will is not to condemn but to save the world and to do so by remaking it after his own heart. This refashioning of creation will so transform the human heart that people will not only desire to live in accord with the law of God but will also be able to live such God-pleasing lives.

We can without much trouble imagine a new Jerusalem, a purified and exalted version of the holy city. We can imagine a new king of Israel following the pattern of David and Solomon but in grander fashion. We can even imagine a new temple, not made with hands, "eternal in the heavens." It is, however, more difficult to imagine a new covenant. For one thing, a body of law is not something to be seen, except as recorded in books. For another, Jews could not imagine replacing or updating the definitive covenant given to Moses. But law is not something to be looked at; it is something to be experienced, to be lived. The psalmist, echoing the prophets, says, "Sacrifice and offering you do not desire, but you have given me an open ear. Burnt offering and sin offering you have not required. Then I said, 'Here I am; in the scroll of the book it is written of me. I delight to do your will, O my God; your law is within my heart'" (Ps. 40:6-8). In Christian devotion this portion of the psalm is used during Holy Week to give voice to the willing obedience of Jesus on the way to Golgotha. The New Testament takes up this idea of the new covenant and is itself sometimes known by that name—a new covenant that does not replace or abrogate the former covenant but clarifies it. The new covenant will not just restrain sin and sinful impulses. It will be a pattern that all will follow without constraint, gladly and willingly living as God in his goodness intended.

Most of all the new covenant comes to a clear focus in the Lord's Supper. Jesus says of the cup, "This is my blood of the new covenant," and "new covenant" has become one of the many titles for the central sacrament of Christianity. The wonderful prayer written in the thirteenth century by Thomas Aquinas for the new feast of Corpus Christi has been taken up by Anglicans and Lutherans as well as Roman Catholics. "O God, in a wonderful sacrament you have left us a memorial of your suffering and death: Grant that we may have such reverence for these holy mysteries, that the fruits of your redemption may continually be manifest in us." The prayer makes the connection between the reception of the sacrament and the way communicants live their lives. The presence of Christ, who by the sacrament now lives in them, will transform the behavior of those who have shared in the Holy Supper. The focus of the meal is the physical action of eating and drinking, but the result of such activity is or ought to be evident in the way those who eat the meal live. Then the words of the prophet will be fulfilled, and the new covenant will indeed be written on their hearts.

RESPONSIVE READING
PSALM 51:1-12 OR PSALM 119:9-16 (RCL); PSALM 51 OR 51:11-16 (BCP); PSALM 51:3-4, 12-13, 14-15 (RC)

For comment on Psalm 51 see Ash Wednesday, for which the psalm is also appointed. This psalm, the church's great song of penitence, expresses a deep sense of sin that opens the door to the mercy that God is eager to extend. As sin is a turning away from God, so we must turn back to the Holy One whom we have abandoned. This penitential psalm, therefore, asks for a restoration of moral health, a thorough transformation, and so is a complement to the First Lesson. "You desire truth in the inward being; therefore teach me wisdom in my secret heart. . . . Create in me a clean heart, O God, and put a new and right spirit within me" (vv. 6, 10). It is also echoed in Eph. 4:23-24, "Be renewed in the spirit of your minds, and . . . clothe yourselves with the new self, created according to the likeness of God in true righteousness and holiness." Such is goal of the discipline of Lent.

Psalm 119:9-16, the second section of the alphabetical acrostic poem, is the RCL alternative responsorial psalm. The emphasis falls on the effort of the psalmist to keep the law of God. "I treasure your word in my heart" (v. 11);

"I delight in the way of your decrees" (v. 14); "I will meditate on your precepts. . . . I will delight in your statutes" (vv. 15-16). It is markedly different from the emphasis of the first reading, which makes the writing of the law in the heart entirely God's doing. The psalm may be understood as an expression of the result of the law that God inscribes in the heart: the joy of doing God's will.

SECOND READING
HEBREWS 5:5-10 (RCL);
HEBREWS 5:(1-4), 5-10 (BCP);
HEBREWS 5:7-9 (RC)

Interpreting the Text

This reading presents the heart of the teaching of the book of Hebrews: Jesus Christ is the high priest after "the order of Melchizedek." There are three qualifications for being a priest. First, the priest is a link between God and humanity. Second, the priest must be one with humanity. Third, the priest is not self-appointed nor appointed by human beings but is appointed by God. Christ fulfills all three qualifications.

First, Jesus Christ is the link between God and humanity. He has come to represent God to the world and to lift the world to God by opening the way back home. He does that by offering sacrifice, but the sacrifice he offers is his obedience, his very self. This high priest is both priest and victim, "himself the victim and himself the priest" as a seventh-century Latin hymn declares inviting communicants to "Draw nigh and take the body of the Lord" (*Hymnal 1982*, 327, 328; *LBW,* 226). This high priest has fulfilled the prophetic ideal by combining in his perfect life both sacrifice and obedience.

Second, Christ is one with humanity, not only because he was born of a human mother, but because he was completely involved in the human situation by living our life as we should have lived it by obedience and prayer, and further, being tested by suffering. He knows our flesh in both its strength and its weakness and is therefore able to sympathize with those whom he represents. The emphasis in this passage is on the humanity of Christ. A priest must be human in order to represent humans before God, and he must share in their sufferings since he must feel compassion for them (Heb. 2:17-18; 4:15). Jesus suffered in this way throughout his life on earth but especially in his passion and death, which on this Fifth Sunday in Lent loom on the horizon. He is thus the perfect example of the new heart and spirit demanded of God's people; he is truly one who has the law written on his heart. He did not need to make an offering for himself (4:15; 7:26), yet he did make a perfect offering, complete and willing obedience to the Father (5:7ff.; Pss. 2:7; 110:4).

Third, Christ is a priest, not as a member of the Levitical priesthood, but by his direct divine appointment from before the foundation of the world, which was confirmed at his baptism in the Jordan. His priesthood is distinctive, for it is "according to the order of Melchizedek," that shadowy and mysterious figure who comes out of nowhere to receive Abraham's offering and then returns to the unknown place from which he came. So Christ, in the way of the argument of Hebrews, is without beginning and without end. He is one of us, and yet at the same time he is from outside this world. The priesthood of Christ is eternal and is associated with his entrance into heavenly glory.

Responding to the Text

The idea of priesthood is difficult. It is a word and an idea that carry a great deal of baggage in theological controversy and denominational self-

> JESUS IS THUS THE PERFECT EXAMPLE OF THE NEW HEART AND SPIRIT DEMANDED OF GOD'S PEOPLE; HE IS TRULY ONE WHO HAS THE LAW WRITTEN ON HIS HEART.

identification. Moreover, the word *priest* calls forth deep archetypal associations and therefore is not easily dismissed. For those denominations with an ordained priesthood, the challenge is to see that in relation to the unique priesthood of Jesus Christ. For those denominations that reject priesthood and sacrifice or boast of "the priesthood of all believers," the challenge is to see the enormous responsibility and high demand of such a calling. It requires perfect obedience, the sacrifice of one's life for the sake of God, constant and unwearied prayer for all the church and for all the world. And all this is to be done in the spirit of Christ, willingly and gladly out of gratitude for the example he has given us.

The work of a priest is the offering of sacrifice, and that is something in which all God's people share. We are called upon to sacrifice ourselves and our time, possessions, hopes, dreams, ambitions, fears, regrets, guilt—all we are and have and do—through the great high priest, Jesus Christ. Jesus Christ, crucified, risen, and ascended, is our great high priest who stands eternally in the heavenly sanctuary ceaselessly interceding for us with God. So when Christians gather on Sunday as the assembly of the baptized, their weekly offerings become Jesus' once and for all offering of himself. Their weekly prayers become part of Jesus' own prayer of intercession. The privilege of being a baptized priest means that Christians who gather to worship on the Lord's Day bring their whole week, their whole life, to the altar on Sunday morning and see it transformed into the risen body of the perfect Son of God.

Such service must be learned. The writer to the Hebrews subtly alludes to the agonizing experience of Jesus in the Garden of Gethsemane as he struggled to embrace the Father's will (Matt. 26:39, 42) with "loud cries and tears" (Heb. 5:7). And after the garden there was the desolate and even terrifying cry from the cross, "Why have you forsaken me?" (Mark 15:34). Jesus' anguished prayer was heard, the author assures us, but the hearing did not prevent suffering and even death.

He was not saved from dying, for that was the whole purpose of his life, as the Gospel for this Sunday makes clear. But his death was not his end; God's hearing of the prayer meant the transformation of suffering into triumph and transitory agony into eternal joy.

THE GOSPEL
JOHN 12:20-33

Interpreting the Text

Now we come to the great mystery of the necessity of death before life. Jesus has entered Jerusalem for the last week of his life. Just as John provided a day-by-day account of the first week of Jesus' ministry (1:29, 35, 39; 2:1), so he does the same for Jesus' last days. And just as Philip and Andrew were prominent in the first week, so they are prominent in these last days. Some Greek proselytes wanted to "see" (in John, a word that usually carries the connotation of believing) Jesus, and so they came to the apostle with a Greek name, Philip, who went to the other apostle with a Greek name, Andrew. Both were from Bethsaida, a city with a diverse population. Greeks represented a large group within the Gentile world of the time who were attracted to the Jewish faith, and although not admitted to full acceptance within the Jewish community, they were nonetheless granted certain privileges of instruction and worship (Acts 10:1-2; 13:16). They were called "God-fearers," converts to the monotheism of Israel who adopted certain specific Mosaic observances.

It was the coming to Jesus (not just to the temple) of these believing Gentiles that caused Jesus to declare that the "hour" had come for him to be glorified. The coming of the Gentiles was a sign of the fulfillment of his mission to all the world. In the Johannine account, Jesus is untroubled by his impending death and goes forward with serene confidence. His being lifted up, his elevation on the cross, is emblematic of his elevation in glory. Indeed, for John the crucifixion is the glorification. All time is concentrated in these great and world-changing events, and so John refers not to the broad "time" of glory but more precisely to the "hour" of Christ. Jesus has come to unite the world, bringing Jews and Gentiles together and uniting all his followers with him in his death and resurrection.

An extraordinary tension is felt in 12:27. The experience is comparable to the experience of Gethsemane in the Synoptics: anguish as the "hour" draws near, the appeal to the Father, acceptance of death, comfort from heaven (Luke 22:43). But there are differences in the way John tells the story. Jesus' prayer for pity is unuttered, nor does he fall to the ground (as in Matthew and Mark) or kneel (as in Luke). In John's portrayal, Jesus is ever the victorious conqueror.

"Father, save me from this hour" (12:27) may be a definite prayer, or it may be, as in the NRSV, a wondering question. However it is interpreted, it was immediately superseded by the great cry, "Father, glorify your name" (v. 28). The glory of the Father's name transcended all other considerations. A voice from heaven declared God's acceptance of the offering of the Son, although the onlookers did not then understand its significance (v. 29).

The "judgment" of the world is literally its "crisis." All human life insofar as it is organized apart from God is under the control of "the ruler of this world," whose defeat must lead his former subjects to reconsider their allegiance. In this crisis they must choose to go down to destruction with the fallen ruler of this world or to gain eternal life through faith in the crucified Savior of the world. When he is "lifted up from the earth," both in the crucifixion and also in the resurrection and ascension, he will with his royal power draw people of every nation to himself. This is the complex answer to the Greeks' desire to "see" Jesus.

> WHEN HE IS "LIFTED UP FROM THE EARTH," BOTH IN THE CRUCIFIXION AND ALSO IN THE RESURRECTION AND ASCENSION, HE WILL WITH HIS ROYAL POWER DRAW PEOPLE OF EVERY NATION TO HIMSELF.

Responding to the Text

This Gospel is an explication of the complaint that the Pharisees have just uttered, "The world has gone after him!" (12:19). They unwittingly testified to the universal appeal and the ultimate spread of Christianity.

The Greeks were well known in the ancient world as inveterate travelers in search of new things and seekers after truth. Homer's hero Odysseus is such a restless inquirer who wanted to meet new people, to see their cities, and to know their minds. It is therefore not surprising that the Greeks in this Gospel came to Jesus to see and understand what he was about. Indeed, they represent the human condition, as Augustine knew. "You have made us for yourself, and our hearts are restless until they find rest in you," he prayed at the beginning of his autobiographical *Confessions.* These Greek searchers also remind us that we do not need to leave our minds behind when we come to faith, and that those with endless questions are at least as welcome in the church as those whose minds are closed and who refuse to think for fear they might lose their faith. We are reminded that at the end of John's story of Jesus, "doubting Thomas," with his hard-headed realism, refused to be taken in by what he wished to be and wanted physical proof of what the others had told him of their encounter with the risen Jesus. The Fourth Gospel was written to present the truth of Christianity in a way that restless, questioning, and even doubting people could understand and identify with.

"The hour has come," Jesus declared (12:23). In that little phrase we may hear the trumpet of eternity sounding, the rumbling of the advancing army of God thundering toward victory, leaving the corpses of the enemies of God in the dust. But in this glorification of which Jesus speaks, it is not seen in the corpses of the enemy but in his own body dying on the tree of the cross. He turns our ideas upside down. Sacrifice is the salvation of life, selfishness its stultification.

The profound mystery of which Jesus speaks upsets our usual assumptions. We think of life as preceding death; it seems obvious. But Jesus looks at the natural world and says that it is in fact the other way around: Death comes before life, as the seed is buried in order to grow. The source of our life is Jesus' death. And because that sacrificial death has given life to his people, those who follow in his train, the martyrs, who like him die in order to gain life, have enriched the church. As the old saying has it, "The blood of the martyrs is [or waters] the seed of the church." Because they died, the church lives.

Not many of us are called to a dramatic giving of our life for Christ. For most it is a quieter service to which we are called. Bishop Reginald Heber's hymn describes how "The Son of God goes forth to war," his blood-red banner streaming afar; then it asks those who sing the hymn, "Who best can drink his cup of woe triumphant over pain?" And the answer is not those who fight in a brave and public and widely watched way, but rather those who patiently and largely unnoticed bear their cross here on this earth. Then comes the challenge: "Who follows in their train?" Those unknown people who have patiently and quietly made their difficult way through life are like the seed that is buried in the soil and then left forgotten—until the time comes when the growth that has been working its hidden way all along is made known and flourishes for all to see.

A few Greeks came to Jesus to "see" him, and Jesus saw in their request the sign for which he had been waiting: The "hour" had come. A few Greeks came to him, but Jesus saw beyond them to a vast company of Gentiles down the centuries. Those who have never seen Jesus with their own eyes must come to know him through those who transmit the living witness (1 John 1:3-4). In the midst of those inquirers and believers long after Jesus' earthy life, we find ourselves following these forerunners of ours into the church and finding there our life.

The road this Sunday leads downhill into the valley of the shadow of death. We who would be Jesus' companions must follow him on his journey to death and beyond. In the valley and in the sunlight that will finally dispel its shadows, we will learn again that the cross is not only the sign of salvation but also the sign of the Christian way of life. This sign calls us to turn from what is ultimately the loneliness and futility of selfishness and self-centered living to a life lived for others, a life characterized by the evangelical counsels with which Lent began—almsgiving, fasting, and prayer.

HOLY WEEK

MARTIN F. CONNELL

Introduction
The Bible and the Liturgy in Holy Week

Aside from the proclamation of a Last Supper narrative—from Paul's first letter to the Corinthians or from one of the Synoptic Gospels—during a celebration of the Lord's Supper, there is not usually a direct correspondence
between the actions of Jesus in the Gospel and the actions of a congregation during its celebration and fellowship. In most celebrations when the Gospel readings
narrate something Jesus or someone else did, the congregation or the presiding
minister is not ordinarily behaving as if in first-century Palestine. (There probably have not been too many occasions during Sunday worship, for example, when
the congregation has witnessed or occasioned an annunciation from an angel, a
virgin birth, a calming of a sea, a multiplication of loaves and fishes, a healing of
a leper, or a cessation of bleeding in a hemorrhaging woman.) The miracles and
healings in our assemblies are usually effected when readings such as these are
applied to our local circumstances and when the strength and support of the risen
Christ in our local assembly enable us, by God's grace, to do more than, without
them, we could have asked for or imagined.

In a unique way, this is not exactly true of the liturgies of Holy Week; for this
reason, among others, this is quite a remarkable span of the liturgical year. On
Passion Sunday, for example, we might take up palm branches and, in so doing,
be reminded in our bodies of what took place in Jerusalem as Jesus arrived there
just before the end of his life. On Holy Thursday, we hear of the foot-washing
story from John's Gospel, and we might then wash feet or have our feet washed,
an action connecting us by our bodies with what Jesus himself and his disciples
did with their bodies many years ago. On Good Friday we hear the Passion
account from the Gospel of John, and we might, depending on the worship traditions of the local congregation, find ourselves venerating the wood of a cross
as a sensory connection between the experience of Jesus' followers during his

own incarnate life and death, and as a way of linking ourselves ritually with the behaviors of Christians who have done this for centuries, indeed, now in the year 2003, for almost two millennia. At the Easter Vigil we hear the proclamation of the resurrection, this year from the Gospel of Mark, and the resurrection is intimately connected to the life of the baptized (as we'll see below), and so we have a liturgical action that bears a ritual bodily connection between the life of Christ and the life of the church.

For this and many other reasons, Holy Week is a unique span in the annual life of the church. During it the church and all of its members are brought to new birth as we are reminded of the events in the life of Jesus that wrought salvation for the whole world, but we are also reminded, liturgically, of our own baptism—however long or short a time ago that was celebrated—into the body of Christ, into God's embrace, and in the power of the Holy Spirit.

The rituals listed above—carrying palm branches, washing feet, venerating the cross, initiating at the Easter Vigil—take a great deal of pastoral and catechetical preparation. If, therefore, a local church is moved to start such ritual actions for the first time, much forethought, planning, and catechesis need to happen before the change is brought to the assembly. Introducing these ritual elements without preparation and education is worse than not doing them at all. Below are some of the theological, liturgical, and pastoral matters that might be considered as these rites are executed. The ritual elements of the readings will be highlighted, especially when they give us some help in interpreting the liturgical elements of the unique rites of Holy Week. This will provide some material and direction for pastoral leaders who would be preparing their congregations for the new elements in the future.

The Theology of Time in Holy Week

The Gospel readings that are proclaimed and preached on in the course of our usual Sunday gatherings for worship are not readily recognized as taking place at a certain time in the relatively brief life span of Jesus of Nazareth. When, for example, we hear the narrative of a healing, like his healing of a blind person; or of his telling of a parable, such as that of the prodigal son; or of his performing a nature miracle, like the multiplication of loaves and fishes; or of his teaching, like the beatitudes or the Our Father, we aren't inclined to consider the place of the reading in the overall course of the life of Jesus. The readings are put before the assembly as a narrative out of the sequence in which the evangelist put it in the Gospel.

Yet the Gospel readings that we hear each year during Holy Week are different from these, for as we listen to them we know that they are drawn from the remembrance of Jesus' last days. More or less, we recognize the chronology of events from his entrance into Jerusalem, as recounted on Passion Sunday, to his death on the cross on Good Friday, the discovery of the empty tomb and the proclamation of the resurrection on Easter Sunday morning.

The Balance of the Gospels of Mark and John in Holy Week 2003

Our three-year lectionary cycle covers the first three Gospels, the Synoptic Gospels (so called because their views and narratives of the life of Jesus are similar), the Gospel of Matthew for Year A, Mark for Year B (the year we are in currently), and Luke for Year C. One might wonder, then, about how the liturgy incorporates the Gospel of John. The Fourth Gospel has a narrative and theology of Jesus' life that are uniquely suited for particular times of the liturgical year because of its high theology, its portrayal of the relationship of God the Father and the Son. So although this Gospel does not have a year dedicated to its proclamation, it is proclaimed often in Lent, as the catechumens are prepared for initiation, and during the Fifty Days of the Easter season.

The Gospel of John is also unique because John's Jesus does a lot of talking. (If you happen to have a red-letter edition of the Bible, take a peak at chapters 14–17 of the Gospel, and you'll readily see just how chatty Jesus is in the Gospel of John!) Holy Week is one of the times of the year when the theology of the Gospel of John is fitting and even needed.

The Gospel enables the community of faith to consider Jesus' experience and feelings of abandonment in the balance with the exaltation of Jesus as one with the Father in all things: "The Father and I are one." The Gospel of John uniquely juxtaposes the abasement and glory of Jesus' final week. As Jesus is about to be taken into custody leading to the crucifixion, for example, the listener is aware of what is to come, yet we find that the soldiers who come to arrest Jesus fall down to the ground in a display of awe before they set about arresting him (18:4-6). Even his enemies fall down before him.

The theology of the Gospel of John has a privileged place in Holy Week; those who attend the liturgies throughout the week will hear the Fourth Gospel on Monday (12:1-11), Tuesday (12:20-36), Wednesday (13:21-32), Thursday (13:1-17, 31b-35), and Friday (18:1—19:42). These five days will be embraced by "bookend" readings from the Gospel of Mark, at the beginning of the week (the Passion account of Mark on Passion Sunday) and at the Easter Vigil, which is also the launching of the Easter season (the account of the empty tomb from the Gospel of Mark [16:1-8]). Throughout the week between Passion Sunday and the Easter Vigil, however, the theology of the Gospel of John reminds the church time and again that suffering is not the only aspect of the Passion story; the Gospel of John maintains the suffering and the glory as two sides of the same Christological coin. In John the victory of the resurrection complements the passion of the cross, for they are inseparable. This Gospel is at the heart of the Word on Monday, Tuesday, Wednesday,

THROUGHOUT THE WEEK BETWEEN PASSION SUNDAY AND THE EASTER VIGIL, THE THEOLOGY OF THE GOSPEL OF JOHN REMINDS THE CHURCH TIME AND AGAIN THAT SUFFERING IS NOT THE ONLY ASPECT OF THE PASSION STORY.

Thursday, and Friday of Holy Week (as it is prominent in the Fifty Days of the Easter season as well).

The victory and glory of the Gospel of John do not displace the passion, however; the two stand together in the theology of Holy Week as they do in the lives of human beings, of families, of communities of faith, and of the world. God is ever near to the dying and the dead, in the life of Jesus and from age to age until our time. In Holy Week this is boldly celebrated in our worship. It makes us face the inevitability of death for all persons, practicing and nonpracticing Christians, baptized and nonbaptized persons.

Past, Present, and Future in the Life of Jesus and the Life of the Church

In the history of Christian worship, there have been periods when one of the three aspects of time in human life—the past as remembered, the present as experienced, and the future as anticipated—has been emphasized over the other two. Some variation of emphasis is natural from time to time, of course, but over the life of a community of faith, a balance of the three is necessary. Holy Week is the period of the liturgical year when "the rubber meets the road" with regard to the Christian experience of time, for communities of faith sometimes expect that the holiest moments are the moments of the most earnest *remembering* of the historical life of Jesus of Nazareth. The prayers of the liturgy and the theology of the proclamation of the Passion according to the Gospels of Mark (on Passion Sunday) and John (on Good Friday) stand as correctives to this inclination to remember only.

Two millennia of Christian life have repeatedly highlighted that our faith would be in vain if its purpose were merely to remember what Jesus did and who Jesus was. Though these past deeds are the keystones of our salvation and of the narrative of our salvation in the gospel (and therefore supremely important as the foundation of Christian faith), mere remembrance—without efficacy for life today or hope for the future—is fruitless. We remember the life of Jesus so that we can be united in the church as the risen body of Christ bearing the good news and the sacraments to the world. And from there we move to renew and transform the face of the earth day by day, Sunday after Sunday, year after year, millennium after millennium.

WE REMEMBER THE LIFE OF JESUS SO THAT WE CAN BE UNITED IN THE CHURCH AS THE RISEN BODY OF CHRIST BEARING THE GOOD NEWS AND THE SACRAMENTS TO THE WORLD.

Of the countless Christian churches in the United States, some communities gravitate naturally toward an interest in the "historical Jesus," toward the *past.* Others, especially those churches engaged in works of charity and social justice, find the presence of Christ most vibrant in the world today, in the *present.* Still others look most expectantly for the final consolation of the life of faith, individually and communally, on the "last day," at the end of the world, in the *future.*

Perhaps we can find hope that in the wide spectrum of Christian traditions and churches all three are part of church life. But each community can itself consider the balance of the past, present, and future in its life and plan its liturgical and pastoral order to keep each of these as living aspects of the life of believers.

Ecumenism and Holy Week

In the past few decades there has generally been a movement toward consensus between Protestants and Roman Catholics in the ways of celebrating the Lord's Supper and other liturgical rites. The lines of distinction between churches and denominations have not been as thick and divisive on liturgical matters as they were not so long ago. Protestants and Catholics who celebrate in one another's churches still often notice differences, but these are not nearly as marked today as they were a half-century ago. We see, then, that some of the goals and experiences of ecumenism have been achieved and are efficacious. Catholic worship in the past thirty years has adopted some of the liturgical changes introduced by Protestant reformers in the sixteenth and seventeenth centuries, yet there has also been movement toward Catholic traditions of worship by many Protestant assemblies.

The Influence of Protestant Worship on Roman Catholics

It took a few centuries for the Roman Catholic churches to begin to follow some of the liturgical reforms the Protestant churches undertook as they reformed worship in the sixteenth century. By the consensus of historians, the Reformation was started officially when Martin Luther nailed his "Ninety-five Theses" on the cathedral door in Wittenberg in 1517 (though the Roman Catholic Church did not cut him off until 1520). But in the last three or four decades of the twentieth century, Catholics made up for centuries of lost time, and its churches have benefited from the reform of the liturgy at Protestant initiative. What Protestant liturgical notions did Catholic churches adopt?

Clearly, the main liturgical contribution of the Reformation churches to the Roman Catholic tradition was putting scripture in a place of primacy in Sunday worship and in all rites. This was done by Catholic parishes in a number of ways. First, and perhaps the most obvious way, was the translation of the Bible into the vernacular for use in worship. (Some Catholics even in our own day wish that the liturgy and the proclamation of the scriptures had remained in the Latin of the Roman tradition for over a millennium.) This gift of the Reformation to Christianity in rendering the Bible and the texts of worship in accessible languages is taken for granted now, but it was a monumental development in liturgical practice when Luther introduced the German vernacular after centuries during which the faithful did not understand what was being said during the liturgy.

Second, Protestant liturgical practice influenced Catholic worship in opening up a wider selection of scripture readings for proclamation at worship. Most impoverished in Catholic worship before Vatican II was the use of the Old Testament, for very few verses of the entire Hebrew Bible were used in Catholic worship during the four centuries between the Council of Trent (1545–1563) and Vatican II (1962–1965).

Third, formerly Catholic clergy were not well prepared for or trained for preaching on the scriptures to their assemblies. The strong witness of preaching from Protestant pastors moved the Roman Catholic Church to begin to develop its own theology of ministry that now includes an emphasis on preaching and seminary training to help future ministers learn the art of proclaiming and preaching the Word of God.

There are surely other ways in which the Protestant liturgical traditions contributed to the Catholic reform of worship after Vatican II, but these ways in which the Word of God was highlighted in Catholic worship are surely the most fruitful mainstay of Protestant influence.

Liturgical Influence of Roman Catholic Worship Traditions on Protestants

The influence of liturgical traditions was not in one direction only, for the reform of the liturgy by Roman Catholics in the late twentieth and early twenty-first centuries has also influenced Protestant worship in recognizable ways. Related to the Word of God just mentioned, while the Protestant traditions influenced the Roman Catholic use of the vernacular in the proclamation of the scriptures, the Roman Catholic Church undertook a revision of the lectionary and came up with the basic plan of the three-year lectionary cycle that is used now by many Protestant communities in the Revised Common Lectionary. Though this has been so for some time now, there are many faithful churchgoers, Protestant and Catholic, who do not know that week after week they hear the same readings as their neighbors of other traditions.

The issue of the mutual influence of the Protestant and Catholic liturgical traditions is introduced here at the beginning of Holy Week because during this one-week span many Protestant pastors and believers get nervous about the traditions of Holy Week that at first sight seem uncomfortably too "Catholic." Among these liturgical traditions one might count carrying palm branches in procession on Passion Sunday; washing feet on the evening of Holy Thursday; and— perhaps most disorienting of all for traditional Protestants—venerating the wood of the cross on Good Friday. In local churches where these practices have not been part of the tradition, grave consideration and preparatory catechesis need to anticipate how the suggestion of using palm branches and foot-washing and cross-venerating might seem foreign to many who have contentedly celebrated the liturgies of Holy Week in their churches and denominations for most of their lives without these ritual ingredients. Such changes are consequential and need to be approached with pastoral care by the leadership and by all church members involved in the planning and execution of the liturgy.

For some churches this exchange of gifts and traditions over denominational and church boundaries has been anticipated and welcomed. For others it is uncomfortable and a little nerve-racking, depending perhaps on the proximity or distance of the two traditions from one another. But whatever the assembly's feelings about the swapping of liturgical developments and traditions, Holy Week is a time when this mutual influence is quite evident and the church membership should be catechized to understand why these changes build the body of Christ even when they are novel.

In the commentary on Holy Week below, therefore, the biblical matters are taken up as they have been for the other times of the year, but particular attention has been given to the light that the scripture readings shed on the liturgical traditions in each service, and of these even more attention to the liturgical recommendations for traditions and behaviors that happen only at this time of the year. We will consider the readings of the day with an emphasis on the ritual gestures that might accompany the proclamation of the Word, in which Jesus himself used such objects or performed such gestures in the accounts of the Gospels.

> WE WILL CONSIDER THE READINGS OF THE DAY WITH AN EMPHASIS ON THE RITUAL GESTURES THAT MIGHT ACCOMPANY THE PROCLAMATION OF THE WORD.

Because of this, the liturgies of Passion Sunday, Holy Thursday, Good Friday, and the Easter Vigil get longer commentary than the liturgies of Monday, Tuesday, and Wednesday of Holy Week for two reasons. First, most churches do not assemble as a community on those first three days; many people are at work; most businesses, schools, and stores are all in full swing. Second, later in the week the readings have often been chosen as the ones proclaimed at the liturgy because of the liturgical actions of that liturgy. Many might think that the actions of the liturgy gravitated to the readings proclaimed, but liturgical studies reveal that the actions were likely in the tradition and that the Gospel narratives were affixed to the ritual element either at the same time or later. For this reason, then, the commentary will consider the interaction of both the biblical and the ritual traditions.

Holy Week is a supremely wonderful opportunity to consider and experience the link between the actions of Jesus as proclaimed in the Word and the actions of our church as proclaimed by the liturgy. The traditions of Holy Week, if carefully planned and if the preaching highlights the unique elements for the benefit of the faithful, strike a deep note in Christian life because they engage the whole of the human person—bodies, emotions, minds, society, and soul—and because they build up the body of Christ at this key time of the church's rebirth and renewal.

SUNDAY OF THE PASSION / PALM SUNDAY

April 13, 2003

Revised Common	Episcopal (BCP)	Roman Catholic
Mark 11:1-11	Mark 11:1-11a	Mark 11:1-10
or John 12:12-16		or John 12:12-16, (37)
Ps. 118:1-2, 19-29	Ps. 118:19-29	
Isa. 50:4-9a	Isa. 45:21-25	Isa. 50:4-7
	or Isa. 52:13—53:12	
Ps. 31:9-16	Ps. 22:1-21 or 22:1-11	Ps. 22:8-9, 17-18,
		19-20, 23-24
Phil. 2:5-11	Phil. 2:5-11	Phil. 2:6-11
Mark 14:1—15:47 or	Mark (14:32-72),	Mark 14:1—15:47
15:1-39, (40-47)	or 15:1-39	15:1-39, (40-47)

Introduction to the Liturgy

Because of the length of the narrative of Jesus' way to the cross in the Gospel of Mark, some Markan scholars came to regard it basically as a "Passion narrative with a long introduction." Far more than in the Gospels of Matthew, Luke, and John, the Passion narrative takes up a relatively large chunk of the Gospel of Mark, and from this comes the somewhat exaggerated, but also apt, scholarly descriptive tag. Some of this can be attributed to the brevity of the Gospel itself, for there are sixteen chapters in Mark, compared to the twenty-eight chapters of Matthew, twenty-four of Luke, and twenty-one of John. Because, on this Passion Sunday of Year B, the assembly will hear two readings from the Gospel of Mark—that of the procession of Jesus into Jerusalem on the donkey (in chap. 11) and the Passion account (chaps. 14 and 15)—this single liturgical day has nearly one-fifth of the Gospel proclaimed in the liturgy, more of a single Gospel in the liturgy than on any other day in the three-year lectionary cycle.

While this is a large chunk of the Gospel of Mark, the description of the Second Gospel as a "Passion narrative with a long introduction" is more than one of quantity; it also captures the character of the Gospel, for the inevitability of Jesus' suffering and death looms heavily throughout this life of Jesus. It is a biblical text filled with the suffering in those whom Jesus encounters as well as with Jesus regularly predicting his own suffering and death and

THE GOSPEL OF MARK IS DESCRIBED AS A "PASSION NARRATIVE WITH A LONG INTRODUCTION."

with him telling his followers that they themselves will encounter suffering and enmity if they choose to follow the Christian way.

From the distance of nearly two millennia, we cannot know what the community of the Gospel of Mark was like in detail, nor can we accurately assess what kinds of suffering that early assembly of faith endured as individuals or as a community. Nor can we know fully how the sufferings of that community were captured in the community's unique narrative of Jesus and his mission. But we can be both appreciative and consoled that the life of faith in the years after Jesus' death (the Gospel of Mark was written about forty years after his death) was not one of joy without suffering. Much like ourselves today—Christians in whose lives is a balance of joy and suffering—those Christians of the first-century community from which the Gospel of Mark emerged had a mixture of joy and suffering in their lives, and they had a Savior who also had this mix in his days.

Apprehension and hesitation at this realization might come to us from this truth, because, though faith brings hope and hope brings new vision and life, for each of us, as for Jesus, suffering and death are likely to be the inevitable accompaniments of the end of human life. Though it would be wonderful if baptism exempted us from suffering and death, the example of Jesus and of Christians from his death to today, sinners and saints alike, forces us to recognize and admit that death is inevitable.

The consolation, however, that comes from that realization is that we have the promise and proclamation of the resurrection, and our lives in the community of faith in each of our churches assures us that death is not the final word. The triumph of new life and the union we share with God today and at the hour of our death, by the power of the Holy Spirit, weighs in the balance with the suffering that is at the center of the sobering narrative of the Gospel of Mark.

As the Introduction to Holy Week tried to make clear (pages 197–203), there can be a pastoral tendency to consider the most well-executed and well-celebrated liturgies of Holy Week to be those in which the last events in the life of Jesus are reenacted. Such a tendency can reign on this day, Passion Sunday, if the pastoral team is inclined to have not a proclamation of the Passion, but a Passion drama, a virtual recreation of the way of the cross and of the crucifixion. (The introduction addresses why, on the theological reasons, this is not usually a good inclination.)

Jesus of Nazareth suffered unimaginably in his human life—the one suffering in which salvation was wrought—and this was so in his last days especially. But the biblical traditions of the New Testament reveal that the suffering of Jesus is carried on in the suffering of the body of Christ, the church. This link between the passion of Jesus and the suffering of the church is reflected too in the prayers for today, as in this collect in the Episcopal *Book of Common Prayer:* "Mercifully grant that we may walk in the way of his suffering, and also share in his resurrection."

Too much concentration on the Passion as a mere remembrance of history ignores the reality of human life, even a human life baptized into the church, fraught as much with sadness and sickness, with misery and melancholy, as with the joy and exaltation of the resurrection. But, fortunately, our prayer tradition does not let the church off the hook with mere remembrance; notice, for example, the movement from past to present (and a tiny bit of the future) here in the prayer for today in the *Lutheran Book of Worship (LBW)*:

> Almighty God,
> you sent your Son, our Savior Jesus Christ,
> to take our flesh upon him and to suffer death on the cross.
> Grant that we may share in the obedience to your will
> and in the glorious victory of his resurrection;
> through your Son, Jesus Christ our Lord,
> who lives and reigns with you and the Holy Spirit,
> one God, now and forever.

This attentiveness to past, present, and future is important on Passion Sunday and on Good Friday in particular but generally for the liturgy at all times and in all places.

Procession with Palms

Many Christians ask, "Why the palms?" Their value is a means to an end, a sign by which we are united in faith with God's church of all times and places who have done the same. The collect of the *Book of Common Worship* of the Presbyterian Church (U.S.A.) captures a theological foundation and warrant for the material gesture of bearing the palms:

> We praise you, O God,
> for your redemption of the world through Jesus Christ.
> Today he entered the holy city of Jerusalem in triumph
> and was proclaimed Messiah and king
> by those who spread garments and branches along his way.
> Let these branches be signs of victory,
> and grant that we who carry them
> may follow him in the way of the cross,
> that, dying and rising with him, we may enter into your kingdom.

The procession with palms should be celebrated, if possible, in fullness, because it is one of the parts of the annual liturgical tradition that is availed only once a year, and because it is one of the few occasions when the assembly is encouraged to move from one place to another as a sign of the movement in Christian life from this world to God's reign. (A brief explanation of the traditions of Passion Sunday can be found in Philip H. Pfatteicher, *Commentary on the Lutheran Book of Worship: Lutheran Liturgy in Its Ecumenical Context* [Minneapolis: Augsburg Fortress, 1990], 233–37.)

The Lutheran practice proposes the following:

The service begins with a procession of the ministers and the congregation commemorating the Lord's entry into Jerusalem. (The procession with palms is as old as the fourth century and appears to have originated in Jerusalem.) In the procession everyone carries palms or other branches. Ritually and symbolically the church becomes Jerusalem for the time of the service, and Jesus again enters his city. The past becomes the present, and the future is foreshadowed when Jesus will lead his people into the new Jerusalem, the heavenly city in which the Easter celebration will find its fulfillment.

For the most dramatic effect, the congregation should gather in a parish house, the church basement, the porch of the church, or, if it is commodious enough, the narthex. From here the procession moves into the church. (The crowds met Jesus outside Jerusalem and accompanied him into the city.) A sufficient quantity of palm branches is placed ready for distribution as people gather for the service. Other branches, especially olive branches [or branches local to the natural environment of the region], may be used instead. . . . The distribution of branches is completed before the service begins.

This describes the unique part of the Passion Sunday liturgy (though making the protracted proclamation of the Passion of Mark engaging and participatory for the assembly is no mean accomplishment either). Careful planning of the procession and its route is necessary before this liturgy is undertaken by the pastoral leadership of the church.

PROCESSION WITH PALMS

MARK 11:1–11 (RCL);
MARK 11:1–11A (BCP);
MARK 11:1–10 (RC)

Complementing the procession, this proclamation starts the community in its movement of remembering the last days of Jesus' life. For most in the assembly, the story is very familiar, but it is only once a year that we remember it together in the community of faith, as inheritors of the church born in the paschal mystery of Christ's passion and resurrection. This triumphal entrance of Jesus into Jerusalem begins a journey of faith, and it is a link to our lives of faith celebrated in the Lord's Supper as the body of Christ. In the Gospel account we find the people spreading their cloaks on the road by which Jesus would pass and taking up palms, "leafy branches," as a signal of their adoration of their Savior.

THIS PROCLAMATION STARTS THE COMMUNITY IN ITS MOVEMENT OF REMEMBERING THE LAST DAYS OF JESUS' LIFE.

While we might be inclined to wistfully imagine that first-century time to have been more privileged in having the incarnate Son of God in their view as he passed by on the donkey, we do well to remember that this was not likely so for most or even all of the members of the community in which the Gospel of Mark was written. The study of this text has demonstrated that it is rather unlikely that this gospel was written by or for a person or persons who knew Jesus face to face.

We know, for example, that even the apostle Paul, writing twenty years *before* the evangelist Mark, was not an eyewitness, and the evangelist Luke tells us also that he was not an eyewitness but a chronicler basing his Gospel on the testimony of eyewitnesses (1:1–4). Rather than lead us to discouragement, this realization raises up our own church experience to one comparable to the experience of those in the churches the apostle Paul found and in the community of Mark's Gospel. We, like them, are not eyewitnesses to the life of Jesus in the flesh, but we, also like them, come together as the church week after week, and there we hear the Word proclaimed and preached, and we find the risen Christ in the life of the community of faith, much like those first-century believers.

The anthem of this gospel narrative of Passion Sunday—"Hosanna! Blessed is the one who comes in the name of the Lord!" (Mark 11:9)—is incorporated into our service of Holy Communion. During the prayer of Great Thanksgiving, after the preface, we sing (or say),

Holy, holy, holy Lord, God of pow'r and might:
Heaven and earth are full of your glory.

Hosanna. Hosanna. Hosanna in the highest.
Blessed is he who comes in the name of the Lord.
Hosanna in the highest.

Now, the event described in the Gospel is based on the life of Jesus, but in the community of Mark's Gospel that life is told in combination with the community's experience of the risen Christ in worship. So it is not unlikely that they, like ourselves today, were also singing "Blessed is he who comes in the name of the Lord" as part of their weekly worship. When the narrative of the Gospel was written down, it was a mix of history (from the thirty-year life of Jesus) and of the church's life (experienced in worship, in the preaching of the Word and in Holy Communion). So when we hear this Gospel, or when we sing this anthem in worship, we are walking in the footsteps of those believers in the first century. Most of them, like us, did not know Jesus personally. Most of them, like ourselves, had heard of him in their community of faith and in the preaching of the Word from their leader (or leaders). Most of them, like ourselves, experienced him in the bread broken and wine poured, shared with the assembly.

The Christian tendency is to think of the experience of all other believers as richer, more powerful, more convincing, and more consoling than our own. But during Holy Week the preacher needs to emphasize for the assembled believers that the tradition of the church counters this, and many things were and are shared in the overlapping experiences of the life of Jesus, the life of the community of Mark's Gospel (from which this narrative of the entry into Jerusalem emerged), and the life of our own church. Among these is the inclusion in the narrative of this liturgical song, still proclaimed in Holy Communion these twenty centuries later. By it we are united in the body of Christ, the risen Savior, and by the paschal experience it expresses we are thus redeemed. As you sing this anthem, keep in mind the life of Jesus (as usual), but also the life of Mark's community and what, in singing, we share with them.

With them we also share in the anticipation of the death of Christ and in the anticipation of our own death. The liturgical experience, in which we are wedded to one another by faith and by singing, puts us in the privileged position, one that transcends time and space and in which we find the body of Christ, the redeemer of the world, then, today, and always.

JOHN 12:12-16 (RCL, alt.);
JOHN 12:12-16, (37) (RC, alt.)

This story is John's version of the entry into Jerusalem, the same basic narrative but with an important detail for the tradition we have inherited and for our imaginations and our liturgical life. Mark has the spectators bearing "leafy branches" (Greek *stibadas,* 11:8), Matthew simply describes "branches" (*kladous,* 21:8), and Luke has no branches at all (cf. 19:36). It is from the evangelist John that we get the specificity of "branches of palm trees" *(phoinikon),* a detail that has engaged the imaginations of believers and artists and worshipers from the first century on.

The narrative of the entry is relatively sparse in John (five verses compared to Mark's eleven), but it is important to emphasize the common element in John and the three Synoptics, which is the liturgical anthem: "Hosanna! Blessed is the one who comes in the name of the Lord!" (Mark 11:9; see Matt. 21:9; Luke 19:38; John 12:13). Yet even with this uniform liturgical anthem, the names by which the gathered people call Jesus reflect the unique elements of each Gospel. So in Matthew he is the "Son of David," in Luke he is the "king" and the bearer of "peace," and in John he is the "King of Israel." This balance of unity and difference in the biblical narrative likely reflects a similar balance of unity and difference in the liturgical experience of the churches from which each Gospel emerged. It might prompt us to consider what our local church would call him based on our faith experience of his risen presence among us. This elbow-room of interpretation is an important component today, for any of us who have visited other churches—of our own communion or not—know that there are some relatively constant components in the liturgical life from church to church and some spots where the liturgy reflects the experience of the local community. The balance of similarity and dissimilarity of our experience has a precedent in the same balance in the biblical stories and in the liturgical experiences the biblical stories reflect.

The Great Thanksgiving for Passion Sunday in the *Book of Common Worship* highlights this balance and the link between the life of Jesus as we know it from the scripture and our own lives these many years later:

> Lead us, O God, in the way of Christ.
> Give us courage to take up our cross
> and, in full reliance upon your grace, to follow him.
> Help us to love you above all else
> and to love our neighbor as we love ourselves,
> demonstrating that love in deed and word
> in the power of your Spirit.

PSALM 118:1-2, 19-29 (RCL);
PSALM 118:19-29 (BCP)

The juxtaposition of praise and passion of the refrain "O give thanks to the Lord, for he is good" and the Passion according to Mark soon to follow it in the liturgy is simultaneously odd and consoling. The oddity might be felt by those who will be saddened by the proclamation of the Passion, yet the praise of Psalm 118 qualifies the gravity of the Passion for believers because they know, and indeed experience, the victory over sin and death won through the passion and death of Christ. The familiar metaphor—"the stone that the builders rejected has become the chief cornerstone" (118:22)—is apt for this celebration of the liturgical year, a sign of hope for Christians whose lives are burdensome. The metaphor of the stone rejected becoming the cornerstone captures the heart of the paschal mystery in the early church and in the church today. God's presence and the life of grace are not often recognized in the most auspicious or likely of persons, places, times, and experiences. This psalm encourages us to look for God in the least predictable circumstances.

> THE METAPHOR OF THE STONE REJECTED BECOMING THE CORNERSTONE CAPTURES THE HEART OF THE PASCHAL MYSTERY IN THE EARLY CHURCH AND IN THE CHURCH TODAY.

LITURGY OF THE PASSION

FIRST READING

ISAIAH 50:4-9A (RCL);
ISAIAH 50:4-7 (RC)

This proclamation from Isaiah anticipates the long Passion narrative that will follow from the Gospel of Mark. Although the Isaiah reading was not applied to Jesus of Nazareth centuries before him when the prophet spoke it, the Christian tradition has found in this prophecy a precedent for the man of God who suffers and yet is vindicated by God. For this reason the tradition of the suffering servant of the prophet Isaiah was integrated into the New Testament theology of Jesus of Nazareth, who suffered and died for the salvation of the world.

Christians can be consoled by this "word to the weary"—as the prophet describes it (50:4)—for all believers, no matter how holy or devout, can be wearied by the burdens and complexities of human life. Though we might not find ourselves insulted and spit upon as did the suffering servant of this passage, we can sometimes feel the weight of the world and feel a disgrace that we had not earned or anticipated. The message of the prophet did indeed pave a theological path that for Christians was fulfilled in Jesus of Nazareth, but we ourselves walk in this same path when we are perplexed and find life burdensome. As members of an assembly that in the liturgy realizes the body of Christ, we are not exempt from suffering. In this Holy Week we can be consoled by the prophet Isaiah and by the example and life of Jesus himself as anticipated and narrated in the scriptures: "I know that I shall not be put to shame; he who vindicates me is near" (50:7-8).

ISAIAH 45:21-25 (BCP);
ISAIAH 52:13—53:12 (BCP, alt.)

These two readings from the lectionary of the *Book of Common Prayer* anticipate the victory that will be claimed in the paschal mystery of the death and resurrection of Christ. We might see the vindication about which they speak as giving us the victory before the narrative of the battle has begun. In the first of these, for example, God declares through the prophet, "To me every knee shall bow, every tongue shall swear" (45:23). This will be echoed in the reading from the Letter to the Philippians on Good Friday in which the cross is the instrument of the victory in Christ.

In the longer reading from Isaiah in the *BCP*, we feel the physical anguish and suffering of this servant of God—"so marred was his appearance," "despised and rejected," "acquainted with infirmity," "as one from whom others hide their faces"—and, like the other readings about this servant and about what happened to Jesus in the Gospel accounts, we might sometimes feel like that suffering servant. Yet in the cross of Christ, proclaimed in the church and celebrated in this Holy Week as our consolation and our victory, we are saved. So when, in the course of our lives and in the decisions that we make in faith that distance us from those around us, we are at odds with the common opinion and common way of acting—such that we ourselves can be despised and rejected, such that we can feel like that ancient one of Israel from whom others hid their faces—we can be buoyed by this proclamation from the prophet Isaiah. As Christians we do not positively seek out suffering for suffering's sake, or as way of imitating Christ, but our convictions made because of faith might result in personal suffering and social ostracism. If so, we can take heart in this suffering servant passage of Isaiah's prophecy.

PSALM 31:9–16 (RCL)

This is a fitting communal song between the proclamation of Isaiah's song of the suffering servant and the long narrative of Christ's passion in the Gospel of Mark. Though the response is not usually taken up in preaching, here the plight of the person speaking might be a fitting vehicle for pastoral care toward those in the assembly, often unnoticed in the last pew or because of spotty attendance, who are themselves suffering. "My life is spent with sorrow, and my years with sighing" (31:10a), the psalmist recorded and we the church sing on this day. "I am the scorn of my adversaries, a horror to my neighbors," captures the situation familiar to those on society's margins. Yet the preacher might counter their possible depreciation of themselves by highlighting the plea that follows— "I trust in you, O LORD. . . . Save me in your steadfast love" (31:14, 16)—such that those who are in distress might turn to the church as the first move out of their plight. Indeed, the progress of Holy Week as a theological and temporal span, embracing the horrors of Passion and the hope of resurrection, would offer a message of strength and hope for the pastoral care leaders and for the persons to whom they minister.

PSALM 22:1–21 OR 22:1–11 (BCP); PSALM 22:8–9, 17–18, 19–20, 23–24 (RC)

Like Psalm 31 above, Psalm 22 here speaks from the tradition of suffering in the history of the nation Israel, and the New Testament picks this up in its theology of the cross. Key for preaching on this text is that the body of Christ still groans in suffering, and that there are many in our assemblies in whom these kinds of responses strike a deep chord. Rhetoric on such biblical passages, however, must be careful that it does not leave people with the impression that the passages are prescriptions or warrants for self-loathing or self-torture.

Most people in the church will hear such a text and wisely appropriate it as a reflection on the agony of Jesus' death. Yet preachers need to hear such texts through the ears of those in dire straits; for example, "My hands and feet have shriveled; I can count all my bones" (22:16–17) in the ears of an unloved young person, or "I am a worm, and not human" (22:6) in the ears of someone experiencing domestic abuse.

SECOND READING

PHILIPPIANS 2:5-11 (RCL, BCP);
PHILIPPIANS 2:6-11 (RC)

This is a privileged text in the Christian tradition because of its antiquity as a hymn. The passage comes from Paul's letter to the Philippians, written in the middle of the first century and therefore among the earliest of extant New Testament books. In addition to the antiquity of Philippians, scripture scholars have come to agree that this part of the letter was probably a hymn from a time even earlier than Paul wrote the letter itself. So the hymn is likely a remnant of the earliest stratum of Christian literature reflecting the theology of communities after the death of Jesus.

Theologically, it is key to understand that because of Christ's obedience, to the point of accepting the ignoble death on a cross, God exalted him. Though this death on the cross won salvation for humanity, then as now and always, we do not participate in salvation by the mere imitation of the acts of Jesus' death. That is, we do not long for crucifixion, but accepting the finality of that paschal event, we like Christ Jesus, listen to God's word in order to discern what our vocation is—as individuals and as a community of faith—and how we also will be obedient as Christ himself was. The opening prayer in the *LBW* weds Christ's and our obedience:

Almighty God, you sent your Son, our Savior Jesus Christ,
to take our flesh upon him and to suffer death on the cross.
Grant that we may share in his obedience to your will
and in the glorious victory of his resurrection;
through your Son, Jesus Christ our Lord.

THE GOSPEL

MARK 14:1—15:47 OR 15:1-39, (40-47) (RCL);
MARK (14:32-72), 15:1-39, (40-47) (BCP);
MARK 14:1—15:47 OR 15:1-39 (RC)

This long story of the Passion moves from the woman anointing Jesus' body in preparation for burial to the Last Supper, the agony at Gethsemane, the betrayal by Judas Iscariot, the interrogation by the chief priests, the denial by Peter, the exchange with Pilate, the release of Barrabas, the way of the cross, the death of Jesus, and finally the burial of his body. It is a very long Gospel story for the Sunday liturgy, one that calls for a clear and evenly timed proclamation. Those who proclaim the Gospel might be inclined to read only a portion or to read it quickly so that less time be taken up with the story. One should seriously consider the losses sustained by the community when time is the primary concern that reigns over the edifying of the church and its members.

The Passion account is key in inviting believers to see their vocation and their own difficulties and sorrows in Christian living as united to the life of Jesus Christ. Who among the faithful, except perhaps the youngest in the assembly, has not known deep sorrow or disappointment or loss? Who has not felt betrayed by someone whom they love and trust? Passion Sunday and its Gospel account, this year from Mark, is a bridge between the life of Jesus and the life of the body of Christ in the church.

Vital to establishing the bridge between Jesus' life and our own are the sacramental traditions of Baptism and Eucharist, which are deep—if not readily apparent—in this Passion account. Since the reading is itself so long, let us concentrate on one particular character and see what his presence reveals about the context of the Holy Week we begin today and about the initiations to be celebrated at Easter. The character is a rather odd and hidden person, yet his odd role is important for understanding the Gospel of this year in the lectionary, the Gospel of Mark.

> THE PASSION ACCOUNT IS KEY IN INVITING BELIEVERS TO SEE THEIR VOCATION AND THEIR OWN DIFFICULTIES AND SORROWS IN CHRISTIAN LIVING AS UNITED TO THE LIFE OF JESUS CHRIST.

This character—though key to Mark's Gospel and not in the scene in any of the other Gospels—never even gets a name; he is merely the *neaniskos* in New Testament Greek, the "young man" in English, and he appears only twice in Mark's story (and, with that, in only two verses here, 14:51-52). We will meet him again at the tomb in the Gospel proclaimed as the last reading at the Easter Vigil, though there in only three verses (16:5-7).

In today's Gospel this is what we hear about this enigmatic character: "A certain young man was following him [Jesus], wearing nothing but a linen cloth. They caught hold of him, but he left the linen cloth and ran off naked" (14:51-52). Quite odd, huh? The signifying and weight-bearing details in this description are the linen cloth and the nakedness. Even though we baptize today with the initiates clothed, the baptismal liturgies in the early church dunked the new members while they were naked, and then, on coming out of the font, they were wrapped in white cloths. So at this point in the narrative of the Gospel of Mark, the passion and death of Jesus is just on the horizon. We can feel the tension in Mark as we start chapter 14, because we know that Jesus' betrayal and arrest, suffering and death are just around the corner.

As we hear this description of the young man, the *neaniskos,* we can think back over the course of our Christian lives—the lives of individuals but also the life of our church community. We can think of the choices we've made and of the difficulties we faced in discerning what the Christian way of life dictated that did not always make life easiest. We can feel our own vulnerability in this young man who does not appear earlier in Mark's Gospel. He approaches Jesus for the first time just as Jesus is being led to the high priest for the death sentence. Perhaps the young man was convinced that the way of Jesus was the truth, but on seeing the suffering that was on the horizon for Jesus—yes, also for himself as a person of faith—he fled, and in his flight he loses his linen garment and goes away naked.

This flight in nakedness can have us recall the course of our Christian lives, and of the suffering and difficult decisions and circumstances we have faced as persons of faith. We, like the young man, might have been tempted to flee. This is the feeling with which we begin Holy Week. We know the suffering and obstacles that will be proclaimed from the Gospel during this week, and the challenge is not just in remembering the life of Jesus, but in recommitting ourselves to the body of Christ and to the joys and difficulties to which such a commitment weds us.

We do not begin Holy Week forgetting the story that is to come throughout the week. The story does not change; in it Jesus will be crucified and he will die. So we do not listen to the story with the hope that the ending might be different, or that this year the story will be edited so that there is less pain, less blood, or a lesser feeling of abandonment. No, we listen because in the community of faith we are able to recognize that the gospel story is our own, and that in the church we are strengthened year after year so that—when we ourselves face problems, perplexities, perhaps even abandonments—we will be upheld by the witness and obedience of Jesus and by the support of the community of faith in the church into which we were plunged unto suffering and death at baptism.

MONDAY IN HOLY WEEK

APRIL 14, 2003

REVISED COMMON	EPISCOPAL (BCP)	ROMAN CATHOLIC
Isa. 42:1-9	Isa. 42:1-9	Isa. 42:1-7
Ps. 36:5-11	Ps. 36:5-10	
Heb. 9:11-15	Heb. 11:39—12:3	
John 12:1-11	John 12:1-11	John 12:1-11
	or Mark 14:3-9	

The prayer of the church for this day in the *Lutheran Book of Worship* is directive as we anticipate what is to be proclaimed in the scriptures in the week ahead:

O God,
your Son chose the path which led to pain before joy
and the cross before glory.
Plant his cross in our hearts,
so that in its power and love
we may come at last to joy and glory;
through your Son, Jesus Christ our Lord.

Mindful of the events in the life of Jesus just recounted in the long Gospel narrative of Passion Sunday and anticipating the familiar narratives of the end of the life of Jesus that are proclaimed in Christian assembly every year on Holy Thursday, Good Friday, and at Easter, many churchgoers will likely take time to read the scriptures, but few churches will celebrate the liturgy on this Monday in Holy Week. Still, the lectionary of the church prescribes the readings to follow for those communities that will conduct services. So it would be a good inclination for those who wish to spend some time in personal prayer throughout these first few days of Holy Week, before the three-day span (Triduum) begins on Holy Thursday, to take up their Bibles and consider prayerfully the scriptures that the lectionary puts forth, as above.

FIRST READING

ISAIAH 42:1-9 (RCL, BCP);
ISAIAH 42:1-7 (RC)

This passage probably sounds familiar to members of the church because similar words come from the mouth of Jesus at the beginning of his public ministry as told in the Gospel of Luke. There Jesus proclaims the "year of the Lord's favor" in which he will "bring good news to the poor" and "proclaim release to captives and recovery of sight to the blind" (4:18-19). As we hear these words, both from Isaiah and from Jesus, this is a good time to consider as a church the relationship of those individuals in the tradition, handed on from the past, to the community of faith listening to the reading in this very Holy Week.

The supreme value placed on individual freedom in our culture makes it difficult for us to imagine that some of the individual characters in the stories of both the Old and New Testaments represent tribes, communities, nations, and churches. The narrative may indeed reflect a historical event in the life of an individual, but often the narratives are reflecting the fates and events of a group. In the New Testament we are perhaps more familiar with this likelihood, since we recognize that the Gospels were written a few decades after the death of Jesus. So they incorporate their memories of events in Jesus' life, but they also include their experiences of the risen Christ in the birth of the church and in the community of faith. Trying to separate the singular person of Jesus from the communal body of Christ within the Gospel narratives can be a contentious and perhaps impossible task.

This balance of individual and communal narratives reflected in the stories about individuals is also true for the suffering servant songs from the prophet Isaiah, as in today's first reading. The Lord speaks in the scriptures of "Israel, my chosen servant." While the suffering servant passages may, therefore, reflect the experience of a person ("He will bring forth justice to the nations"), they also reflect the experience of the people Israel.

Today's passage is one of the loveliest and most poetic passages in the Bible, a consolation to members of the church whose lives have been difficult, to members rescued by the power of God. Speaking of the servant, the Lord declares through the prophet that he will not break a bruised reed nor quench a dimly burning wick (v. 3). These are beautiful metaphors that picture God's love for those most vulnerable in our midst. Our God is near to those who are hurting, and the church must similarly attend to those in need, not just in charitable acts of the church toward the needy, but because God is to be found in the "bruised reed" and the "dimly burning wick." The needy reveal the face of God to us. Because of such a theology, individual church communities, however great or small, and the Christian church as a whole must be unshakable advocates for the weakest in our society. The church stands as a sign of contradiction to the dog-eat-dog culture on which our society is founded. These images in today's reading must be ever-present to us so that this fundamental basis for being engaged in the world is not lost.

The advocacy is more explicit in the last few verses: "I have given you as a . . . light to the nations, to open the eyes that are blind, to bring out the prisoners from the dungeon, from the prison those who sit in darkness" (vv. 6-7). The theology of the church that sees us as "in the world but not of the world" enables us to support those whom the "world" has broken, those who are without bread, without shelter, without companionship, without love. Mindfulness of such people is important as we remember the suffering of the Son of God as it is proclaimed and remembered during Holy Week.

SECOND READING
HEBREWS 9:11-15 (RCL);
HEBREWS 11:39—12:3 (BCP)

In these days between two Passion narratives—the Passion of the Gospel of Mark yesterday and the Passion of the Gospel of John on Good Friday—the sacrifice offered by Christ for our salvation is uppermost in our thoughts and prayer. This reading from the Letter to the Hebrews is clear about the sanctification won for us in the death of Christ. It is a great relief for Christians to know and experience the freedom of the cross, such that we, sanctified by Christ, do not have to be overcome by the scrupulosity that would plague us if salvation were contingent on our actions and on our holiness. The blood of the redeemer frees us from such a burden so that, as this reading proclaims, we might "purify our conscience from dead works to worship the living God!" (9:14). Our works flow out as our response to God's unimaginable love, rather than our works occasioning God to act on our behalf or in our favor.

THE GOSPEL
JOHN 12:1-11 (RCL, BCP, RC);
MARK 14:3-9 (BCP, alt.)

Already we find someone ministering to Jesus at this crucial time before his death. Mary, the sister of Lazarus, whom Jesus had raised from the dead, comes to him and anoints his feet. This gesture might bring to mind other moments in the Gospel of John that contribute to the theological context of this narrative in the liturgy. First, we know that just a few verses earlier Jesus arrived at the tomb of Mary's dead brother, and in utter faith she knelt before Jesus and said, "Lord, if you had been here, my brother would not have died" (11:32). Her confidence, even in the rawness of her grief at the death of her brother, is amazing.

Second, on Holy Thursday, three days from now, we will hear the proclamation of the account, also from the Gospel of John, in which Jesus himself ministers to others by washing their feet. This is a unique sequence, in which on Monday we hear of Mary ministering to Jesus by anointing his feet, and then on Thursday, in the very next chapter of the Gospel, we hear that Jesus ministers to his followers by washing their feet. (See the commentary on the foot-washing passage of Holy Thursday, pages 228–31 below.)

Third, another association can be made, as we knit together the narratives proclaimed in this week, between Mary's anointing of Jesus' body in life with Nicodemus's anointing of the dead body of Jesus after his crucifixion. As we consider these people ministering to the *body* of Jesus, alive and dead, we might bear in mind an important question that Paul asked of the Corinthians: "Do you not know that your body is a temple of the Holy Spirit within you, which you have from God, and that you are not your own?" (1 Cor. 6:19). That letter of Paul was written a while before the Gospel of John, and the "body" about which Paul writes is not the body of an individual, but the body of the church. (When Paul says "your body" here, the possessive "your" is plural in number, not singular.) So when, during this week, we hear about the body of Jesus, and his sufferings and passion, we can be mindful also of the sufferings and passions of those in the "body" of Christ in our church. And we, like Mary and like Nicodemus, are called to minister to that body of Christ.

THE "BODY" ABOUT WHICH PAUL WRITES IS NOT THE BODY OF AN INDIVIDUAL, BUT THE BODY OF THE CHURCH.

We might traditionally think of the healing ministry of Jesus and his followers as one-directional, that is, that Jesus healed those in need. Yet there are a number of places in the Gospels where we find others ministering to the body of Jesus. Here this woman anoints his feet, an unimaginably intimate gesture and one the disciples objected to vehemently.

The key juxtaposition in these apostolic objections is that of this woman (whose service Judas objects to) and Judas himself. On the one hand, there is Judas, one of the chosen Twelve, who is about to hand Jesus over to the authorities; on the other hand, there is Mary, who, like all women in the social world of the first century, would not have been considered one of the "chosen." Yet she offers this service and physical consolation to Jesus in the hour of anxiety and reckoning by the authorities. The social world of first-century Palestine would have looked on this gesture with repulsion, and the Gospels are filled with such scenes in which the Savior is in the company of the society's most objectionable people. Such associations lead to the social pressure put on Jesus and contribute to the plotting against his life, as are narrated in this first half of Holy Week.

TUESDAY IN HOLY WEEK

APRIL 15, 2003

REVISED COMMON	EPISCOPAL (BCP)	ROMAN CATHOLIC
Isa. 49:1-7	Isa. 49:1-6	Isa. 49:1-6
Ps. 71:1-14	Ps. 71:1-12	
1 Cor. 1:18-31	1 Cor. 1:18-31	
John 12:20-36	John 12:37-38, 42-50	John 13:21-33, 36-38

FIRST READING
ISAIAH 49:1-7 (RCL); 49:1-6 (BCP, RC)

This reading has a lovely theology of light and darkness, one particularly poignant as the church anticipates its rebirth at Easter and the lighting of the Easter candle. The prophet Isaiah proclaims the word of the Lord to the servant, "I will give you as a light to the nations, that my salvation may reach to the end of the earth" (v. 6).

We can be consoled by this message and we can relax that this salvation has been offered to us in the Lord and in the gift of Baptism. Yet, too, we must recognize the part we are called to play in carrying this light "to the end of the earth." Living in a culture in which success and acceptance are predicated on our performance, we might be reticent to receive God's lavish love, a love that we cannot and do not earn, a love that is pure gift. But having received the gift of God, we are bearers of this love to the ends of the earth. So we proclaim God's Word and God's love not in order to earn God's favor but, having been so lavishly loved by God, we feel compelled to share that gift with those it has not reached.

The prophet declares the measure of this gift when he says, "Kings shall see and stand up, princes, and they shall prostrate themselves, because of the LORD, . . . who has chosen you" (v. 7). Although this word was fulfilled in the life and ministry of Jesus of Nazareth, whose final days and death we remember especially this week, we ourselves are incorporated into that life by the mysteries celebrated during these days and during the Easter season. By our baptism we were brought into that saving body of Christ. That word of the servant in the prophecy, "I am honored in the sight of the LORD, and my God has become my strength," is therefore also spoken to us in the church. For we carry on that life in the church and, through it, to the ends of the earth. We listen attentively to God's Word, we discern our part in the mission of the church, and we face our vocations squarely at this holy time of the liturgical year.

RESPONSIVE READING
PSALM 71:1-14 (RCL); 71:1-12 (BCP)

The psalmist and the community sing these words, which are a balance of sobering recognition of the difficulties of human life and of the trust in God that sees us through. The vocation of the speaker is certain when he says to the Lord, "Upon you I have leaned from my birth; it was you who took me from my mother's womb" (v. 6). But this did not spare him from difficulty: "I have been like a portent to many" (v. 7).

These days between Passion Sunday and Holy Thursday are not often days when the congregation assembles in church to worship. But meditation on the readings and perhaps singing responses like Psalm 71 are ways to sustain a prayerful posture in the span between the times when the church is at prayer together.

SECOND READING
1 CORINTHIANS 1:18-31 (RCL, BCP)

In the middle of the first century, as nascent Christian churches struggled to be born, Paul made a powerful case for the ways of God. In his first letter to the Corinthians, he wrote, "God's foolishness is wiser than human wisdom, and God's weakness is stronger than human strength" (v. 25).

We, perhaps like that first-century community in Corinth, are surprised that the work of God is mediated in the likes of us, twenty-first-century Christians, as weak and foolish as were those Greek Christians to whom the apostle sent his letter. The fragility of our life—as individuals and as a community of faith gathered Sunday after Sunday, year after year—might instigate doubts about our worthiness to do the work of God in this world. In the face of this, however, we hear, with peace and hope and consolation, that God knows us better than we know ourselves, that God's foolishness and weakness are more powerful than our own wisdom and strength. Each of us in the church can hear the apostle Paul, whose words are no less wise or efficacious to our own ears than they were to the Corinthians two millennia ago: "Consider your own call, brothers and sisters."

We pause to think about how we came to be where we are; we think of how the work of God goes on in us in spite of our own depreciation of our gifts. For

God is wiser than we are. As individuals and as a church, we hear that "God chose what is foolish in the world to shame the wise." We know that Jesus was despised and rejected and that he suffered and died for his convictions and in obedience to the Father. Today we carry on that call to holiness in the church, to "foolishness" in the world's assessment, to sanctity in the church, and to "weakness" in the world's eyes. The standard was set in the life and passion of Jesus Christ, the "source of your life" (v. 30). And we are undeterred, for he is our "righteousness and sanctification and redemption" (v. 30), because he loved us while we were still sinners.

The Gospel
JOHN 12:20-36 (RCL);
JOHN 12:37-38, 42-50 (BCP);
JOHN 13:21-33, 36-38 (RC)

We continue the narrative from the Gospel of John leading toward the death of Jesus. Here we find a complement to the light imagery of the first reading from the prophet Isaiah and in anticipation of the new light of the Easter Vigil. The Gospel of John is not the only Gospel to use light as a compelling sign of God's presence, yet this evangelist uses this metaphor boldly in his theology of exaltation.

> THE GOSPEL OF JOHN IS NOT THE ONLY GOSPEL TO USE LIGHT AS A COMPELLING SIGN OF GOD'S PRESENCE, YET THIS EVANGELIST USES THIS METAPHOR BOLDLY IN HIS THEOLOGY OF EXALTATION.

At the very start of John's Gospel, still in the prologue, we find the image of light applied to Christ as the Word come into the world: "The light shines in the darkness, and the darkness did not overcome it" (1:5). Then, later, on the very lips of Jesus, we find this assertion: "I am the light of the world" (8:12). In this passage we hear Jesus speaking again of himself as the light: "The light is with you for a little longer. Walk while you have the light. . . . Believe in the light, so that you may become children of the light" (12:35-36). This passage is well suited for the church just four days before the Great Vigil.

As we anticipate the observance of the vigil, it is good to remember that the church requires it be celebrated in the dark so that the symbol of Christ as the light conquering darkness will be *experienced* by those in attendance. Light conquering darkness is not just an idea at the vigil but an experience of the senses, and the church ardently proclaims "The Light of Christ!" as the burning candle is borne into the darkness. We cannot overemphasize the importance of light during the Holy Week to prepare the church in anticipation of its rebirth at the vigil and during the fifty-day season of Easter.

WEDNESDAY IN HOLY WEEK

APRIL 16, 2003

REVISED COMMON	EPISCOPAL (BCP)	ROMAN CATHOLIC
Isa. 50:4–9a	Isa. 50:4–9a	Isa. 50:4–9a
Psalm 70	Ps. 69:7–15, 22–23	Ps. 69:8–10, 21–22, 31, 33–34
Heb. 12:1–3	Heb. 9:11–15, 24–28	
John 13:21–32	John 13:21–35	Matt. 26:14–25

The prayer from the *LBW* for this day in the middle of Holy Week reminds us of the purpose of recounting the last days of the life of Jesus each year just before Easter:

> Almighty God,
> your Son our Savior suffered at the hands of men
> and endured the shame of the cross.
> Grant that we may walk in the way of his cross
> and find it the way of life and peace;
> through your Son, Jesus Christ our Lord.

Jesus Christ suffered once for the redemption of all; we have been won at a price, as the scriptures say. But once brought into the body of Christ, the church, we are destined to follow his life and, as the prayer suggests, to "walk in the way of his cross." The Christian vocation is not to imitate Jesus physically, but to listen for the voice of God in the new place and time in which God animates the world. Jesus was one with God the Father and hastened to obey the voice of the Father even as an itinerant and revolutionary Jew in first-century Palestine. Almost twenty-one centuries later, we find ourselves in a completely different place, yet God is still speaking, still present in the life of faith. We therefore attend to God's word and call in our time.

The prayer is sobering, however, because it reminds us that the way of the cross continues in the world, in the church, and in our lives today. By our baptism we are called to discern God's word and presence, but God's life calls us and continues to call us to a life of challenge and at times to a life of discomfort. Still, as the prayer concludes, we trust that we will "find [the cross to be] the way of life and peace." This is both sobering and consoling, and the community of faith with which we celebrate helps strengthen and support us as we answer God's call.

FIRST READING
ISAIAH 50:4-9A

The prophet Isaiah speaks with the strength of faith in the Lord, and he is courageous in recognizing the gifts the Lord has given him in the face of opposition: "The Lord GOD has given me the tongue of a teacher" (v. 4). On hearing this passage, the example that is put before us is the historical Jesus, who faced his end in the adversity resulting from his steadfast willingness to obey God's call, his willingness to be an advocate for the weak in the court of a hostile crowd, in the hearing of the satisfied. The Gospels describe Jesus as familiar with the words of Isaiah. These words are on his lips in his last days, as he would pray "that I may know how to sustain the weary with a word" (v. 4). The community of faith in which we observe and indeed celebrate Holy Week and Easter sustains us, as it does week after week, Sunday after Sunday through the year.

Even though Isaiah describes what will happen to the opposition—they "will wear out like a garment; the moth will eat them up" (v. 9)—we know that such vindication is not readily evident. Yet it must also have been intensely difficult for Jesus to have faced an opposition so strong that it eventually took his life. Perhaps his opposition was also "worn out" and "eaten up," but not before it had set the demise on him who had caused them to question, who had sought help for the needy.

RESPONSIVE READING
PSALM 70 (RCL);
PSALM 69:7-15, 22-23 (BCP);
PSALM 69:8-10, 21-22, 31, 33-34 (RC)

Like Jesus nearing his passion, the speaker in each of these psalms is despised and rejected, taunted by those who seek his demise. The taunts in Psalm 70 are not as striking as those in Psalm 69, but in both songs the speaker remains resolute even while facing rejection and suffering. Each speaker trusts that, no matter what the taunts, God will be generous with love and help: "In the abundance of your steadfast love, answer me," he prays (69:13), even as he is ostracized and the subject of gossip.

WE MIGHT NOT BE ABLE TO TELL HOW MANY PEOPLE IN OUR ASSEMBLIES ARE BROKEN; THERE MAY BE SOME IN OUR CHURCHES FOR WHOM SUCH FEELINGS WEIGH DOWN THEIR LIVES DAY AFTER DAY.

As were some of the psalms in the liturgies earlier in the week, these words might speak to members of our congregations in ways that pastoral leaders cannot imagine. We might not be able to tell how many people in our assemblies are broken or how many say with the psalmist, "I have become a stranger to my kindred, an alien to my mother's children" (69:8). There may be some in our churches for whom such feelings weigh down their lives day after day. So the preacher might take the opportunity of Holy Week to raise up these members so that they may be strengthened by the closeness of their circumstances to Jesus' own, and with that strength perhaps they will seek help and be made whole.

SECOND READING
HEBREWS 12:1-3 (RCL)

In the Apostles' Creed we profess, "I believe in . . . the communion of the saints," those who have gone before us marked with the sign of faith, as well as those who go with us in the present, those in our own church and neighborhoods and families who are baptized into the life of God or are inquiring about the life of faith. This communion is the group described in this reading from the Letter to the Hebrews: "We are surrounded by so great a cloud of witnesses" (12:1). The metaphor of the "cloud" for those with whom we share the faith is keen, for it captures not only that each believer stands among other believers, but that together believers permeate the world in which they live, move, and have their being. Faith irradicably sinks into every nook and cranny of human life.

As part of this cloud of witnesses, believers are able to be strong in the face of temptation and sin, for it is in the context of the local assembly and its unique "cloud" of witnesses that a church is born in a particular time and place. The church fortifies believers so that they can say "no" to sin. The example for this life is Jesus himself, who is, as the reading says, "the pioneer and perfecter of our faith" (v. 2). He, like us in all things but sin, was glorified because he took on our human condition.

In the middle of Holy Week, the reading reveals the simultaneity of Christ's debasement in the hands of his persecutors and murderers and his glorification in having "taken his seat at the right hand of the throne of God" (v. 2). These are the two aspects of the paschal mystery, suffering and glorification. As followers of him, we do not seek suffering for its own sake, but we are able to be strong in the face of whatever suffering might be ours for having followed the call of the gospel and of the church. The communion of saints continues to put before us this simultaneity of suffering and glorification, and we members of the church at the beginning of a new millennium join in the cloud of the saints and witnesses. And it is on account of their witness that we do "not grow weary or lose heart" (v. 3).

JOHN 13:21-32 (RCL);
JOHN 13:21-35 (BCP)

The juxtaposition of suffering and glorification continues from the second reading to the Gospel. In the Gospel of John the scene of this reading comes after the foot-washing scene, though in Holy Week the liturgies transpose them. In the Gospel we recognize that the foot-washing precedes this scene of revealing Judas as the betrayer, but the liturgical tradition marks them in the other order. Such changes and transpositions prompt us to wonder about the chronological relationship of the Gospel and of the chronology as proclaimed in the readings. The transposition of Wednesday's and Thursday's Gospel remind us again that the primary reason for Holy Week is not mere historical reenactment. We do not wash feet on Holy Thursday merely to imitate what Jesus himself might have done; that is an important ritual ingredient but not, in the end, the determining or efficacious factor. More important is the witness of faith in the risen Christ in the church today, and the experience of Holy Week and Easter are not just recollecting of the past but participating in the future. The ritual actions are not ends in themselves, but they ground us in the tradition that makes us who we are and whose we are. We are members of the body of Christ, and by baptism we belong to God.

Another element in the Gospel for this Wednesday is the presence of a unique disciple, "the one whom Jesus loved" (v. 23). He is not well known in the tradition, for he appears only in the Gospel of John. (The Gospels of Matthew, Mark, and Luke do not label any of the disciples as "the one whom Jesus loved.") In his few appearances in this Gospel, he is not named, and he is usually juxtaposed to Peter: In this scene (chap. 13), Peter asked him to get some information from Jesus about the betrayer; at the tomb there is actually a foot race between Peter and this beloved disciple (20:1-8). The beloved wins the race but is gracious enough to let Peter go in first anyway! And after the resurrection, after having been fishing (first things first!), they share breakfast with the risen Jesus on the shore (21:4-14).

> THIS DISCIPLE INVITES US TO IMAGINE OURSELVES AS THIS FOLLOWER WHOM JESUS LOVED SO UNIQUELY. EACH OF US, LIKE HIM, HAVE HEARD THE CALL, AND WE CONDUCT OUR LIVES AS MEMBERS OF HIS BODY, WORKING IN THE WORLD TO REALIZE THE KINGDOM.

Some theologians have suggested that the anonymity of this disciple invites us, the hearers of this narrative in Holy Week, to imagine ourselves as this follower whom Jesus loved so uniquely. Each of us, like him, have heard the call, and we conduct our lives as members of his body, working—though perhaps not with nets so full of fish—in the world to realize the kingdom.

MAUNDY THURSDAY /
HOLY THURSDAY

April 17, 2003

Revised Common	Episcopal (BCP)	Roman Catholic
Exod. 12:1-4, (5-10), 11-14	Exod. 12:1-14a	Exod. 12:1-8, 11-14
Ps. 116:1-2, 12-19	Ps. 78:14-20, 23-25	Ps. 116:12-13, 15-16bc, 17-18
1 Cor. 11:23-26	1 Cor. 11:23-26, (27-32)	1 Cor. 11:23-26
John 13:1-17, 31b-35	John 13:1-15 or Luke 22:14-30	John 13:1-15

Although the span of time in the liturgies of Holy Week—from Passion (Palm) Sunday to Easter Sunday—is quite an ancient observance in the history of Christian worship, a shorter span of time—from the evening liturgy of Maundy Thursday until Easter Sunday evening—is older yet. Even though by our reckoning it seems like four days (Thursday, Friday, Saturday, Sunday), the span was called the "Three Days," the *Tri-duum,* by its Latin name in the early church, perhaps marking three twenty-four-hour spans: Thursday to Friday, Friday to Saturday, Saturday to Sunday.

The liturgy of Maundy Thursday was the start of this very ancient three-day span at the heart of the liturgical year, as the evening of the same day is for us centuries later. In a way the Triduum is in itself one liturgy over three days, rather than a series of individual celebrations. One sure indicator that the church intends it to be so is the "soft" beginnings and endings of the liturgies.

For our usual celebration of the Lord's Supper, the presider declares, "Go in peace. Serve the Lord." And the congregation responds, "Thanks be to God." The assembly is able to recognize the end of the rite just before it leaves. During the Triduum, however, the end is not so clear. The *LBW* indicates that at the end of the Maundy Thursday liturgy "there is no benediction. All leave the church in silence." It is a relatively soft ending, unlike that of the usual celebration of the Lord's Supper, which ends with a benediction and a hymn. This absence of a definite end is complemented by a "soft" beginning of the liturgy for Good Friday, for the liturgy instructs, "The ministers enter in silence and go to their places." There is no rousing hymn to mark the beginning, and the usual greeting, "The grace of our Lord Jesus Christ, the love of God, and the communion of the Holy

Spirit be with you all," and its response, "And also with you," are omitted. These soft endings and beginnings wed the rites of the Triduum as one liturgical and calendrical span, with the weight of Easter borne by the whole span as a movement toward the Fifty Days of the Easter season, from Easter to Pentecost, rather than by a sum of the parts.

"Maundy" is a weird word, brought into English from Latin, one that centuries ago would have immediately signified the liturgical action at the center of the Gospel reading, the foot-washing. It is a modification of the Latin word for "commandment" in early Christianity, *mandatum*. It is taken from the same chapter of the same Gospel account in the lectionary for the day, John 13. The commandment to which the word refers is well known in the tradition: "I give you a new commandment, that

THE DAY BECAME KNOWN AS "MAUNDY THURS-DAY," FROM THE COMMANDMENT TO LOVE, AND THE RITUAL ACTION OF WASHING FEET ITSELF RECEIVED THE TAG THE *MANDATUM*.

you love another. Just as I have loved you, you also should love one another" (13:34). So the day became known as "Maundy Thursday," from the commandment to love, and the ritual action of washing feet itself received the tag the *mandatum*.

The *mandatum* is a unique ritual action, about which we hear in the proclamation of the reading from the Gospel of John, and the ritual is connected to the love about which Jesus speaks in the Fourth Gospel. The *mandatum* of washing feet is related to the commandment to love: "For I have set you an example, that you also should do as I have done to you" (13:15). So we hear in the opening prayer *(LBW)*:

Holy God, source of all love,
on the night of his betrayal,
Jesus gave his disciples a new commandment:
To love one another as he had loved them.
By your Holy Spirit write this commandment in our hearts;
through your Son, Jesus Christ our Lord,
who lives and reigns with you and the Holy Spirit,
one God, now and forever.

In the Lutheran and Episcopal liturgical traditions, the foot-washing rite is recommended; in the Roman Catholic tradition it is required. The *LBW* instructs: "The WASHING OF FEET may follow. The minister lays his vestments aside, puts on an apron or a towel, and washes the feet of a representative group of the congregation. During the washing of the feet, 'Where charity and love prevail,' hymn 126, is sung. Other hymns may be sung also" *(LBW,* 138).

The foot-washing is a key gesture of love and service, and it is possible that in the late first century, when the Gospel of John was written, it, like baptism as we know it, was the ritual by which newcomers became members of the church. Look in your Bible closely at John 13:10 and you will see: "Jesus said to him [Peter], 'One who has bathed does not need to wash, except for the feet, but is entirely clean.'" Near that verse you will likely see a reference or textual note letting you, the reader, know that in some ancient manuscripts of that verse the phrase "except for the feet" is missing. What that note teaches us is that there were two textual traditions regarding the meaning of the foot-washing, and the two traditions are revealed in the two versions of the manuscripts of 13:10. Two verses earlier Jesus had said, "Unless I wash [your feet], you have no share with me" (13:8), with its clear suggestion that the foot-washing was a rite of initiation or a rite of having a share in Christ in the church.

The manuscript versions of 13:10 in which Jesus says, "One who has bathed does not need to wash, except for the feet" probably come from those communities in which the foot-washing was the initiation rite, before the discourse of Jesus in 13:12-20—likely added later, according to biblical scholars—in which the gesture is interpreted as one of service rather than of initiation. This is the most obvious meaning of Jesus' gesture of foot-washing before one searches more closely the differences in the ancient manuscripts of the Gospel. The ancient manuscripts with the phrase "except for the feet" missing, as the note might indicate, were communities in which initiation happened by baptism.

What this complex consideration reveals, in the end, is that there was more than one way to have been initiated into a Christian community in the churches of the late first century. This is surely a consolation to us today, for in the church universal and in the many churches of our society we find a number of different ways that initiation happens and even a number of different theologies of initiation, as in the early church. The diversity of our ritual traditions and our liturgical theologies has a precedent, a forerunner, in the diversity of traditions evident in the New Testament, like this one in the manuscript evidence of the Gospel of John.

A church's decisions about its liturgical traditions can take the deep meaning and history of the foot-washing into account and perhaps, if not done before, see the ritual action as a way of deepening the life of the members of the community. If done well and meditatively, the foot-washing will change a community, because it is a new way of discovering one's neighbor; indeed, if the testimony of the Gospel of John is accepted, foot-washing is a new way of loving one's neighbor.

IF DONE WELL AND MEDITATIVELY, THE FOOT-WASHING WILL CHANGE A COMMUNITY, BECAUSE IT IS A NEW WAY OF DISCOVERING ONE'S NEIGHBOR; INDEED, IF THE TESTIMONY OF THE GOSPEL OF JOHN IS ACCEPTED, FOOT-WASHING IS A NEW WAY OF LOVING ONE'S NEIGHBOR.

Another reason why the foot-washing rite will deepen the life of faith in a church is because the exchange is, after all, such an awkward one. Few of us attend to our own feet, and most of us are embarrassed to have another person even see our feet, let alone touch and actually bathe them in a public ceremony during the gravity of Holy Week's Three Days. If you are going to wash or be washed and you are a little anxious about it, be consoled by knowing that it is a commandment, indeed the commandment, *mandatum,* that lends its name to the day "Maundy" Thursday. And trust that, in the tradition of the Gospel of John, the rite of washing feet is linked to the Lord's commandment that we love one another.

Social reasons and practical matters of space and preparation—Who should be asked to wash? Who is to be washed? Do we have enough basins? Where is the nearest water source? How many towels will we need? How many washers and how many to be washed?—need to be attended to. But the primary impetus for considering the rite is the scriptural tradition and the depth of the liturgical tradition. If space, time, and numerous basins are available, the ideal celebration of the rite is to have all who are willing and able be both washers and washed.

Depending on the design of your parish church, the "choreography" of the foot-washing might take some planning. It might be a procession toward the front with an adequate number of basins and a large supply of towels at each basin. Or the flow might work best with a basin at the main aisle or at the outside end of every other pew, so that a circular procession of two pews will bring each person to the basin to be washed and then that person turns to wash the next person in line: "Love one another as I have loved you." As the community gets used to the ritual action and the discomfort is overcome by expectation and even excitement (especially in the children), the effort the pastoral staff has expended will be well worth it. It will take a few "practice" years to get the kinks out of the system, and with a rite that happens only once a year, the "few" practices might take up to a half-decade before it happens smoothly and without a hitch.

Notice that the altar is left completely bare by the end of the Maundy Thursday celebration. The *LBW* instructs that after communion "the stripping of the altar follows: Linens, paraments, ornaments, and candles are removed." At the end of Thursday the church instructs this so that the remembrance of Christ's death on Good Friday will be faced in the starkness and sobriety with which believers recognize the inevitability of their own deaths.

These are among the many unique and revelatory details of the liturgies for Holy Week and for the Triduum. The community of faith is being renewed and reconstituted by its observance of the liturgical tradition, revealed in these most ancient traditions. They are at the heart of the faith.

FIRST READING
EXODUS 12:1-4, (5-10), 11-14 (RCL);
EXODUS 12:1-14a (BCP);
EXODUS 12:1-8, 11-14 (RC)

The Gospel of John has a deep theology drawn from the Jewish tradition of slaughtering a lamb for the annual Passover. A liturgical tradition in the Lord's Supper drawn from this tradition is the prayer before reception of communion, "Lamb of God, who takes away the sins of the world." The image of the lamb in the Christian tradition—in the New Testament, in liturgy, in art—comes primarily from the Jewish tradition of the Passover meal. This meal is described in the first reading of Maundy Thursday, in which we hear of the close prescriptions for the slaughtering of the lamb: how old it was to be, how it was to be prepared, how it was to be cooked, how it was to be eaten, and even how those eating it were to be dressed. The meal was—and still is—a ritual reenactment of the exodus of the Israelites from Egypt millennia ago: "This is how you shall eat it: your loins girded, your sandals on your feet, and your staff in your hand; and you shall eat it hurriedly. It is the passover of the LORD" (Exod. 12:11). The way time is configured in the description is important, for the event itself had already happened when the book of Exodus was written. So the details of cooking and eating and dress are to make a time out of time for Jews who survived the Passover and for the generations to come.

In heeding the detailed prescriptions of the author of the book of Exodus, Jews who mark the Passover are tied into not only the family or families with whom they eat the meal and celebrate ceremony in the current year, but they are also linked to the families who ate and celebrated the rite in the exodus itself and in the centuries of strife and blessings between then and today. Ritual traditions, words spoken and gestures unde rtaken, can in this linkage transcend time. In this way the details of the rituals of the lamb centuries later vivify the community of faith, for the ritual actions of Jews connecting with their ancestors in this annual meal dispose them for discovering and experiencing the presence of God in their lives in the tradition today. And the ancient traditions of the Jews remembered today by Jewish families millennia later set an example of crossing the boundaries of time.

In this way the proclamation of Exodus 12 in the Christian tradition puts forth this strong precedent for ritual behavior and the formation it delivers to human beings. Christians who preserve ritual traditions—including Maundy Thursday's foot-washing and bread-breaking—are, like the Jews with their forebears, able to connect with their ancestors in the tradition who observed the same rites.

The Jewish ritual traditions of the Gospel of John cannot be taken up without also acknowledging the anti-Jewish rhetoric of this Gospel. The preacher and the pastoral team should address these elements, expecting that they will be heard by the local assembly and perhaps cause puzzlement at best, prejudice at worst. While the theology of this Gospel makes it a fitting Passion proclamation, the anti-Jewish content should be unpacked and contextualized for the community so that silence not be taken as tacit consent. Many pastoral resources can be of help in this regard, and an essay in the church bulletin might be supplied as an educational tool for parishioners who want to know more about how the Christian tradition came to be marked by anti-Jewish polemic.

Responsive Reading
PSALM 116:1-2, 12-19 (RCL);
PSALM 116:12-13, 15-16bc, 17-18 (RC)

We feel a slight shift in the psalm responses now at the beginning of the Triduum. They move from descriptions of the plight of those in need and in difficulty toward a recognition of God's response to the plight of the afflicted. Indeed, here, at the start of Psalm 116, the church sings, "I love the LORD, because he has heard my voice and my supplications" (v. 1). The celebrations of the Triduum, with its climax in the baptisms, make the connection between the life of Jesus and the life of the church as explicit as they will be at any time in the liturgical year. This shift in the psalm responses signals the closeness of God to those who celebrate the salvation won in the gift of the Son, Jesus Christ.

PSALM 78:14-20, 23-25 (BCP)

The psalm verses remind the assembly of God's presence and promises even in the midst of difficulty and despair. "He has heard my voice and my supplications" (116:1) is recalled in the Passion from Mark that was proclaimed on Passion Sunday, and in anticipation of the Passion from John to be proclaimed the very next day, Good Friday. The water image of Ps. 78:20—"He struck the rock so that water gushed out and torrents overflowed"—reminds us of our own baptism. The food image of v. 25—"Mortals ate of the bread of angels; he sent them food in abundance"—evokes the eucharistic emphasis of the Maundy Thursday liturgy, foreshadowing the gift of the bread and wine whose institution is recalled on this "night he was betrayed."

SECOND READING

1 CORINTHIANS 11:23-26 (RCL, RC);
1 CORINTHIANS 11:23-26, (27-32) (BCP)

MARTIN F.
CONNELL

Even though the four Gospels are given priority of place in the Bible because the tradition put them at the beginning of the New Testament, they are not chronologically in the first stratum of Christian literature. That chronological priority goes to the letters of Paul, written just a few decades after the death of Jesus, whom Paul never met. Among the most well known of Paul's letters is First Corinthians, which contains the earliest extant biblical account of the Last Supper before Jesus' death, the second reading of Holy Thursday.

AMONG THE MOST WELL KNOWN OF PAUL'S LETTERS IS FIRST CORINTHIANS, WHICH CONTAINS THE EARLIEST EXTANT BIBLICAL ACCOUNT OF THE LAST SUPPER BEFORE JESUS' DEATH, THE SECOND READING OF HOLY THURSDAY.

What is extraordinary about the account is the amount of detail here, for elsewhere in Paul's letters we learn little of the early life of Jesus. He was, by Paul's account, "born of a woman" (Gal. 4:4), but there is little historical detail about Jesus of Nazareth in Paul's writing between that brief mention of birth and the event recounted in this passage of the Last Supper. There are no miracles and few teachings of Jesus in Paul's letters, but there is a concentrated and deep theology of the death and resurrection of Jesus. And those events are preceded by this, Paul's account of the Last Supper, which took place "on the night he was betrayed." Though only a few sentences long, this narrative supplies more detail about Jesus' life than does any other portion of Paul's corpus, so we attend to it closely.

Paul wrote his first letter to the Corinthians in 53 or 54 C.E., and this segment about the supper begins with Paul's indication of this tradition: "I received from the Lord what I also handed on to you" (11:23). Our word *tradition* means a "handing on," and so here it would have been only twenty years or so since Jesus' death. That Paul establishes the "pedigree" of tradition "from the Lord" is significant. The apostle was handing on to the church at Corinth what the Lord had handed on to him. Because the church has included this letter in the canon of the Bible, we on Maundy Thursday act in the stead of the Lord and of Paul and, like them, hand on the tradition to the church today.

Hearing the reading proclaimed on Maundy Thursday is both wonderful and ominous: wonderful because the Lord is sharing a meal of bread and wine as he faces his own imminent death, and ominous because he expects us to do likewise, that is, share the eucharistic meal with our communities of faith even as we ourselves face reality day after day and finally at the end of our life. As Paul wrote: "For as often as you eat this bread and drink the cup, you proclaim the Lord's death until he comes" (11:26).

JOHN 13:1-17, 31b-35 (RCL);
JOHN 13:1-15 (BCP, RC)

Apart from the initiation significance in the rite of foot-washing as described in the liturgy of Maundy Thursday, one can find in this passage from the Gospel of John much that is fitting to this action, to participation in the Last Supper, and to the overall theology of the Three Days. As mentioned earlier, the *LBW* recommends that hymn 126, "Where Charity and Love Prevail," be sung during the foot-washing. In that hymn we hear:

Where charity and love prevail, there God is ever found;
Brought here together by Christ's love, by love we thus are bound.

With grateful joy and holy fear, God's charity we learn;
Let us with heart and mind and soul now love God in return.

Let us recall that in our midst dwells Christ, God's holy Son;
As members of each body joined, in him we are made one.

Let strife among us be unknown; let all contentions cease.
Be God's the glory that we seek; be his our only peace.

First, the hymn (vv. 1-4) ties the ritual action to the fruits of our baptism and incorporation into the body of Christ by that sacrament. Where love and charity are, there is God. Yet the life in love and charity does not exempt us from difficulties, for we still learn from love *and* fear, and we need to face the contentions and strife that inevitably visit our faith communities. In themselves fear and difficulty, contention and strife are not signs of God's absence, but the way these are faced squarely and bravely will reveal the presence of God in the faith of the assembly.

> IN THEMSELVES FEAR AND DIFFICULTY, CONTENTION AND STRIFE ARE NOT SIGNS OF GOD'S ABSENCE, BUT THE WAY THESE ARE FACED SQUARELY AND BRAVELY WILL REVEAL THE PRESENCE OF GOD IN THE FAITH OF THE ASSEMBLY.

The Three Days are an occasion for much joy, but they are also an occasion for facing the inevitable end of human life, suffering and death. In this we know what we share with Jesus Christ, our Savior and Teacher, whose holiness did not exempt even him from suffering and death. We are made one in the body of Christ, the church, so that we, following his example, might face the inevitable with nourishment from the Lord's Supper and consolation from the body of Christ we joined at baptism—and with which we reacquaint ourselves each time we celebrate the Lord's Supper, eating the body and drinking the blood of Christ "until he comes" (11:26).

LUKE 22:14-30 (BCP, alt.)

This account of the Last Supper in the Gospel of Luke is a complement to the second reading with its account of the same from First Corinthians. It surprises us to hear that, even at this late stage in Jesus' earthly life, the disciples are still disputing as to which one of them was the greatest. Having just shared in the body and blood of the Lord, the disciples still dispute.

As the church hears this reading, it might be puzzled that Jesus' closest followers would be engaged in dispute at this time before his death. But we can also be consoled as we think about the brokenness of the church over theological and disciplinary disputes through the centuries. And, lest we be left off the hook by considering only through the lens of history, we can hear this passage with our own local community of faith in mind. No church is exempt from or above the fray of disagreements and disputes; indeed, we might even be encouraged by knowing that this is constitutive of church life. The tough vocation of Christian life in community, however, is sitting at the table of discussion and at the table of the Lord's Supper and facing those with whom we have serious disagreements, so that—if not always agreement—charity and love prevail.

The second reading from 1 Corinthians recounts the Last Supper, but Paul wrote that account to the church in Corinth fully aware that the church there was filled with divisions and disagreements (see esp. 1 Cor. 1:10-13; the whole letter to the Corinthians captures major issues of division in this church of the first century). This passage from Luke with the disciples arguing about "who's the greatest" at the hour of Jesus' suffering and death is both hard to hear and a consolation when there are disputes in our own church, at the local and denominational levels.

We can also be consoled by knowing that Jesus reminds them that "I am among you as one who serves" (v. 27). Like the interpretation of the footwashing as a gesture of service, this passage reminded the disciples then and reminds us disciples now that service in the church and in the world is the fruit of our lives of faith.

GOOD FRIDAY

APRIL 18, 2003

REVISED COMMON	EPISCOPAL (BCP)	ROMAN CATHOLIC
Isa. 52:13—53:12	Isa. 52:13—53:12 or Gen. 22:1-18 or Wisd. of Sol. 2:1, 12-24	Isa. 52:13—53:12
Psalm 22	Ps. 22:1-21 or 22:1-11 or Ps. 40:1-14 or Ps. 69:1-23	Ps. 31:2, 6, 12-13, 15-16, 17, 25
Heb. 10:16-25 or 4:14-16; 5:7-9	Heb. 10:1-25	Heb. 4:14-16; 5:7-9
John 18:1—19:42	John (18:1-40), 19:1-37	John 18:1—19:42

In the introduction to Holy Week (pages 197–203), we considered the ecumenical exchanges that have taken place between Protestant and Catholic churches during the reforms of worship in the past few decades. All Catholic churches have benefited immeasurably from the centuries of Protestant biblical scholarship and preaching, and many Protestant churches are much richer for the fruit borne by Catholic liturgical traditions of the lectionary and the liturgical year. The issue of Catholic influence on Protestant worship is quite concentrated in the liturgical complexities of the services of Holy Week, but the "rubber meets the road" particularly in the liturgical element of the veneration of the cross during the rite of Good Friday.

The ritual gesture of veneration can make many Christians uncomfortable when it is introduced without much catechesis or ritual practice. A church whose liturgy committee decides that it will introduce this ritual gesture into the Good Friday service must plan well in advance so that the community is prepared for what will happen and what it means.

Key for the catechesis is how the salvation of the members of the church was won by the cross of Christ and, because of that victory, they as members of the church by baptism are today the body of Christ. The veneration is not only a ritual gesture to recall the suffering of Jesus (though this is an essential part of

> THE CROSS IS CARRIED TO REFLECT THE SIMULTANEITY OF THE CHURCH'S REMEMBRANCE OF THE PASSION OF JESUS AND ITS MINDFULNESS OF GOD'S INTIMACY WITH SUFFERING IN THE CHURCH AND THE WORLD.

the experience), but it is also a call to make the church more able to recognize the suffering body of Christ in the assembly and in the world in which the church ministers and gives witness. The cross without the image of Jesus' body is a symbolic expression of this, for the body of Christ is the assembly at prayer. The cross is carried to reflect the simultaneity of the church's remembrance of the passion of Jesus and its mindfulness of God's intimacy with the suffering in the church and the world.

The *Manual on the Liturgy: Lutheran Book of Worship* (Minneapolis: Augsburg, 1979) instructs the church about how the veneration might be executed:

> A large, rough-hewn wooden cross should be provided for use. . . . The cross may be placed in front of the altar before the service begins; tall, lighted candles may be placed on stands on either side of the cross. The cross may rest against the top of the altar or against the communion rail or it may be placed upright in a stand. It is more effective, however, showing more clearly the divisions of the service, if the cross is carried in procession, following the Bidding Prayer. The cross may be kept in the narthex or sacristy or other convenient place. The presiding minister carries the cross into the church; the cross may be accompanied by two torchbearers. The verse and response is sung (to one of the psalm tones) or said as the procession begins; it is repeated as the procession is halfway to the altar; it is repeated again as the procession reaches the altar. . . .
>
> If there is no procession, the verses are simply sung or said in sequence.
>
> The adoration of the crucified . . . is not unlike the homage paid to a sovereign at a coronation. The cross is a throne, and the people show allegiance to Christ and his rule as they kneel before the sign of salvation.
>
> Silence is kept for meditation on the mystery of the crucified Savior, the mystery of redemption. The congregation may come forward to bow before the cross, to touch it, or to kiss it as a further sign of devotion.

Because for most Christians this is so different from any other church ritual behavior of the liturgical year, the introduction of the rite requires pastoral attention and care, yet it is well worth the time and attention. The readings, as below, surely support the theological wedding of the life, suffering, and death of Jesus to the lives, sufferings, and deaths of the members of the congregation. In fact, without that connection made vibrant for the faithful, the veneration of the cross can veer toward the medieval "Passion play," which was not as much a worship service as a dramatic reenactment.

ISAIAH 52:13—53:12

The portrait that we take from this proclamation fits into the Triduum's juxtaposition of the suffering of the servant at the hands of humanity and God's vindication of him. We hear both that "he was despised and rejected," "a man of suffering and acquainted with infirmity" (53:3), and that "my servant shall prosper; he shall be exalted and lifted up, and shall be very high" (52:13). The tradition of the suffering servant from the Hebrew scriptures was adopted into the religious tradition in which Jesus and his followers were formed and was even part of the theology that contributed to the early church's understanding of the suffering and death of Jesus himself. It is a wonderful theology adopted by Christianity from the Hebrew tradition, and today's proclamation is incomparably constitutive of the tradition about Jesus Christ and about the efficacy of the cross for salvation.

SECOND READING

HEBREWS 4:14-16; 5:7-9 (RCL, alt.; RC)

The complex rhetoric and vocabulary of the Letter to the Hebrews makes this a hard book of the Bible to read and hear, but there are some really important ways in which it can shape our life of faith and spirituality. This passage, in particular, corrects the omnipresent Christian tendency to distance our lives today from the life and experience of Jesus two millennia ago.

Referring to Jesus Christ, the author of the Letter to the Hebrews states so clearly, "We do not have a high priest who is unable to sympathize with our weaknesses, but we have one who in every respect has been tested as we are, yet without sin" (4:15). Though the effect of sin in Christian life is of no mean consequence, the reflection of this writer brings the life of Jesus much closer to us than most of us usually imagine it to have been. In preaching it is difficult to take the foreign and elaborate vocabulary and rhetoric of Hebrews

THAT CHRIST IS ONE WHO SYMPATHIZES WITH OUR WEAKNESSES AND IS LIKE US IN ALL THINGS BUT SIN IS A THEOLOGICAL CORE THAT EVER NEEDS TO BE PROCLAIMED AND PREACHED, ON THIS DAY ESPECIALLY BUT AT ANY TIME OF THE CHURCH YEAR.

and make it accessible and appreciable for the congregants, but at this time in the liturgical year, on this day when the death of Jesus and the gravity of this sacrifice for human existence is remembered and marked, the time spent in explaining the relevance of the theology of Hebrews is well worth the effort. That Christ is one who sympathizes with our weaknesses and is like us in all things but sin is a theological core that ever needs to be proclaimed and preached, on this day especially but at any time of the church year.

Moreover, the point that Christ, the high priest, "learned obedience through what he suffered" and was thus "made perfect" (5:8, 9) is also important, because there is an inclination in pastoral life to think of sickness, suffering, and social ostracism as signs of failure. Jesus explicitly excludes this interpretation of sickness in the Gospel of John when, in the narrative of the man born blind, his adversaries asked about the source of the man's ailment: " 'Rabbi, who sinned, this man or his parents, that he was born blind?' Jesus answered, 'Neither this man nor his parents sinned; he was born blind so that God's works might be revealed in him' " (9:2-3).

Christians, indeed all people, are chastened and challenged by sickness and suffering. Faith holds up a theology by which we can face suffering squarely and, like Christ, learn through what we suffer rather than be crushed by self-doubts about whether something we did occasioned God's wrath and punishment. Good Friday is a day of the liturgical year when such complexities are close to our thoughts and hearts, and the readings prompt us not to sugar-coat such perplexities but to see them in the light of the scriptural and theological interpretations offered by the church and its preachers.

THE GOSPEL
JOHN 18:1—19:42 (RCL, RC);
JOHN (18:1-40), 19:1-37 (BCP)

A believer coming to worship on Good Friday might wonder at hearing yet another long proclamation of the Passion only five days after having heard another Passion narrative. Why does the liturgical tradition repeat the Passion story twice in the same week when it does not do this at any other time in the liturgical year?

There is a three-year cycle for the Passion reading on Passion Sunday. This year the reading was from the Gospel of Mark, letting us know that on Passion Sunday last year it had been from Matthew and that next year it will be from Luke. But the Good Friday Passion reading is the same year after year, coming from the non-Synoptic Gospel, John. So why is the Passion of the evangelist John heard in the liturgy three times more often than any of the others.

First, what is the difference between the synoptic Passion accounts and that in John? The word *synoptic* is used to describe the first three Gospels as a group, and it means "to see" *(-optic)* something together *(syn-)*, or similarly. The portraits of Jesus in the Gospels of Matthew, Mark, and Luke, though not identical, are, when juxtaposed to the Gospel of John, much more alike than different. So they are called synoptic more to emphasize the singularity of the Gospel of John than to highlight their own similarities with one another.

John's portrait of Jesus is theologically higher than that of the Synoptic Gospels; scripture scholars call the theology of John a "high Christology." Indeed, its theological lofty portrait of Jesus is more exalted. Even in the Passion account proclaimed on Good Friday, there are moments in which there is an irony in the simultaneity of portraying a man being killed for violating the law and a man exalted and raised up as the Son of God. This irony is especially apparent in the Passion narrative antecedent to Jesus' death.

The high Christology of this Gospel is readily revealed at the start of the Passion, where the evangelist reveals that Jesus "knew all that was to happen to him," an omniscience of Jesus in this Gospel that is not characteristic of him in the Synoptics.

Next, the Gospel of John is unique for the number of statements that Jesus begins with the phrase, "I AM." Hearers and readers of this Gospel would be familiar with many of these: "I am the bread of life" (6:35), "I am the light of the world" (8:12; 9:5), "I am the gate for the sheep" (10:7), "I am the good shepherd" (10:11), "I am the resurrection and the life" (11:25), "I am the way, and the truth, and the life" (14:6), and "I am the vine, you are the branches" (15:5). These place the Christology of the Gospel in high relief. At the beginning of the Passion account, the soldiers approach Jesus, and he asks them, "Whom are you looking for?" They respond, "Jesus of Nazareth," and Jesus answers them, "I am he" (18:3-6a). Then the evangelist supplies a detail that is not included in any of the other Gospels, one that is quite revealing about the theology of this Gospel: "When Jesus said to them, 'I am he,' they stepped back and fell to the ground" (18:6b). If this story were not itself so sorrowful and ominous, this juxtaposition or irony would be almost humorous, for the soldiers, the very ones who come to take Jesus away to kill him, are worshiping him. They bow down and fall to the ground when he says, "I am he."

Because John's Gospel has Jesus expressing all of the "I am" statements before this point, one can think of the "I am" at the scene of his betrayal and arrest as a summary of all the others, in the face of which the soldiers are in adoring awe. Without a predicate—good shepherd or true vine or bread of life, etc.—this "I am" wraps all those together, and the summary forces even the soldier-enemies to worship him, the Son of God. The result is a Christology so high that even the soon-to-be-murderous antagonists bow down before him.

Next, although there are not many similarities between the Gospel of John and the other Gospels, Peter's threefold denial of being a follower is one of the few stories in all four Gospels. Yet the Fourth Gospel puts a unique ending to this denial that rehabilitates the portrait of Peter in a way that the other Gospels do not. In the very last chapter of John's Gospel, we find a threefold profession of love of the risen Jesus on the lips of Peter, a counter to his threefold denial. Peter tells Jesus twice, "You know that I love you," and then a third time, in exasperation, and you can almost picture him slamming his foot against the ground as he says, "Lord, you know everything; you know that I love you" (21:15, 16, 17). This is a rhetorical device, of course, to leave the last image of Peter in the Gospels as one that casts him into Christian posterity with a more positive portrait than that in which he is left in the synoptic traditions.

Next, we find an exchange between Jesus and Pontius Pilate himself, and oddly enough, their words dwell on the meaning of "king." As in the exchange between the soldiers and Jesus, there is an irony in hearing this bout between the ruler with all the power and the accused criminal with absolutely no power at all. Pilate, a king himself in the temporal realm, turns to Jesus, powerless in the temporal realm yet supreme in the eternal, for a deep understanding of the meaning of "king."

Last, why is this unique Christology in the Passion according to John the one that it is singled out for proclamation on Good Friday? In the introduction to the liturgy of Holy Thursday, we saw that these days from Thursday evening to Easter Sunday are more aptly considered one liturgy over three days rather than individual liturgies. With that concatenation in mind, we might appreciate the church's placement of the Passion according to John within the Three Days, for the juxtaposition of death and resurrection in the narrative of Jesus Christ ennobles death and prompts us to see it not as punishment, not as the result of sin, but as the sobering end of all human life, including that of Jesus himself.

Jesus' death is recorded in 19:30, but the Passion proclamation continues for another few paragraphs. From our perspective two millennia later, we might consider the possible symbolism in how Jesus' dead body is treated and the bearing this might have on our worship today.

Because we do not know exactly when or even how the communities of the New Testament initiated members into their communities, we need to be a little cautious in attributing liturgical meaning to biblical vocabulary. Nevertheless, here at the end of the Passion in the Gospel of John we find a number of potential baptismal symbols. The reason why such an interpretation might be warranted is that the Gospels were not written contemporaneously with the events they describe. So when the Gospel speaks of the "body" of Jesus, as in this Passion account, it has a two-layer meaning reflecting what was happening to the body of the historical Jesus as well as what was happening to the body of Christ in the church when the narrative of the Gospel was being written. (See Paul's theology of the body, 1 Cor. 12:12-31, in particular, as a warrant for this ecclesiological interpretation of the "body" of Jesus in the Gospels.)

In this Passion account, when we hear that "one of the soldiers pierced his side with a spear, and at once blood and water came out" (19:34), we cannot be absolutely sure that the "water" here is a symbol for the waters of initiation, but it is a possibility. This is further highlighted when we hear that the body of Jesus was wrapped in linen cloths. In many churches today the baptized are clothed in white linen when they "are baptized into his death," and they rise from the waters with their bodies, like the body of Jesus in this Gospel, wrapped in linen cloths.

So what, then, might this Passion narrative reveal to us today? It is true of human life that we often learn most from the predicaments and intricacies of life that we may try to avoid. While we do not seek out trouble or complexity or vulnerability, we often find that it is at such times and in such situations that the presence of God is found and is most comforting. The mystery and paradox of the cross, as a historical reality in the life of Jesus and as a symbol in the tradition, are that there are power and life in vulnerability and death. It is important, however, to distinguish the inevitability of being hurt and of dying from seeking these out when they might be avoided. The former is powerful, the latter simply crazy. The ritual gesture of the veneration of the cross unites our lives of faith today, as the suffering and rising body of Christ, with the life of the historical Jesus of Nazareth.

> THE MYSTERY AND PARADOX OF THE CROSS, AS A HISTORICAL REALITY IN THE LIFE OF JESUS AND AS A SYMBOL IN THE TRADITION, ARE THAT THERE ARE POWER AND LIFE IN VULNERABILITY AND DEATH.

THE GREAT VIGIL OF
EASTER / HOLY SATURDAY

REVISED COMMON
First Reading: Gen. 1:1—2:4a
    Response: Ps. 136:1-9, 23-36
Second Reading: Gen. 7:1-5, 11-18; 8:6-18; 9:8-13
    Response: Psalm 46
Third Reading: Gen. 22:1-18
    Response: Psalm 16
Fourth Reading: Exod. 14:10-31; 15:20-21
    Response: Exod. 15:1b-13, 17-18
Fifth Reading: Isa. 55:1-11
    Response: Isa. 12:2-6
Sixth Reading: Prov. 8:1-8, 19-21; 9:4b-6 or Bar. 3:9-15, 32—4:4
    Response: Psalm 19
Seventh Reading: Ezek. 36:24-28
    Response: Psalm 42 and Psalm 43
Eighth Reading: Ezek. 37:1-14
    Response: Psalm 143
Ninth Reading: Zeph. 3:14-20
    Response: Psalm 98
Tenth Reading: Jon. 3:1-10
    Response: Jon. 2:1-3, (4-6), 7-9
Eleventh Reading: Deut. 31:19-30
    Response: Deut. 32:1-4, 7, 36a, 43a
Twelfth Reading: Dan. 3:1-29
    Response: Song of the Three Young Men 36-65

Rom. 6:3-11
    Response: Psalm 114
Mark 16:1-8

EPISCOPAL (BCP)
Gen. 1:1—2:2

Ps. 33:1-11 or 36:5-10
Gen. 7:1-5, 11-18; 8:8-18; 9:8-13
    Psalm 46
Gen. 22:1-18
    Ps. 33:12-22 or Psalm 16
Exod. 14:10—15:1
    Canticle 8
Isa. 4:2-6
    Psalm 122
Isa. 55:1-11
    Canticle 9 or Ps. 42:1-7
Ezek. 36:24-28
    Ps. 42:1-7 or Canticle 9
Ezek. 37:1-14
    Psalm 30 or Psalm 143
Zeph. 3:12-20
    Psalm 98 or Psalm 126

Rom. 6:3-11
    Psalm 114
Matt. 28:1-10

Roman Catholic
Gen. 1:1—2:2 or 1:1, 26-31a
    Ps. 104:1-2, 5-6, 10, 12, 13-14, 24, 35 or Ps. 33:4-5, 6-7, 12-13, 20-22
Gen. 22:1-18 or 22:1-2, 9a, 10-13, 15-18
    Ps. 16:5, 8, 9-10, 11
Exod. 14:15—15:1
    Exod. 15:1-2, 3-4, 5-6, 17-18
Isa. 54:5-14
    Ps. 30:2, 4, 5-6, 11-12, 13
Isa. 55:1-11
    Isa. 12:2-3, 4, 5-6
Bar. 3:9-15, 32—4:4
    Ps. 19:8, 9, 10, 11
Ezek. 36:16-17a, 18-28
    Pss. 42:3, 5; 43:3, 4 or Isa. 12:2-3, 4bcd, 5-6 or Ps. 51:12-13, 14-15, 18-19

Rom. 6:3-11
    Ps. 118:1-2, 16-17, 22-23
Mark 16:1-7

Though not all churches follow the ritual suggestion of the *LBW,* the service book for the Easter Vigil begins with a Service of Light: "The congregation gathers, preferably in a place other than the interior of the church itself. A large fire may have been prepared" (*LBW,* 143). It is a striking recommendation for the liturgy, usually so predictable and tame. What could the church intend in suggesting that this peak of the year begin with a fire? An answer is provided in the first reading of the vigil.

As baptism is the time when an individual leaves behind the world of the past and moves to new life in Christ, so is the Easter Vigil a time when the local community similarly leaves the past behind and is reborn in the faith. The fire and the candles lit from the fire, for a procession into the dark space of the church about to be reborn, are symbols of Christ, who was like a fire destroying the old creation and giving birth to the new. Communities of faith, like each of us as individuals, have lives, and some of the decisions and experiences of the community are later found to be not of God. People in the church have been hurt and ignored resources have not been used with wisdom, or any of myriad other ways in which the church, like each of us, has not lived up to its vocation.

> AS BAPTISM IS THE TIME WHEN AN INDIVIDUAL LEAVES BEHIND THE WORLD OF THE PAST AND MOVES TO NEW LIFE IN CHRIST, SO IS THE EASTER VIGIL A TIME WHEN THE LOCAL COMMUNITY SIMILARLY LEAVES THE PAST BEHIND AND IS REBORN IN THE FAITH.

The instinct of the church at the Easter Vigil is that this is a time for leaving the past behind and for being reminded of the core of our vocation. The old ways have passed; the life of faith renews us and gives us another chance, a new liturgical year for the realization of the kingdom of God in our midst. The fire at the start of the vigil is a preparation for the proclamation of the first reading about God's creating the world in seven days. The vigil gives each church and its pastor an opportunity to cast the old ways on the pyre, with the responsibility to learn from the mistakes and be strong in the face of trouble in the future.

FIRST READING
GENESIS 1:1—2:4a (RCL)

This first account of the creation of the world does not follow a destruction of the world. Yet the conflagration at the start of the vigil suggests the destruction of the old such that this account of the order of creation, of making the world from chaos, follows a time of reckoning. Indeed, as we hear that "the earth was a formless void and darkness covered the face of the deep" and see the remnants of the Easter fire (the ashes and charred fragments) after the vigil, we might understand the latter as a sign of this dark and formless void.

This would speak deeply to individuals in the assembly whose lives, between last Easter and this, have been difficult and challenging, and it might also speak to the assembly as a whole if the year as a church has not been without difficulties and disagreements.

The patterned rhetoric of the account—"there was evening and there was morning, the first day" (1:5), "there was evening and there was morning, the second day" (1:8), etc.—is best proclaimed by a patterned recitation. Things are being ordered by God to help humanity again find its place in the order of created things.

The creation of male and female, the familiar second creation story (2:4b—3:24), has the woman subordinate to the man, her mate. In fact, her very creation is derived physically from the man, for the Lord takes a rib from the male and with it brings forth the woman. Juxtaposed to this is the first creation account (1:1—2:4a), proclaimed at the vigil, in which the male and female are created at the same time: "So God created humankind in his image, in the image of God he created them; male and female he created them" (1:27). For better or worse, these two versions of the relationship of male and female have stayed vibrant in the tradition, and individual churches and traditions have had to reckon how this mixed message would be interpreted in their church life.

In the first creation account, creation is made in order and harmony, and when it is finished, we read, "God saw everything that he had made, and indeed, it was very good" (1:31). With this as our theology of creation and with the first reading proclaimed as the church is reborn at the vigil, we as Christians should work hard to keep the preservation of and care for the world as a priority in our values and lives of faith.

Fourth Reading
EXODUS 14:10-31; 15:20-21 (RCL)

We noted in the commentary for Maundy Thursday that the earliest narrative from the book of Exodus to have been read at the Easter Vigil was the immolation of the Passover lamb (chap. 12). This reading was used at the vigil in the centuries before the span of the Three Days—Holy Thursday, Good Friday, Holy Saturday—was introduced into the liturgical tradition. Once Easter evolved in the fourth century from just the vigil to the three-day span, the reading about the immolation of the lamb was affixed to the Holy Thursday liturgy—likely because the Passover meal was for many early church leaders a typology from which they developed preaching on the Last Supper. When Exodus 12 was taken from the Easter Vigil, the reading that was introduced into the Christian tradition was Exodus 14, the narrative of the Israelites crossing the Red Sea. This has been a deep narrative in paschal theology since the fourth century.

The primary connection between the narrative of Exodus and the Easter Vigil is the water, *lots* of water, the entire Red Sea, through which the Israelites walked "dry shod," as it used to be translated, that is, without getting their feet muddy, an engaging image. The water common to the reading and to the sacrament of baptism is the material link, but there are also the history of Israel and the key role of the Red Sea narrative in Israel's tradition. In this reading the people of Israel are reconstituted as the people of God; they are reminded of their vocation and of their election as God's chosen.

Ecclesially, this is a wonderful image for the church at the Easter Vigil and through the Fifty Days of the Easter season. As was Israel in the exodus, so the church is in the celebration of baptism renewed and reborn in the experience of initiating new members. Since many in the church were baptized as infants and today have no memory of the time when they were brought into the body by the sacrament of baptism, the celebration of baptism at the vigil is the ritual way that they can consciously experience the gift of grace and new life that comes from the rite. The preacher at the vigil would do well to highlight the connection between the exodus and the baptism so that those who are about to be baptized and those already baptized can appreciate the gift of grace and community wrought in this rite.

> AS WAS ISRAEL IN THE EXODUS, SO THE CHURCH IS IN THE CELEBRATION OF BAPTISM RENEWED AND REBORN IN THE EXPERIENCE OF INITIATING NEW MEMBERS.

RESPONSIVE READING
EXODUS 15:1b-13, 17-18 (RCL)

In some vigils this response is done as a response incorporated into the proclamation of the narrative. If this is so, Exod. 15:20 can follow 14:31, so that the transition from reader to community response is seamless. The verses would then be proclaimed in this order: 14:31, 15:20, 15:1, and then the canticle. The end of the cutting and pasting would read as follows: "Israel saw the great work that the LORD did against the Egyptians. So the people feared the LORD and believed in the LORD and in his servant Moses" (14:31). "Then the prophet Miriam, Aaron's sister, took a tambourine in her hand; and all the women went out after her with tambourines and with dancing" (15:20). "Then Moses and the Israelites sang this song to the LORD" (15:1a). This ends the reader's proclamation, and the assembly then participates in song with the other part of the verse (Exod. 15:1b): "I will sing to the LORD, for he has triumphed gloriously . . ." and what follows in the canticle. Done well, this is a great liturgical experience to complement the deep imagery of water in the Christian tradition for Easter.

ISAIAH 55:1-11 (RCL, BCP, RC)

This solicitation to all to come to the waters does not advance the story of Israel as have the four readings so far in the vigil: the creation account, Noah and the flood, the sacrifice of Isaac, and the exodus from Egypt. So why—in this kind of "greatest hits" survey of readings presenting the history of Israel—does this reading appear?

First, one of the key images of this beautiful passage from Isaiah is the water. "Come to the water," the prophet solicits, and the image is empowered by the connections the prophet makes with nature and its fruits: "For as the rain and the snow come down from heaven, and do not return there until they have watered the earth, making it bring forth and sprout, giving seed to the sower and bread to the eater, so shall my word be" (vv. 10-11). The poetic specificity of the prophet's description can make the readers and hearers of this passage feel the water on themselves, mnemonically transporting them to the life-restoring water of their own initiations. This water would be the ordinary water of bathings, cleansings, plantings, and growings, and also the extraordinary water of our own baptism. Most of us don't remember our baptism, yet our unconscious participation made it no less efficacious. We were and are saved by God's goodness and God's grace day after day, even when we may not be aware of these. God is steadfast in love and in life, and this is not conditional on our solicitation or works. These waters of Isaiah remind us of our entrance into God's life at baptism and our deepening in that life, whether we are mindful of this or not.

Second, the call of Isaiah to the water is open to all. This passage is a social leveler, for the prophet emphasizes that the gift of God is without cost: "Everyone who thirsts, come!" You don't have money? Still come, buy without money, and eat as much as you want. No prices, and you can still buy wine and milk. Like the waters of baptism, available to all who approach, so is God's love: Come without money, without price!

The prophet could well be speaking to us in our own day, for the lures of the world around us are indeed distracting. He asks, "Why do you spend your money for that which is not bread?" Clearly, the prophet had witnessed the lure of things and values that were not of God, and he calls the people to discernment so that they will recognize the real thing when they find it. "Why spend your labor for that which does not satisfy?" In contrast, Isaiah speaks to us of the vigilance needed to recognize when God comes.

There is a tension here in discerning where God will be found. On the one hand, the prophet commands, "Call upon [the LORD] while he is near," yet, on the other hand, the Lord says, "My ways are higher than your ways and my thoughts than your thoughts" (vv. 6, 9). One might wonder, then, what the truth is: Is God nearby or far away? The ways of God are not of this world; this we know. But we can be sure of God's presence in the lives of those baptized and, most particularly at Easter, in the wedding of those whose baptisms are celebrated in the vigil and the community whose faith and witness has attracted them to make this commitment.

The waters of baptism have an effect on the church similar to that of water on fields and gardens. They encourage new life and growth. We see plants languishing from no water and witness their revival when the rain (or garden hose) arrives. This is an apt parallel to baptism in the church. The rite of initiation is not simply something done for those being baptized; as important as that is, revitalization and growth and inspiration come to the whole community of faith, locally and universally, from the witness of those who are reborn in the waters of baptism.

> THE WATERS OF BAPTISM HAVE AN EFFECT ON THE CHURCH SIMILAR TO THAT OF WATER ON FIELDS AND GARDENS. THEY ENCOURAGE NEW LIFE AND GROWTH.

SEVENTH READING
EZEKIEL 36:24-28 (RCL, BCP)

Christian life and faith are experiences not of individuals alone, but of a community. The history of Israel with its ups and downs demonstrates again and again how central was the identity of the nation, the people, the community of Jewish faith. The "people" of Israel were, to borrow a word from this passage, a "body" (see 1 Cor. 12:12-26). This is a brilliant metaphor for teaching about the community of faith, because each of us knows what having a body is like and how attentive we must be to it to keep ourselves healthy.

In Ezekiel's prophecy, the community is renewed by "clean water." The image of the water sprinkled to renew the nation Israel can be an inspiration for communities of faith in the celebration of baptism. The water is connected to receiving "a new heart." So, in parallel, is the effect of the initiation of new members into the church. Such initiations enliven Christian faith, taking hearts weary of life, "hearts of stone," and reminding them of the gift of baptism, when we were and are given "hearts of flesh," living hearts, beating hearts of feeling, compassion, and love.

TENTH READING
JONAH 3:1-10 (RCL)

The story of Jonah and the big fish has an eerie wonder about it. The whole story has few words—two or three pages in most Bibles—yet has had a profound effect on many lives of faith through the centuries. Pictures of Jonah coming forth from the mouth of the "big fish" (the story never identifies it as a whale) abound through history, confirming the deep place the narrative has had in the marginalizations of communities of faith and of individual believers.

The association of this passage with the vigil is clear from a few elements. A simple narrative fact is that "Jonah was in the belly of the fish three days and three nights" (1:17), a ready link to the span of the three days between the death of Jesus on Friday and his rising from the dead on Sunday, according to the Gospel narratives, as well as a link to the Three Days we mark from Holy Thursday to Easter Sunday.

More relevant for the experience and theology of baptism, of course, is the sea into which Jonah is cast in the story just before the vigil's reading. The verse before the vigil reading begins reveals that "the LORD spoke to the fish, and it spewed Jonah out upon the dry land" (2:10).

ROMANS 6:3-11 (RCL, BCP, RC)

The experience of adult initiation in our churches at the Easter Vigil brings this wonderful passage from Paul to life quite literally. The passage was prescribed for the Easter Vigil for centuries after initiation had been separated from the vigil. It is remarkable that the reading from Paul had such staying power; the instinct of faith maintained the initiation meaning of Easter even when the action itself of being plunged into the waters was no longer observed.

By God's grace, the gift of baptism weds us individuals into a community. Paul's declarations are in the first person—not the first-person singular, "I," but the first-person plural, "we": "we were baptized into his death" (v. 3); "we have been buried with him" (v. 4); "we walk in newness of life" (v. 4); and "we will be united with him in a resurrection like his" (v. 5). Baptism is a celebration of the community and of the church; as we witness the Easter baptisms, it might feel like we are passive spectators of what is being done to an individual, but the building up of the body of Christ, the fruit of the initiation ceremonies, is a cause célèbre by the whole church, local and universal.

Paul's inquiries and declarations highlight the drama of baptism in the early church. This ceremony has less of a transforming influence on those baptized and those witnessing when the quantity of water used is only a few drops. The depth of this reading is experienced more profoundly when the baptismal font is closer to death, burial, and resurrection—being dunked into the water, submersion, and coming up out of the water—as described in Paul's letter. Going from a minimal font to an immersion pool in a church building—if possible according to the space and design of the church—is not done without great expense, much debate, and long-term catechesis. But the testimony of believers in churches in which the change has happened is itself enough for a community to see the fruits. In the early church, as known from readings such as this from Paul and from the synoptic descriptions of the baptism of Jesus in the Jordan River, initiation was a total body experience to complement the total change of life in the person baptized and in the church.

RESPONSIVE READING
PSALM 114 (RCL, BCP)

The psalm connects the passage of the Israelites through the Red Sea with the sacrament of baptism celebrated at the vigil. The Jordan River is mentioned, a link, symbolically and geographically, between that river of the land of Israel, the baptism of Jesus in the Synoptic Gospels (Matt. 3:13-17; Mark 1:9-11; Luke 3:21-22), and the initiations celebrated at the vigil. However grand or simple, however prolonged or brief the baptisms in your church will be at the Easter Vigil, this psalm gives a precedent for their importance, for it commands the world:

> Tremble, O earth, at the presence of the LORD,
>   at the presence of the God of Jacob,
> who turns the rock into a pool of water,
>   the flint into a spring of water. (114:7-8)

The church employs this imagery both for the water image included in the psalm and for the cosmic ramifications of the rite of initiation into the Christian faith.

PSALM 118:1-2, 16-17, 22-23 (RC)

This psalm is in the order of the vigil only in the Roman Catholic lectionary, but for Catholic churches its theology is important for the feast and for the Easter season to follow for the Fifty Days. The metaphor of "the stone that the builders rejected" becoming "the chief cornerstone" (v. 22) has been a key image for understanding the paschal mystery—the juxtaposition of abasement and glory, death and resurrection in the preaching tradition and in the experience of the faith at the key moment: before the woman came to the empty tomb and discovered that the body of Jesus was not there, and before proclamation of the resurrection.

MARK 16:1-8 (RCL); MARK 16:1-7 (RC)

Perhaps your Bible, like many, notes that the original ending of the Gospel of Mark was at 16:8. So this last reading for the Easter Vigil liturgy of the Word is the finale of the Gospel of Mark's testimony about Jesus Christ, the Son of God (see 1:1). Let us first attend to the time frame: "very early on the first day of the week, when the sun had risen" (16:2). This first day of the week was Sunday, and so the narrative of the empty tomb, the recognition of the missing body of Jesus of Nazareth, took place on the same day of the week as our weekly celebration of the Lord's Supper two millennia later. As then, so now do we come together in faith to be marked by the word and sacraments celebrated through the ages. The protagonists in the visit to the tomb were Mary Magdalene, whom tradition has called the "apostle to the apostles," for the role she plays in the vigil's Gospel, and the other women, Mary the mother of James, and Salome.

I do not exaggerate in writing that I could think of no biblical passage that would be more fitting for proclamation and preaching before the initiations at the Easter Vigil than this passage in the Gospel of Mark. After the women who come to the tomb to anoint the dead body of Jesus, the key character in the account is one met in the scriptures a week ago (Passion Sunday), the young guy without a name, the *neaniskos,* though here he is described as "dressed in a white robe, sitting on the right side" (16:5). (Note that though he does not have a name from the evangelist, we do receive details of what he wears and what he was wearing before stripped; see commentary for the Gospel on Passion Sunday.)

Although anonymous, the young man would not be unfamiliar to those in the community out of which the Gospel of Mark sprang, for the young man appeared before the account of Jesus' death in Mark's Gospel, in a short passage that remains somewhat inscrutable centuries later. A week ago we heard about the scene in which Judas handed Jesus over, and then: "A certain young man was following him, wearing nothing but a linen cloth. They caught hold of him, but he left the linen cloth and ran off naked" (14:51-52).

> I DO NOT EXAGGERATE IN WRITING THAT I COULD THINK OF NO BIBLICAL PASSAGE THAT WOULD BE MORE FITTING FOR PROCLAMATION AND PREACHING BEFORE THE INITIATIONS AT THE EASTER VIGIL THAN THIS PASSAGE IN THE GOSPEL OF MARK.

We Christians no longer baptize naked people; we are more inclined to keep them clothed in some liturgical garment even as they are about to enter baptism, the source of their new life. But if in the first century the baptized entered the font (or river) naked and were wrapped in a robe as a signal of the new life, then this "young man" (neophyte) is an example of the courage and conviction of the faith of the baptized, especially in these days when the ancient model of initiation is being reintroduced to churches in the United States.

It is hard to know the reason why the author of the Gospel of Mark would have left this young man nameless, but perhaps it was so that he might represent the baptized people to come into the church later, perhaps even embracing symbolically the persons who in your particular church became members at the liturgy. In this way the young man would not be primarily a historical figure in the Gospel story, but a model for the life of those whose faith has led them to the church and to full incorporation into it. That the young man, after the betrayal of Jesus by Judas, fled the scene is an important detail, for he is an example of the complexities, doubts, and fears that might be experienced by those entering the process of the catechumenate and the rites of initiation.

No matter, really, who this young man was, why he appears in only a few verses, or even how he came to have such a small yet important role in the Gospel of Mark. He embraces the theology of baptism that incorporated us into the body of Christ at our baptism and that day after day calls people forth in the service of the church. For this year's celebration of Holy Week, the young man—the *neaniskos* as a character of Mark, the Gospel throughout this Year B—forms a kind of bracket around this key span of the church year, Holy Week. He was part of the narrative of Jesus' suffering at the beginning of the week, on Passion Sunday, and his proclamation at the Easter Vigil, "Jesus of Nazareth has been raised; he is not here" (Mark 16:6), greets the church at the beginning of the Fifty Days of the Easter season.

Also worth mentioning about the Gospel of the vigil is the final posture of the believers at the tomb in the original ending of Mark (16:8). Even after hearing from the young man that Jesus had been raised, the women and the disciples were seized with fear and amazement. This is perplexing to us today, perhaps, because we imagine that those earliest believers, as eyewitnesses, would have been convinced beyond all doubt. Yet, much like ourselves at times, the faith called them to convictions and changes of life and living that left them frightened and insecure, even in those early days of Christian faith and fervor. Initiation into a community of faith and into Christian life at baptism does not erase all doubt and fear; rather, it gives us a stronghold to bear us up and carry us through in difficult times, now as then. For, in spite of the trouble, the church survived, and our faith is not in vain. As they and the *neaniskos* proclaimed, so we continue to proclaim the life, death, and resurrection of Christ in our homes, in our churches, and throughout the world.

DECEMBER 2002

Sunday	Monday	Tuesday	Wednesday	Thursday	Friday	Saturday
1 1 Advent	2	3	4	5	6	7
8 2 Advent	9	10	11	12	13	14
15 3 Advent	16	17	18	19	20	21
22 4 Advent	23	24 Christmas Eve	25 Christmas Day	26 Boxing Day (Canada)	27	28
29 Christmas 1 / Holy Family	30	31 New Year's Eve				

JANUARY 2003

Sunday	Monday	Tuesday	Wednesday	Thursday	Friday	Saturday
			1 Name of Jesus New Year's Day	2	3	4
5 Epiphany	6	7	8	9	10	11
12 1 Epiphany	13	14	15	16	17	18
19 2 Epiphany	20	21	22	23	24	25
26 3 Epiphany	27	28	29	30	31	

FEBRUARY 2003

Sunday	Monday	Tuesday	Wednesday	Thursday	Friday	Saturday
						1
2	3	4	5	6	7	8
4 Epiphany Presentation of Our Lord						
9	10	11	12	13	14	15
5 Epiphany						
16	17	18	19	20	21	22
6 Epiphany						
23	24	25	26	27	28	
7 Epiphany						

MARCH 2003

Sunday	Monday	Tuesday	Wednesday	Thursday	Friday	Saturday
						1
2 8 Epiphany Presentation of Our Lord	3	4	5 Ash Wednesday	6	7	8
9 1 Lent	10	11	12	13	14	15
16 2 Lent	17	18	19	20	21	22
23 3 Lent	24	25	26	27	28	29
30 4 Lent	31					

APRIL 2003

Sunday	Monday	Tuesday	Wednesday	Thursday	Friday	Saturday
		1	2	3	4	5
6 5 Lent	7	8	9	10	11	12
13 Palm Sunday	14 Monday in Holy Week	15 Tuesday in Holy Week	16 Wednesday in Holy Week	17 Maundy Thursday	18 Good Friday	19 Holy Saturday Vigil of Easter
20 Easter Sunday	21	22	23	24	25	26
27	28	29	30